Edward John Goodman

The Best Tour in Norway

Edward John Goodman

The Best Tour in Norway

ISBN/EAN: 9783337191986

Printed in Europe, USA, Canada, Australia, Japan

Cover: Foto ©Andreas Hilbeck / pixelio.de

More available books at **www.hansebooks.com**

THE BEST TOUR IN
NORWAY

BY

E. J. GOODMAN

AUTHOR OF 'TOO CURIOUS,' 'THE ONLY WITNESS,' ETC.

WITH 34 ILLUSTRATIONS

AND ROUTE MAP

THIRD EDITION

LONDON
SAMPSON LOW, MARSTON & COMPANY
LIMITED
St. Dunstan's House
FETTER LANE, FLEET STREET, E.C.
1896

Dedicated to
CHARLES HENRY WILSON, Esquire, M.P.

OF WARTER PRIORY, POCKLINGTON,

CHAIRMAN OF THOS. WILSON, SONS AND CO. (LIMITED), HULL,

WHOSE LINE OF STEAMERS

HAS MADE THE GERMAN OCEAN A PLEASANT PATH

BETWEEN ENGLAND AND NORWAY.

PREFACE TO FIRST EDITION

I OUGHT perhaps to apologise for the seemingly presumptuous title which I have given to this book. Let me say at once, then, that I do not for a moment claim for my narrative of travel any superiority to any other work that has been written about the beautiful land in which I spent four weeks in the summer of 1890 and three weeks in that of 1891, except in one respect. Having read many other books on the same subject and examined all the guide-books; having compared notes with many fellow-travellers and consulted the most competent resident authorities, both native and British, I have come to the conclusion that the route, which it was my good fortune to be enabled to follow in 1890, is the very best that can be adopted by those who wish to see as much as possible of the beauties of Western Norway within the space of three or four weeks, which is about the average holiday-time of most people.

And in claiming for this round that it is the best

that can be taken, I freely recognise the fact that it leaves many interesting places unvisited. For instance, it does not extend to Trondhjem with its ancient and splendid cathedral, the coronation place of all the Norse kings; nor does it even afford a glimpse of the curious Laplanders with their sledges and reindeer; or comprise a voyage to the North Cape with its midnight sun.

My 'best tour,' in fact, is simply a tour in Western Norway, covering the ground most frequented by other tourists, but differing from the ordinary beaten track in certain important particulars. It forms a complete circuit, which is very rarely made, and which, indeed, has been accessible only within the last few years. The completion of new roads, however, has at last rendered this route practicable for carriage traffic, opening up several beautiful districts not often visited, while enabling the traveller to touch all the most attractive points in this part of the country without going over the same ground a second time.

The journey I made by land and water in the space of four weeks in 1890 took me over nearly 900 miles in Norway itself, and formed a sort of ellipse. Starting from Stavanger, I made my way in a serpentine track through the country northward as far as Molde, and thence returned by the coast southward *via* Bergen and Stavanger. Those who follow my route on the map will see how complete is this circuit, and how many places of interest it includes, even if no divergence be made from the main course, while for those who have more time at their disposal than the ordinary tourist with his short month's holiday, the same route will serve, as at easy distances from it, here and there, many by-excursions may be taken, and many interesting points reached.

In the summer of 1891 I again visited Norway, partly to improve my knowledge of the country and correct my first impressions, and partly to explore new ground. On this occasion I went to Christiania and traversed the new land and water route through Telemarken, besides visiting many of the scenes of my former tour, and repairing unavoidable omissions.

Hence I am now enabled to supplement 'the best tour' with one more extended which may be combined with the other by such as are able to devote, say, six weeks to their journey, or intend to visit Norway a second time.

It is the latter course rather than the former that I recommend to those who wish to 'do' Norway very thoroughly indeed. I cannot but think it a mistake to attempt too much at once in a country where there is so much to be seen. The eye wearies at last of such a rapid succession of fine landscapes as are here presented; the mind is, as it were, glutted with objects of beauty; in short, excess in travel begets satiety as in everything else.

The preferable plan would be, in my opinion, to take that which I call 'the best tour' for a first visit. On the second occasion I would recommend a voyage to Christiania and a tour through Telemarken and Sætersdal. A third trip might be devoted to Trondhjem and the North Cape. And even then there is something left to be done, for a second visit might be paid to Christiania, and then a journey north be made through Valders and the Filefjeld to the Sogne fjord, whence the traveller might proceed by water direct to the Romsdal and return *via* the Dovrefjeld and the Gudbrandsdal to Christiania.

These are routes open to the ordinary tourist, to him or her who does not care to 'rough it,' who prefers driving to walking and is not inclined to cross mountains over rough bridle-paths on horseback. For those who are prepared for the more enterprising sort of travel there is still much to be done in Norway. The district known as the Jotunfjeld, most readily reached *via* the Sogne fjord, is a paradise for the hardy mountaineer, for here is to be found the wildest and grandest of all Norwegian scenery, here are the biggest mountains and the most romantic lakes, and here the tourist proper is conspicuous by his absence.

It is not for such enterprising travellers that this volume is intended. They do not like to be 'personally conducted,' and prefer to go their own way. But for one person of this way of thinking and acting there are hundreds, if not thousands, who want advice; who, bewildered by the alternatives submitted to their choice by the various guide-books, which of course are bound to tell them all about every road and by-road in the country, would 'give anything,' as the saying goes, for a safe and intelligible direction.

It is for such travellers that this little work is intended, and if they find it useful, as showing them which way they should go, it will not have been written in vain.

I cannot close these prefatory remarks without expressing my obligations to Messrs. Valentine and Sons of Dundee for the use of some of their many beautiful photographs of Norway, from which I have been enabled to supply all the illustrations for this volume, except those in the Telemarken district, for which I am indebted to Mr. Axel Lindahl.

LONDON, 1892.

PREFACE TO THIRD EDITION

THE favour with which this book has been received, not only in England but in Norway, has seemed to justify the issue of a new edition. Although originally published in 1892, it is still in demand, and I hope that it may be found still useful. There is reason to believe that such will be the case, as the Norway of 1896 is practically the same as that of 1890, when I made my first tour in the country. There have no doubt been some changes since then, but by the year last named, the routes opening up the most attractive parts of the land were practically completed, and little has yet to be done, save to improve the accommodation here, make a new road there, and so forth. Meanwhile the 'Best Tour' remains what it was, and is likely so to remain for some time to come. Nor has it been found necessary to make any material alteration in these pages. Widely as the book has been read and keenly as it has been scanned by critical eyes, I am gratified to find how very little fault has been found with it, how few have been the errors pointed out to me. The more important of these have been corrected, and some supplementary information has been added to certain chapters. For the rest 'The Best Tour in Norway' stands as it was when first written.

E. J. GOODMAN.

LONDON, 1896.

CONTENTS

CHAP.		PAGE
I.	THE VOYAGE OUT	1
II.	STAVANGER	10
III.	MY FIRST FJORD	24
IV.	SAND	34
V.	A TRIP BY BOAT	43
VI.	THE SULDAL	51
VII.	THROUGH THE BRATLANDSDAL TO BREIFOND	61
VIII.	A DRIVE TO THE HARDANGER	73
IX.	ODDE AND ITS 'LIONS'	81
X.	SLEDGING ACROSS THE FOLGEFOND	92
XI.	ON THE HARDANGER	111
XII.	FROM EIDE TO VOSSEVANGEN	120
XIII.	STALHEIM	131
XIV.	GUDVANGEN	141
XV.	ON THE SOGNE FJORD	149
XVI.	VADHEIM TO THE JÖLSTERVAND	160
XVII.	BY MOLDESTAD TO THE NORD FJORD	171
XVIII.	HELLESYLT AND THE GEIRANGER	180

CHAP.	PAGE
XIX. BY THE HJÖRUND FJORD TO AALESUND . . 193
XX. THE ROMSDAL 203
XXI. MOLDE 220
XXII. BY THE COAST TO BERGEN . . 236
XXIII. BERGEN 243
XXIV. A SECOND TOUR—CHRISTIANIA . . . 259
XXV. SKIEN TO THE VRANGFOS 275
XXVI. TELEMARKEN BY WATER . . . 288
XXVII. TELEMARKEN BY LAND 299
SUMMARY OF THE TOUR 309
FISHING IN NORWAY 322
INDEX 331

LIST OF ILLUSTRATIONS

ROUTE MAP	at beginning of book
STAVANGER FROM THE WATCH-TOWER	facing page 10
IN THE SULDAL	,, 52
SULDAL LAKE—THE PORTAL	,, 58
IN THE BRATLANDSDAL	,, 62
TUNNEL IN BRATLANDSDAL	,, 64
THE HORRABRÆKKER NEAR RÖLDAL	,, 74
THE LAATEFOS	,, 76
ODDE AND THE SÖRFJORD	,, 82
THE SKJÆGGEDALSFOS	,, 86
BUARBRÆ	,, 90
VOSSEVANGEN	,, 124
NÆRÖDALEN	,, 132
GUDVANGEN	,, 142
THE NÆROFJORD	,, 150
LÆRDALSÖREN	,, 152
BALHOLM	,, 154
ROAD NEAR VADHEIM	,, 162
SANDE	,, 164
FÖRDE. (SÖNDFJORD.)	,, 166
JÖLSTERSVAND	,, 168

LIST OF ILLUSTRATIONS.

FALEIDE	*facing page* 176
LOEN LAKE	„ 178
KJŒJ ON HORNINGDAL LAKE	„ 182
THE GEIRANGERFJORD. PULPIT ROCK AND SEVEN SISTERS	„ 188
ÖIE ON THE NORANGFJORD	„ 196
AALESUND	„ 200
THE ROMSDALSHORN	„ 212
MOLDE	„ 220
HORNELEN	„ 240
BERGEN, FROM FLÖIFJELDET	„ 244
GOLSKIRKE AND OLD HOUSES	„ 268
LÖVEID—TELEMARKEN CANAL	„ 284
BANDAK LAKE	„ 294
HAUKELI-SÆTER	„ 304

THE BEST TOUR IN NORWAY.

CHAPTER I.

THE VOYAGE OUT.

I HAD for many years resolved, if ever I should be fortunate enough to be able to take it in June or July, to spend my annual holiday in Norway. In the summer of 1890 circumstances favoured the execution of this long-cherished design, and to my great satisfaction I found myself with leave of absence for some time in the latter part of June. Accordingly I at once decided to go to Norway, as the early summer is the best season that can be chosen for a tour in the 'land of the midnight sun.'

Not that I intended to visit the North Cape or any of those other points of the Norwegian coast where the god of day reigns supreme during the whole twenty-four hours. A voyage to the North Cape is a more serious, and let me admit also, a more expensive undertaking than I contemplated. The fare by the Wilson line from Hull to Christiania, Bergen, or Stavanger and back is from £6 to £7, first class, or £4, 10s. second. But it costs half as much again to get to Trondhjem, and thrice as much to perform the voyage to the North Cape. The perusal of books written by previous travellers, and of the various guide-books issued by Baedeker, Bennett, Beyer, Nielsen, and others, told me that I should have quite enough to do in exploring the beautiful region of Western Norway within the space of one short month, without attempting to combine with the tour a voyage to the Arctic Circle. That must be left for another occasion, and meanwhile I resolved to content myself with a journey among the Hardanger, the Sogne, the Nord, and the Molde fjords, with their offshoots.

In these districts lies at any rate most of the more picturesque scenery of Norway. There is much that is interesting in Christiania and Telemarken, which I visited in the following summer, and in the country north of Molde, embracing Trondhjem, the Lofoden Isles, the North Cape, and Lapland; but just as one cannot in a short space of time unite with a tour in the Bernese Oberland a trip to the Tyrol and the Engadine, so one cannot wander into other parts of Norway without rushing through the western district.

Now if there is one thing I hate to do in a beautiful country it is to 'rush.' While being a moderately active traveller, I am certainly not a feverishly energetic one. I like to linger—some may say, perhaps, to dawdle—over a particularly fine scene; to lie for a while by the roadside in view of some romantic combination of wood and water, of hill and valley; to retrace my steps through some lovely region that has especially charmed me; and, above all, it is my desire to find myself in some pretty spot, where, with a 'pleasing prospect' before me, I may bask in the sunshine after breakfast, and smoke my early morning pipe and dream. To my mind these are among the chief luxuries of a holiday tour; the tit-bits of travel, so to speak, which your 'rusher' can never enjoy.

And that I was enabled to extract the greatest possible amount of enjoyment out of my two tours will be readily understood when I say that on both occasions the weather was all but perfect. Some people are under the impression that Norway is a particularly rainy country. It may be sometimes, but I did not find it so. Of the twenty-eight days which I spent in the country in June–July 1890, twenty were brilliantly, faultlessly fine. The rest were what may be called 'broken' days, with alternate rain and sunshine, or cloudy, or drizzling, but only one was absolutely and irredeemably bad, when it rained from morning till night. It was also a little chilly when the sun was not actually shining. But during my second visit of three weeks in 1891, I enjoyed that which I can only call 'weather of Paradise,'—days of brilliant sunshine and balmy nights, when one could sit out in the open air without the protection of wraps, while on this occasion also I had only one really downright wet day.

Let me further correct another mistaken notion. People are afraid of going to Norway because of the evil reputation of the North Sea. But in the summer months its terrors are reduced to a minimum. Indeed it is, I was assured, often as calm as I found it during all my four voyages out and home. On the first occasion, for at least three-fourths of the distance, there was so little motion in the waves that the rapid *Eldorado* forged through them as though scorning to be shaken by such paltry ripples. It was the same during the return voyage to Hull, while the weather was if possible even finer still all through the second passage of two days in the *Tasso* from Harwich to Christiania; and though on the return we rolled a little for a few hours after leaving Stavanger, the rest of the transit was made on waters almost as calm as a lake. Indeed, I was rather disappointed than otherwise at being unable to 'feel the sea under me.' But it would have been worse than ungrateful to complain of such weather as that in which we crossed from Hull to Norway. With the sun bathing the deck in genial warmth, with a stern breeze which we hardly felt, and which drove the light smoke from our funnel straight ahead of us, with such a deep green-blue sea, crested with snowy foam, as Hook delights to paint, what more perfect voyage could be desired or imagined?

To be all day at sea in such glorious weather as this is a luxury that can be enjoyed only by those who pass their lives hard at work amidst the dust and turmoil of London and other great cities. You feel the benefit of the 'change' at once; your health already in a few hours seems to be improving, and your spirits are sensibly rising. You are never for a moment bored; the sameness of the scene, the sight of that vast expanse of green water and that almost unclouded blue vault of heaven, has no monotony for you. You are never weary of watching the waves tumbling and tossing into foam, and the creamy sweep of the surge rushing past from the bows to the stern of the vessel. The very smoke that belches from the funnel, rolling forward in light fleecy clouds, graceful and shapely in their contour, seems an object of beauty, and every detail and arrangement of the great ship is curious, novel, and interesting.

The *Eldorado* carried a tolerably full complement of passengers, without being at all overcrowded. Thus there were about eighty saloon voyagers, with berth accommodation amidships for over a hundred, while the small second-class cabin aft contained only about a dozen sleepers for sixteen berths. So there was plenty of room for everybody. It was a wise arrangement to berth the first-class passengers amidships, as they were thereby well away from the noise of the engines and the screw.

Having had no experience of other lines I can say nothing about them, but of Messrs. Wilson's steamships I can speak from personal knowledge. The *Tasso*, in which I made my second voyage, is a new and comfortable boat, but the accommodation provided on board the *Eldorado* is luxurious. Numerous as the berths are, there is ample space in all of them, and by an ingenious contrivance, the lower deck cabins are perfectly ventilated by a current of air which passes over them without creating the slightest draught. The provision of the electric light in this noble ship is also a great luxury, enabling you to make light or darkness, as you please, in your berth by merely touching a switch within easy reach, while the latest and most efficient sanitary appliances are provided in every part of the vessel.

To those who now and then went aft to ascertain the progress of the steamer, as recorded by the mechanical 'Cherub' log rigged up on the taffrail, that little machine was a constant source of amusement. A brass cylinder contains a sort of clock, the figures of which represent intervals of ten miles and their units, with hands that move gradually round, and a bell that gives a little 'ting' every few minutes, denoting that another mile has been made. From the cylinder there passes a chain and a stout cord, penetrating a wheel which revolves with it, and this line is trailed along the depths of the sea, where the screw-shaped log twirls rapidly and works the apparatus. The *Tasso* is also provided with an automatic log, which, in place of the periodical 'ting,' utters a most comical shriek or wail, like that of some living creature in acute agony. These machines are very useful in keeping us constantly informed as to how we are 'getting on.' The *El-lorado's* 'Cherub' marked capital time, indicating that we were doing a steady average of some fourteen miles an hour, a pace that we kept up till we reached the Norwegian coast.

Then there were pleasant sociable chats by the side, or in comfortable corners of the deck, or in the smoking-room and bar, often between persons who met for the first time. There was, on the whole, a good class of people on board—great folks going, with their long salmon-rod boxes, to fish in the rivers they leased, far up in the interior of the country; less wealthy and ambitious anglers with their modest bundles of trout-rods; tourists under the sheltering wing of one of Messrs. Cook's personally conducting agents; middle-aged maiden ladies travelling in couples; college undergraduates and divinity students also consorting in pairs, some with ice-axes and alpen-stocks for the glaciers; young men with knapsacks and knickerbockers, who were going to 'walk'; two or three daring bicyclists with their machines; an artist with his sketch-book and umbrella tent; an amateur photographer with his camera and set of lenses, not to speak of the miscellaneous crowd of ordinary tourists, who had no special purpose in view except to see the country and generally enjoy themselves.

Deck quoits of course. What steamer voyage in anything like decent weather is ever made without this indispensable aid to amusement? And what fun it is to see it played by persons of all ages and both sexes, from the clumsy novice who tries it for the first time, and never makes a ring, but declares that he is 'a little out of practice,' to the demon quoiter who, with unerring aim, drops ring after ring on the protruding peg! Then you can also throw rope rings into a bucket, or try to do so, but this sport, after all, is only another sort of quoits.

However, we are in no great want of amusement during our comparatively short voyage. The fascination of the sea and sun leads us away from every recreation and occupation. We try to carry out our resolve to study our *Bennett* and our *Baedeker*, but do it only fitfully, and in the same way we dip now and then into Mrs. Stone's *Norway in June*, or Lester Arnold's *Summer Holiday in Scandinavia*, and cannot get on even with the lively and delightful adventures of *Three in Norway: by Two of Them*. Yet the time passes pleasantly and fast in this eminently tranquil and prosperous voyage.

It was not until sunset, when we saw the crimson globe sink, inch by inch, bodily into the horizon, without a cloud about it, that the proud vessel was compelled to acknowledge the influence of the waves around her. Then, being in the latitude of the Orkney Islands, the Atlantic rollers came tumbling in, and the good steamer recognised the fact by slowly oscillating from side to side. It was an unpleasant motion no doubt for some of the people on board, though others were only gently rocked to sleep by it. Such was my good fortune, and, after having enjoyed several hours of refreshing rest, I awoke to find by a glimpse through the port-hole above my head that I was in still waters and in Norway!

CHAPTER II.

STAVANGER.

YES. There could be no doubt about it. Through the port-hole I could perceive the green-blue water, calm as the surface of a lake, but still unmistakably that of the sea, and close at hand long stretches of rugged grey rock. It was a brilliant sunny morning, and the hour was exactly six o'clock. Rapidly dressing, I was soon on deck, and there I had further evidence of the fact, otherwise difficult to realise, that I was in that land so long dreamed of and made to some extent familiar by books and pictures.

The steamer was moored alongside the quay of Stavanger, and the outline of the pretty town lay stretched before us. There was nothing strikingly imposing in its appearance, but it looked neat, homely, and comfortable, with its plain, but by no means commonplace, wooden houses, and the spires of a church or two peeping over them. There was something very novel in the aspect of Stavanger, but if it could be compared with anything I had seen elsewhere, it might be said to have rather a Dutch look about it.

But before saying anything about Stavanger itself

STAVANGER FROM THE WATCH-TOWER.

I think it right to relate how I came to select it as the starting-point of my tour in Norway. It is not often thus chosen. Most tourists make their way to the north and west from Christiania over the Filefjeld or the Dovrefjeld, or go direct to Bergen. It had been my intention to adopt the last-named route, which has much to recommend it, as it conveys you at once into the very heart of the best scenery of Western Norway, and has a conveniently central situation. But, however carefully you may plan a tour of this sort, seeking what seem to be the best sources of information, it is surprising how much better you may do by making local and personal inquiries on the spot than by relying merely upon guide-books and travellers' tales. Many a time have I been 'put up to a good thing' by some good-natured and well-informed native, who has directed me to a locality or route unknown to the ordinary tourist, and much superior to the usually frequented road. And it was so in the present instance.

I happened to share a cabin in the *Eldorado* with a person who proved to be beyond all others the sort of man most likely to be of service to me in such a tour as I was about to make. In the first place I found him a very interesting and congenial acquaintance. He was an old Norwegian sea-captain, by name C. H. Pedersen, rough and weatherbeaten, but with all the modest frankness and natural dignity which is so characteristic of the typical sailor. He had been nearly half a century at sea, and for about half that time had had command of his ship, and now he was going home to his wife whom he had not seen for two years, and intended to settle down for good in his native town, Stavanger. A brave, honest, shrewd old fellow he seemed to be; a man who had seen much of the world with his eyes wide open; familiar, more or less, with every topic of social and public life, and speaking half a dozen European languages, including English, with fluency. He enjoyed, moreover, the special distinction of being decorated with a silver medal conferred upon him by the Japanese Government for saving a shipwrecked crew under circumstances of great gallantry. It will be seen, therefore, that Captain Pedersen was a more than ordinarily interesting fellow-traveller, and I found him also a useful one.

He persuaded me to land at Stavanger instead of proceeding to Bergen, not only in order that I should see his native town, of which he was naturally proud, but because he represented it to be the commencement of the best route in Norway. He pointed out that by taking this course I should be enabled to see the beauties of a road which had but very recently been opened. He was eloquent about the charms of the Suldal and the Bratlandsdal, which until then had been unknown names to me. He declared that there were no finer scenes to be viewed in all Norway than these valleys presented, and altogether so provoked my curiosity that I resolved to take his advice. Nor did I regret having done so. On the contrary, I regard it as a most fortunate circumstance, as I am thereby enabled to be the first to describe to the English public a route at present unfamiliar to most travellers, but destined beyond doubt to be hereafter the favourite avenue of entrance to Western Norway.

Having landed on the quay at Stavanger, I proceeded at once to an hotel bearing the imposing title of 'The Grand.' The name is suggestive of a *caravanserai* of vast and stately dimensions, a huge building of many stories, reached by lifts, and externally magnificent in its architecture. But the Stavanger ' Grand ' is not so pretentious. A long, low-built house of some three floors, it is substantial rather than splendid, but within it affords as good cheer and as comfortable accommodation as could be desired. It has a most lady-like and attentive hostess in Mrs. Jorgensen, and a very intelligent and civil *portier*, who speaks English perfectly. Here I had my first experience of a Norwegian hotel, and I never had a more pleasant one. It was here, too, that I ate my first meal on Norwegian soil, and, considering the early hour at which I required it to be served, it was of a very satisfactory character. At any rate it was breakfast, and not merely the *café au lait*, with roll and butter, which in nearly all other parts of the Continent constitutes the first repast of the day.

The Norwegians, in fact, breakfast as we do, partaking of substantial viands as soon as they rise, a fashion which is very acceptable to those Englishmen who cannot readily give up their old habits.

After breakfast I looked up my friend, Captain Pedersen, and found him settled down once more in his home, a snug, neat dwelling in the Helmigade, where everything seemed ship-shape, as a sailor's home should be. How often the good man must have thought of that quiet, cosy little house in distant Norway when beating about in the stormy seas of the South and West! Not that Captain Pedersen had experienced much of the worst perils of the deep, for he told me that he had never been shipwrecked or even overtaken by a tempest of the most violent sort all the years he had been at sea. An ingenious man, too, was the captain, for he had a wonderful invention, of which he had made a model in wood, for applying the screw propeller to sailing ships. I cannot clearly explain the contrivance, and perhaps, with due regard to his patent rights, it is not desirable that I should do so, but it seemed novel and practical, and I hope the good man will reap all the advantages he expects to gain from it.

Meanwhile he showed me, and allowed me to copy, the diploma he had received from the Japanese Government with his medal, and, as it is quite a unique document, and reflects such high credit on this worthy Norwegian ancient mariner, I have no hesitation in reproducing it here in the French translation :—

'Certificat d'une médaille de l'Empire de Japon.

'Le gouvernement japonais décore Monsieur C. H. Pedersen, Capitaine du Coronae, bateau Norvegien, d'une médaille d'argent avec ruban rouge, d'après l'ordonnance impériale du 7 Décembre de la 14e Année de Meiji (1881), parcequ'il a sauvé avec beaucoup de courage le 9 Avril de la 17e Année de Meiji (1884) à coté du Sud d'Okinawa Ken, les Japonais Tatchizumi Tokumatsu et quatre autres habitants du Village Futamote, arrondissement de Shiôdo, département d'Elumé, province de Sanouki, qui étaient très dangereusement naufragés.

'Le 13 juin de la 17 année de Meiji. D'Après l'ordonnance impériale.

'*Cachet de* M. Tanagiwara Sakinitu, *chef du bureau de décoration.*

Cachet du bureau de décoration de l'Empire du Japon

'*Cachet de* M. Ogiû Uzuru, *sous-chef du bureau de décoration et conseiller du sénat.*

'Après examen de ce diplôme, nous l'avons porté au registre de décoration avec le No. 8.

'*Cachet de* M. Hirai Kishiô *directeur du bureau de décoration.*

'*Cachet de* M. Tokota Kanaé *premier scerétaire du bureau de décoration.*

'For correct translation.

'(Signed by the Netherlands Consul),

'8th November 1888.'

After having shown me all the cherished relics of his home, his simple collection of family portraits, the picture of his ship, which he had turned over to the care of his eldest son, his stuffed birds, and so forth, the captain kindly volunteered to accompany me in a ramble about the town and neighbourhood. Everybody seemed to know him, and to respect him, and our walk was frequently interrupted by some friend or neighbour stopping to greet him, and welcome him home again.

The streets of Stavanger are narrow, but very clean, presenting none of those signs of bad drainage which often offend the senses in other foreign towns. A smell of fish certainly does pervade the shore and quays, for a great trade in herrings is carried on here, but in other respects the 'odour' of Stavanger is by no means unpleasant, coming as it does from the resinous and aromatic pine-wood of which the houses are built, and which the inhabitants use for fuel. Those wooden houses, too, are pleasing to the eye. They are plain and neat, and their outer walls consist of planks laid vertically and overlapping after the fashion of an ordinary railway signal-box in England. They are generally painted in soft colours of different tints which harmonise well with the red tiles of the roofs. The pavements are of stone, and are a little rough for walking, but there is also a narrow trottoir of smooth slabs here and there to relieve the pedestrian's feet. Stavanger stands for the most part on uneven ground, some of the streets being built on a steep incline, and it is surrounded by undulating country on the land side, which rises to loftier hills in the distance.

The cathedral is a conspicuous object from all parts of the town, standing as it does on rising ground; and not far from it, perched on the summit of another mound, is the Valbjergtaarne, a tower which serves as an outlook for the fire brigade and other purposes. It is open to the public as a bellevue, and, of course, I took an early opportunity of ascending it. It commands a fine prospect of Stavanger and its vicinity, and the view of the Bukke and Ryfylke fjords, with their numerous rocky islands reminded me not a little of Clew Bay on the west coast of Ireland. The landscape, in fact, has nothing of that savage grandeur which one is promised in Norway. For that sort of scenery we must look elsewhere. Here everything is soft, smiling, and cultivated. Green fields and meadows spread wide beyond the confines of the town, and only in the far distance does the eye discern those masses of bare, grey rock of which the mountains of Norway are composed.

This watchtower is made of wood, like every other structure I had yet seen, and it was my inexperience of Norwegian ways that led me heedlessly to enter the edifice with my pipe in my mouth. But I only mention the circumstance to recognise the extreme courtesy with which the attendant in charge delicately hinted that smoking was not allowed in the building. There was a notice put up to that effect, but it was in the native tongue, and therefore unintelligible to me, and the man only directed my attention to it with a smile, and a polite wave of the hand.

Our walk afterwards lay among the pleasant fertile fields we had surveyed from the tower, and a winding road led us up to the Vaalandspipe, a

B

more elevated point, commanding similar but wider views of the surrounding country. Then we descended, and on the way back passed through the public cemetery. Very unlike the trim well-kept grounds in which we bury our dead was this wild uncultivated piece of wood and undergrowth; yet it did not look altogether neglected. In the midst of this tangle of trees and bushes and bracken, left to grow as they listed, there were enclosures evidently tended with the most loving care—the graves, in fact, of the departed. It was all wild without, but here in the heart of the wilderness were spots which bore unmistakable signs of sorrowing recollection. These 'mouldering heaps' were planted with flowers and evergreens; the headstones, or rather the crosses and monuments of wood, were well kept, and neatly-made gravel paths intersected each enclosure. But that which touched me most was the suggestiveness of the bench or seat placed near every grave. In all the enclosures there were these resting-places, where doubtless the mourners came from time to time to sit and think sadly of the days gone by and the beloved dead.

I was next conducted to the museum, situated just outside the town. It was a large plain wooden building of three floors, on each of which were several rooms, containing an excellent representative collection of Norwegian antiquities and natural history. My conductor was pardonably proud of the fact that he was one of the founders of this interesting museum, and I am sorry that I had not time enough left to do it justice. So I was obliged to content myself with a hurried inspection of its contents, and merely glance here and there at the flint implements and runic crosses, and the stuffed bears and wolves, foxes and lynxes, and wildfowl of endless variety which are here displayed.

We now made our way back to the town, and paid a visit to the Cathedral. It might readily be taken for a building of extreme antiquity, but as a matter of fact it is a remarkable example of clever restoration. Externally it is plain enough, not to say ugly, but the interior is very handsome, the nave and choir being excellent specimens respectively of early and later Gothic styles. The original building dated from the twelfth century, but it was burned down in the thirteenth, and when reconstructed was damaged and desecrated again and again. The final restoration was effected in 1866, and this preserves the Anglo-Gothic character of the pillars and arches, the resemblance of which to those of Winchester is due to the fact that the original architect was Bishop Reinald, an Englishman, who had been a monk in a monastery of that city. The means by which this bishop was enabled to build the Cathedral were derived from a curious source. In the twelfth century, King Sigurd Jorsalafarer divorced himself from his lawful wife, and wanted to marry a younger and comelier woman, by name Cecilia. The Bishop of Bergen refused to perform the ceremony, but the Bishop of Stavanger was less scrupulous, and tied the royal nuptial knot. As a reward for his complaisance the king bestowed large gifts upon him, and these the good Bishop used for the completion of the Cathedral.

Perhaps the most notable feature of the interior is the wonderful pulpit of the seventeenth century, painted and gilded all over, which for ornate decoration and elaborate carving surpasses, or at least equals, anything of the kind to be found in that country *par excellence* of ornamental pulpits—the Netherlands.

Hard by the Cathedral is an unenclosed public pleasure-ground, neatly kept, with fine trees, smooth paths, a little refreshment-house, and a lake, Bredevandet, the view of which with its background of neat, delicately-tinted houses, piled up the hill-side in irregular masses, is extremely picturesque. There is a homely, comfortable look about this simple pleasaunce, which, even in the early morning when it is quite deserted, is suggestive of friendly gatherings on Sunday evenings, of meetings and greetings, and gossiping between neighbours, and of lovers' walks and children's romps and gambols.

The suburbs of Stavanger are very pretty, and contain the residences of many well-to-do people, some being beautifully situated on high ground commanding charming views of the distant fjords and mountains. In the course of a walk in this part of the town, we came upon that rarity in Norway, a highly-cultivated vegetable garden. This is the property of a Mr. Monsen, who also owns in the same neighbourhood a handsome park containing a greater variety of trees than one is accustomed to see elsewhere. These things, common-places in other countries, are noticeable in Norway, where high farming and ornamental planting are the exception rather than the rule. I saw very little of either in other districts.

My next proceeding was to provide myself with a supply of Norwegian money at a local bank. They gave it me chiefly in notes and silver—eighteen *kroner* for a pound sterling, the *krone* being equivalent to one shilling, a penny and a third. Very little gold is current in Norway, but I asked for and received one gold piece of ten *kroner* to keep as a specimen. It is rather smaller than our half-sovereign, but somewhat thicker. The notes most commonly used are little pieces of paper of the value of ten and five *kroner* respectively, and for small change they give you silver coin of two and one *krone*, and of fifty, twenty-five, and ten *öre*, respectively one-half, one-fourth, and one-tenth of a *krone*. The coinage is thus as easy to calculate as *francs* and *centimes*, and for all ordinary purposes you may look upon a *krone* as a shilling, and ten *öre* as three halfpence, in reckoning your expenditure. Everything is so cheap in Norway that one ought not to complain of the fact that the *krone* is sometimes a little misleading. You are apt to allow it to take the place of the more familiar *franc*, and dispense it accordingly. But to do this is a mistake. In all small items of outlay it is quite sufficient to pay half a *krone* or fifty *öre*, where in other countries you would expend a *franc*. As a 'tip' it is universally regarded as ample, and indeed liberal. But there is so little disposition on the part of the natives to impose upon the traveller that he is, if not an incorrigibly mean person, never inclined to be excessively exacting in the matter of small change.

Indeed I never could find it in my heart to be too precise in my dealings with the village lads, who occasionally asked me to give them native money for English coppers that had been presented to them by good-natured tourists, and I have readily handed them a ten *öre* piece for a penny. As a strict matter of fact I ought not to have given more than seven and a half *öre* for it, but that precise amount is not always forthcoming. A small supply of copper money of the value of one, two, and five *öre* is also found useful as 'tips' to the little urchins who run out of the villages to open the gates for you, and who, as they hardly ever ask for any compensation, have for that reason an irresistible claim. Now and again one of these small urchins requests you to give him a copper, but the Norwegian lad is evidently little skilled in the art of begging, and will take the familiar 'no' for an answer at any time. In fact there is very little begging in Norway. The law against it is extremely strict, and is very rarely broken. About the strongest appeal for assistance is that made now and then by some poverty-stricken old man, who puts himself in your way and conveys to you a hint by looks rather than language that, on the whole, all things considered, you might as well give him something as not. What a blessing to travellers would such very mild begging be found in Ireland!

Stavanger, it may be useful to explain, is pronounced with the accent on the second syllable, *vang*, and as though it rhymed to *hanger*. It is the same with Har-*dang*-er, Gei-*rang*-er, and so forth. I may also remark that 'aa' is pronounced 'o' as in 'hope,' and 'sk' something like 'stch,' while the modified ö, which is thus marked here, but is printed in Norsk with an oblique line drawn across the letter, resembles the sound of the vowels in the French word 'œil.' The definite article 'the,' represented by *et* and *en*, is placed at the end of a name. Thus Folgefonden is 'the Folgefond,' and Bredevandet 'the Bredevand.'

CHAPTER III.

MY FIRST FJORD.

I HAD had a good seven hours for 'doing Stavanger, and it was really worth doing. True, it fulfils few of the conditions that go to make other continental towns interesting. It boasts but little in the way of art or of antiquity, for it has been burned from end to end and rebuilt in quite modern times. But it is one of the most characteristically Norwegian towns to be found in the country, and as such it is worth some study. It has, besides, a peculiar beauty all its own, and presents picturesque combinations deserving the attention of the artist, who can hardly fail to admire its variety and harmony of colour and composition.

Those who arrive by the *Eldorado* will usually have time to spend a few hours at Stavanger, but it would be a mistake to hurry away from it. Some day it will acquire an importance for the tourist which it does not possess at present, for, as I have said before, there can be no doubt that sooner or later Stavanger will be the starting-point for, at any rate, the first tour in Norway. Meanwhile its surroundings are too attractive to be passed by, and it has in its neighbourhood at least one very fine fjord, the Lyse, which is not often visited, but is of an imposing character, being very narrow and flanked by lofty mountains.

It was a fortunate circumstance that the fjord steamer *Rogaland*, which was to convey me into the heart of the country, was timed to start at the convenient hour of 1 P.M. As it lay alongside the quay it looked a neat, serviceable little boat, worked by the screw, like all the fjord steamers, and evidently well finished and supplied with all the latest improvements. These steamers are made at Christiania, but are fitted, as a rule, with English machinery. The captains and officers are invariably civil and communicative, and generally speak our tongue well.

We took several passengers on board, nearly all natives, as few tourists alight at Stavanger, because, as I have already said, the attractions of the route from this point are at present too little known. The first-class passengers who occupied the after-deck all seemed respectable, well-to-do people, presenting nothing peculiar in their appearance to distinguish them from persons of the same rank in other nationalities, but I was struck at once by their quiet, orderly demeanour, and their complete self-possession. There was no hurry to get on board, no pushing or crowding, no fuss or excitement of any kind. And in conversing with one another I observed that these good Norwegian folk usually talked in a gentle, subdued tone, very different from the noisy chatter of ordinary middle-class Frenchmen and Germans. I may say at once, for my first impressions were confirmed by subsequent experience, that the Norwegians are a grave people—not sad or sullen, but little given to loud laughter or practical joking. They can be animated enough if you 'draw them out,' but vivacity on their part is not spontaneous. And I have always found them courteous and kindly, ever ready to oblige in a good-natured, but undemonstrative manner, as though it were quite a matter of course that they should render you the service you had asked of them, and accepting any courtesy on your part with the simple but grateful acknowledgment of the national '*mange tak*'—'many thanks.'

The fore and lower parts of the steamer were second-class, and were occupied by a few peasants, who were returning to their villages on the fjord. All were decently dressed, but it was a little disappointing to notice in their apparel nothing that could pretend to the character of 'costume.' For that I had to look elsewhere, as will hereafter be seen. There was, in fact, nothing remarkable about these passengers, except perhaps their luggage, in some instances, which consisted of wooden boxes, painted in various rude designs and in the most gaudy colours. A favourite companion of the Norwegian peasant woman is her *tine*, a box of special construction, oval in shape, and secured at one end by a piece of wood fitting into a sort of groove, and opened at the other by a wedge, which turns in a slit in the lid, while the box is carried by a handle inserted in the middle of the lid. The *tine* likewise, if not profusely ornamented in bright colours, is adorned with figures and designs burnt into the plain wood.

When I say that there was nothing specially noticeable among my fellow-passengers I must make an exception. There was one traveller on board who must have attracted attention wherever he might have been met. Tall and of massive build, with manly, regular features, clear, blue eyes, with a look of command in them, fair hair, moustache and beard, and a dignified, military bearing, this imposing stranger struck me as presenting, in his physical appearance, the most perfect type imaginable of the old Norse heroes that we read of in song and story. He was, in fact, a Norwegian gentleman, and a captain of engineers. I easily made his acquaintance, and found him as polished in manner as he was comely in person. He spoke English fluently and with accuracy, and I am indebted to him for a large amount of information, which I afterwards found extremely useful.

The companionship of Captain —— added greatly to the pleasure of my first voyage in the inland seas of Norway. For some distance from Stavanger our course lay among the wide waters of the Ryfylke fjord, across which the eye encountered long ranges of grey rock, some hundreds of feet in height, with here and there a barren island, or one scantily clothed with herbage, and bearing only a hut or two. Now and then we came upon a piece of land, where a few scattered houses made an apology for a village, but there was no cluster of habitations anywhere in these wild waters having the compactness and populousness of an ordinary European hamlet. It was, in fact, a first sight of those savage solitudes which are the most characteristic features of Norwegian scenery.

But great as was the attraction of the views to be obtained from the deck of the steamer, there was a counter attraction elsewhere which could not be resisted. I allude to the *middagsmad*, or dinner, to which we were summoned by bell. The meal was served in the small saloon below, there being room for only some twenty diners at the three tables spread for the repast. I formed one of a party of about half a dozen, including my friend the magnificent engineer-captain, at one of the smaller tables, where we were waited upon by an attentive damsel who spoke a little English. It was an excellent dinner, and I reflected that if this were an average specimen of Norwegian fare, I should not do badly thereafter. A pleasant light soup was followed by two courses of fish, including some of the freshest and sweetest salmon I ever tasted. This last was boiled and served with a sort of oily sauce. Afterwards there was stewed veal, nicely cooked, and eaten with a fruit preserve, and the meal wound up with a palatable light pudding, with a red syrup. They gave us no fruit, and the only vegetables supplied were rather inferior frost-bitten potatoes and cauliflower. In fact this lack of vegetables is the weakest point of the Norwegian table. Hardly anywhere do you get anything except potatoes, and these are usually of very poor quality. Beans and peas are sometimes supplied, but they are always of the 'tinned' sort. There was wine on the table, both French and German, and large and small bottles of that Norwegian beer or *öl* which is so well known in England, and which differs in no way from that imported into this country, except that it is somewhat cheaper.

By the time our meal was finished,—two *kroner* only being charged for it,—we found ourselves, on returning to the deck, nearing that part of the fjord which resembles more closely the pictures of those waters which have been made familiar to us at home than anything we had yet seen during our voyage. A vast range of solid mountain seemed to bar our way, but presently there appeared a crevice in the mass which widened as we approached it, and then we found ourselves indeed among the fjords. As the waters became narrower the mountains on either hand appeared loftier and more precipitous, and again and again we seemed land-locked by these stupendous giants of stone. After a time we arrived at a point where the main fjord was intersected by two branches to right and left, through the vistas of which we looked down far into the distant land. Here our steamer was brought to a standstill, as we had reached what on a railway line would be called a junction, or, in other words, this was the point at which we were to correspond with another steamer from one of the branch fjords. The latter, however, was not punctual, and kept us waiting a full hour ere it arrived.

This I found was not unusual with local steamers in Norway, which have a pleasing habit of starting and arriving an hour or two either before or after their time. To the tourist this is frequently a source of delay, and a serious one, especially in places where there is only a single steamer two or three times a week, missing which you are hopelessly stranded sometimes in an uninteresting locality for a day or two or more. It was happily never my fate thus to be left high and dry, but other travellers I found were less fortunate. There is an ingenious publication known as the *Norges Communicationer*, which in some measure answers to our *Bradshaw*, but is even more bewildering than that misleading and distracting guide. For while *Bradshaw* at any rate is fairly accurate, and the trains do run as a rule at the hours named in its pages, the times of the steamers as stated in the *Communicationer* and the times kept by the steamers themselves by no means agree. Thus, after exhausting your brain in the painful attempt to plan a route by ascertaining where and when the steamers correspond, and flattering yourself that you have 'got it all right,' you find on arriving on the spot, to your utter despair, that the steamer you fondly expected to catch started yesterday, or, more maddening still, an hour ago!

To the foreign tourist this is very annoying, but the natives take things easily. They never seem to be in a hurry, and they appear to think it matters very little when they get away, as long as they get away at some time or other. Thus, on the present occasion, everybody took the delay in the arrival of the corresponding steamer quite coolly. There was no impatience at this hour's detention. The captain and officers lounged about with an air of supreme indifference, nor were those in charge of the tardy boat assailed with any reproaches when it at last put in an appearance. It crept slowly alongside, and was made fast; the gangway was lowered, and half a dozen peasants with their baggage, and a horse and cow or two, were taken on board, and then we were off again.

As we steamed along the fjord I was struck by the extremely beautiful colour of the water. It was of the most delicate pale green, resembling the hue of those lakes and rivers in Switzerland which are fed from the glaciers that show in their profound crevasses the same rich tints. At first I supposed that the colour of this fjord water was due to a like cause, strange as it would seem if so vast a surface could be affected by the drainings of the snow and ice fields. But I was told that this was not the case. Nor had the reflection from the blue sky above anything to do with the aspect of the waves, for these bore the same emerald tints under cloud, as I perceived on another occasion. When, however, I traversed those fjords again under the same atmospheric conditions, the colour was changed to a slatey grey. The water is green only at certain times of the year, for a month or so after midsummer, and no one seems to know what is the cause of it. Some attribute it to the temporary presence of myriads of minute insects, but this theory is discredited by others. The verdant appearance of the fjords is in fact as great a mystery as the strange phosphorescent light that gleams upon the waves at night in the open sea.

The waters gradually contracted as we steamed along, and the grey mountains rose higher above our heads—long ranges of them with flat or rounded tops, here and there flecked with streaks of snow in mottled patches, while now and then we caught a glimpse of the vast snow-fields with which the table-lands on their summits are covered, and frequently we descried milky torrents pouring down their rugged sides, and presenting to us the first examples, though as yet on a comparatively minor scale, of the mighty fosses or waterfalls of Norway. We were not yet in sight of the magnificent scenery for which the country is famous, but this foretaste or sample, as it were, of its splendours was very fascinating. It looked like Norway, the Norway of the books and pictures, and every mile of the voyage tended to realise more vividly the scenes which imagination had promised. And now, an irregular line of gabled houses with white or tinted fronts and red roofs, softened in tone by time and weather, was seen spread along the shore, and I was told that it was the little town or village of Sand, the station for which I had taken my ticket, situated some forty miles from Stavanger.

[It is under melancholy circumstances that I now find myself free to mention the name of the gallant and courteous gentleman whom I met on my way to Sand. For he, Captain Georg Heyerdahl, is, unhappily, no more. He had been transferred to the district of Trondhjem, and there, in the summer of 1894, I visited him, to receive a cordial welcome and a hundred kind attentions. But his health was broken, his noble figure was shrunken and wasted and he looked prematurely aged. Yet I was greatly surprised as well as shocked to hear, not many months afterwards, that he had passed away. Never since have I met with so grand a specimen of the true Norwegian gentleman as my lamented friend Georg Heyerdahl.—May 1896.]

CHAPTER IV.

SAND.

It was still early in the afternoon when we landed. Sand is a very fair specimen of a Norwegian village, consisting of one long irregular street running abreast of the fjord which takes its name, the houses, like those of Stavanger, of timber, and neat and trim-looking rather than picturesque. In fact I may say at once that in no part of Norway does one ever come across domestic architecture presenting those features so beloved of the artist, the quaint gabled roof, the mullioned window, the whitened wall, with its black cross-beams, and the dilapidated, tumble-down, half-ruined aspect which comes of antiquity. Here and there you see by the fjord or lake side rows of black boathouses, with pointed roofs, which may have been in use for centuries, while, in the interior, the battered old saw-mills at the feet of waterfalls are decidedly picturesque objects. So, too, are the *staburs*, where wood and fodder for the winter are stored, and which are built somewhat in the style of *chalets*, with overhanging eaves and railed galleries. These structures are often of considerable antiquity. But there is nothing that looks ancient in most Norwegian towns and villages. The appearance of these places suggests the idea that they must have been often rebuilt either as the result of fire or decay; yet there is nothing offensively new or raw or vulgar about them. The tone of their colour is subdued and pleasing to the eye, and at least it may be said of them that they always look well at a distance.

Sand contains two or three small hotels, and that at which I put up, Rasmussen's, was not surpassed for homely comfort by any which sheltered me during my tour. It has a pretty wild bit of garden-ground in front of it, and a nice cosy porch overshadowing its front door. It would have a pleasant look-out on the fjord, but that the view is partly intercepted by a shop and a boathouse. The entrance-hall is conveniently fitted up, so that it may be used as a common lounge or sitting-room, for it is provided with a table and chairs. On the walls are posted various useful notices in the shape of time-tables, lists of fares, and other valuable information. There are rooms right and left. One is the *spise-sal*, or dining-room, a bright, cheerful apartment, containing a long table at which about twenty persons could sit down, while the other chamber on the ground-floor is the drawing-room, comfortably furnished, and provided with a piano, and a very fair stock of books. Indeed in most Norwegian hotels there is usually a liberal supply of literature for the amusement of visitors on wet days. Many of these are in the native tongue, but the collection always includes a considerable number of English works, either provided by the proprietor or left behind from time to time by British tourists. Wherever you go, too, you always find large albums of photographs of Norwegian scenery, by Valentine and others, besides maps and guide-books of the country, so that you never need be at a loss for instruction and amusement.

Speaking generally, I would say that the minor hotel accommodation of Norway is neither splendid nor luxurious, but it is essentially home-like and comfortable. These remarks, of course, apply only to the regular tourist track. Elsewhere you have to put up with the much inferior quarters provided at the *skydstations* or posting-houses; but it is quite a mistake to suppose that in Norway you must necessarily 'rough it.' The hotel at Sand was a very fair average specimen of its class. Everything about the house was neat and clean, and its porter or boots was a civil young fellow who had been in America, and spoke English well. The hotel was kept by a widow. She never appeared, but was well represented by two charming daughters, one of whom—the prettiest girl it was my lot to meet in Norway, and somewhat resembling Christine Nilsson in appearance—was shortly to be married to some fortunate barrister at Stavanger. These young ladies did much to render our visit agreeable, for one of them at least spoke English perfectly, and seemed well acquainted with our literature and social customs. There were not many visitors in the house, but among them was an English family who had been residing there for several weeks. In fact, Sand is a place that tempts one to stay, for it is snug and comfortable, besides being the centre of a very beautiful district. In front of it stretches the main fjord, and from this two branches diverge, so that three distinct arms of the sea, overshadowed by grey mountains, some hundreds of feet in height, are visible from elevated points on the shore.

At Sand we had our first experience of a *table-d'hôte* on land, and it proved a sufficiently favourable example of Norwegian living. *Aftensmad*, or supper, was served at seven o'clock, and consisted partly of hot and cold fish, chiefly salmon, including that smoked sort which some people do not like, as they regard it quite mistakenly as 'raw,' but which others pronounce delicious, myself among the number. During my visit to Norway I always availed myself of every opportunity of enjoying this delicacy. It is, when bought in the shops, cheaper by at least two-thirds than in London, the price being, as a rule, one *krone* a pound. Sardines *à l'huile*, such as we get elsewhere, were also supplied; but there was another sort of tinned fish, flavoured with bay-leaves, which was not so much to my taste. Besides the fish we had meat minced and rolled into balls with rich gravy. There were two or three sorts of bread, white and brown; the latter has a sour flavour which some may like, but which did not please me. Even the ordinary white bread is not very palatable, being heavy in quality and not too sweet. But another, a finer sort in rolls and crusty little loaves, is also generally supplied, and with this no one could find fault. The Norwegian butter here and elsewhere is fair, but by no means first rate; nor can I say much for the native cheese, the most popular of which is a red sort, something of the Dutch character, and made up like it in large globes, and another of goats' milk of a curious coffee-colour, and in shape a square block. The latter is usually cut up in very thin slices, one of which at least every Norwegian invariably takes at breakfast.

At *aftens* you are offered the choice of tea or coffee, and tea is more often supplied in Norway than in most continental countries. Sometimes it is very good, and sometimes it is not. And hereby hangs a comical incident which occurred at this same *table-d'hôte* at Sand. An English traveller, who had come over with me in the *Eldorado*, had taken the precaution to bring with him a small supply of tea from England, having heard that the decoction brewed in Norway is not always up to the mark. On arriving at the hotel he had handed over his packet to the head waitress, with directions, so far as he could explain them, to the girl—whose command of our Anglo-Saxon tongue was limited—to 'make' enough of it for his personal consumption. He openly avowed his proceeding at the supper-table, and was commended for his foresight, because, a lady present observed, the tea there was by no means good. When supper was served most of us had tea, and every one noted that it was of excellent quality. Indeed, the lady who had previously spoken declared that the tea at that hotel had never been so good before, and our traveller, I thought, looked as though he felt that he had been rather premature in thus using up a portion of his small and precious supply. He was so indeed, for the sequel, of course, will be guessed. The waitress, misunderstanding his directions, had simply made tea for the whole party out of his packet, and there was not a leaf of it left!

The sun was still high in the heavens when, after supper, at about eight o'clock, some of us sallied forth from the hotel for a walk and a smoke by the fjord-side. And in thus rambling through the one straggling street of Sand, and by the bank of the river that comes roaring down through the Suldal, a valley which opens up to the left at one end of the village, we passed our first evening in Norway. And what an evening it was! The term, as we recognise it in our more southern latitude, when dusk sets in, even on the longest day of the year, at about 8.30 P.M., is here a misnomer. In June and July the evening in Norway is practically no evening at all, but only the latter part of the day. Thus the sun was still shining brightly at past ten o'clock when we turned in, and indeed was only just about to set. It was a novel experience, this broad daylight at bedtime, and it was one that I enjoyed as keenly as any among the pleasures of my tour. I never could get quite used to it, but the occasional embarrassment that it caused me was by no means of a disagreeable kind. Many a time after supper I would take a stroll with some fellow-traveller, and as we walked and chatted there would at last come a period when one experiences a sense of fatigue and sleepiness. Then the thought would cross my mind that, tired as I was, I could not think of retiring to rest for some two or three hours at least. The sun was only just setting, the birds were singing their last song before going to roost,—it could not be later than eight o'clock,—and then I remembered that I was in Norway, and was not surprised to find my watch telling me that the time was just one hour before midnight! The perpetual day is truly one of the greatest delights of Norway at or about midsummer. One must go much further north than any point which I expected to reach to see the midnight sun itself, but sunset at eleven P.M. is a phenomenon hardly less remarkable.

So I went to bed by daylight and availed myself of the dark blinds, with which most Norwegian hotel bedrooms are provided, to exclude the rays of the declining sun. In spite of this precaution I could not sleep, but that was not due to any discomfort in the accommodation provided for me. I never can sleep for a night or two after leaving home, wherever I may go. The Norwegian bedrooms, so far as my experience went, were comfortable enough, and all their fittings scrupulously clean. I had heard that they were often dirty and infested with insects, but I found none deserving this character. Nor did I find the Norwegian beds so small as I had been led to expect. They are said by many travellers to be uncomfortably short, but I should think that none save abnormally tall men would have any cause to find fault with them. Certainly those I occupied were never less than six and a half feet in length.

But there is one detail in the construction of the Norwegian bed which is not quite so satisfactory. Every one in which I slept during my tour is made in the same way, that is, on what may be called the box system. A small upright board runs along each side as in a berth, and this ridge is not comfortable to sit upon when one is unrobing. In all other respects the beds are cosy and snug enough; the sheets are perfectly clean and dry, and, as a rule, a nice eider-down quilt is provided, which is often very welcome, as the nights in Norway, even in summer, are apt to be rather cold. The pillow or bolster is of peculiar shape, being thick at the top and gradually narrowing down so as to form a slope. I did not find it uncomfortable, though some people object to it.

The Norwegian views as to the water-supply necessary for the traveller are somewhat limited, and the jugs might certainly be larger than they are; nor is it always easy to get your morning 'tub' unless you are hardy enough to be able to go out and take a header in the fjord, the waters of which are usually rendered very cold by the melting snows that come down from the mountain-tops. On the other hand, they always supply you with soap, which, as every one knows, is not the custom elsewhere on the Continent. And this soap is invariably of the same kind, a white tablet, which lathers freely, probably owing to the quantity of soda contained in it.

CHAPTER V.

A TRIP BY BOAT.

WHEN I rose, at about 6 A.M., the sun had acquired greater power than it attains at the same hour in our more southern clime. It was indeed a delicious morning, and after a good substantial *frokost*, or breakfast, of which salmon, in various forms, constituted an important feature, I enjoyed my favourite luxury of a pipe, smoked in a pleasant place, on this occasion, in a seat under the portico before the hotel, and in view of the fine fjords which unite at this spot. One of these is the Sand fjord, the others are the Saude and Hylen fjords, narrow branches which penetrate the heart of the country in different directions.

It was a happy thought on the part of a fellow-traveller, who had accompanied me from Stavanger, to explore one of these mysterious waters before proceeding further on our way. So we engaged a boat, with a couple of rowers, to take us to Saude, a distance of some fourteen miles. The boat was soon ready, and it was of a type very common in Norway, modelled almost exactly on the lines of those used by the old Vikings, of which a very perfect specimen is to be seen at the University in Christiania. Of light draught, but strongly, if roughly, built, it terminated in a sharp prow at each end, and was wholly devoid of anything in the shape of a rudder. Sitting accommodation was provided simply on the thwarts not used by the rowers, but my companion and I found it more comfortable to lie down fore and aft respectively in the bottom of the boat, having first made couches for ourselves with rugs and wraps. They were two fine stalwart men who rowed us, using oars worked against a peculiar kind of single rowlock, broad at the base, and terminating in a point, a wisp of rush or piece of rope being used to encircle and secure the oar.

It was a delightful trip, as we lay there in our snug quarters surveying the scene, which became gradually unfolded in panoramic fashion while we glided along on the waveless waters of the fjord. Not a breath of wind was stirring, and the mountains stood reflected as on the surface of a lake. Huge masses of rock rose around us on every side, and now and then our way seemed closed in by them, until a narrow cleft appeared, and we found ourselves in a new reach. Here and there we passed an opening, forming a branch within this branch fjord, and presenting a grand view of snow-capped mountains and forests of fir and pine. Hardly a habitation came in sight for miles, and the sense of the utter desolation and profound stillness that pervaded the scene was as impressive as it was soothing. As the morning advanced the sun became more powerful, but the heat, though fierce, was tempered by the delicious freshness of the air, cooled alike by the waters below, and the snow-fields above.

During this trip we came upon the first waterfalls of any magnitude that we had yet seen. These were mere driblets for Norway, but in almost any other country they would have been regarded as stupendous. They fell from heights of many hundreds of feet in streaks of milky whiteness, sometimes down the bare sides of the rock, sometimes in deep, dark ravines, and assuming, as they fell, all sorts of strange, fantastic forms, now descending in mighty volumes of foam and spray, now like veils of fine lace. The largest and handsomest of the fosses came in sight as we neared our destination, and at one point two or three of them were visible at once.

At the head of the fjord stand two small villages, Saude and Sövde, about a couple of miles apart, and it was at the former that we disembarked. It cannot be said that these villages present a very picturesque appearance—and the same remark may be applied to pretty nearly all the smaller groups of dwellings that one encounters on the fjords. They are simply a few houses scattered about the shore, all detached, and having plenty of space around them. This arrangement is doubtless made as a precaution against the spread of fire, as it is hardly possible but that in the event of a conflagration breaking out in one of these dry pine-wood houses, the whole village, if more compactly built, must fall a prey to the flames. As it is, Norway has suffered terribly from the ravages of fire, and is as yet but ill-provided with modern appliances for contending with the 'devouring element.' The absence of foliage also contributes to give a bare and cold appearance to these Norwegian villages. The houses and cottages are rarely embowered in trees, and, probably owing to the shortness of the summer, which hardly lasts three months, the inhabitants do not seem to be encouraged to cultivate gardens about their dwellings. Wherever, indeed, I saw a bit of garden-ground, I found it generally in the same wild condition that was presented by the cemetery at Stavanger and the hotel garden at Sand.

It was about 1 P.M. when we landed at Saude, and the long voyage from Sand had given me a good appetite. Whether I should be able to appease it by a regular meal at the small and unpretending hotel—Rabbe's—to which we resorted for refreshment was uncertain. Saude is such an out of the way place, and apparently so little visited by ordinary travellers, that one might have thought there was not much to be expected from it in the way of cookery. When therefore I asked whether I could have anything to eat I was quite prepared to hear that nothing more substantial than bread and cheese or eggs was to be obtained. The waiting-maid, however, seemed to take my request in a very matter of course sort of way, as though the demand for dinner were nothing out of the common there. It was all settled in two words. 'Middagsmad?' I asked. 'Ya,' replied the waitress, and without inquiring 'What would you like?'—that aggravating question so often put in country inns at home where they have nothing to give you but ham and eggs—she at once retired.

I had to wait nearly three-quarters of an hour before the promised dinner was ready, but it was worth waiting for. My attendant began by placing on the table a mysterious brown dish filled with what looked like about a quart of white-wash. What this was, and where would be its place in the forthcoming banquet, I was wholly at a loss to guess. It might be some sort of cold soup, or the sauce for some other dish, but doubtless I should be informed of its purpose in due course. As a matter of fact, it was reserved as a wind-up to the repast, which proved to be a most excellent one, and included salmon boiled and fried, a 'hacked' steak, and as good an *omelette aux confitures* as ever I tasted in my life. Then the brown dish was put before me, and it appeared that the white surface was a layer of thick cream covering a stratum of sour milk, and the compound was to be eaten with sweet bread-crumbs and fruit syrup. This dainty somewhat resembled a Devonshire junket; and the fact that I helped myself three times from the brown dish speaks for itself. For this repast I was charged 1 *krone* 50 *öre*, or about one shilling and eightpence.

There is a pretty walk through pine-woods from Sande to Sövde, in the course of which several fine waterfalls are to be seen, and further along the road on the way to the copper mines of Almannajuvet, and for a distance of some six miles the scenery is really magnificent. The place altogether is well worth visiting. The steamer that conveyed us to Sand afterward proceeds to Saude, stays there for the night, and returns *viâ* Sand to Stavanger in the forenoon. It was our intention on reaching Sand that afternoon to go on further by road, but circumstances prevented the carrying out of this plan. We set out in our boat on the return journey at three o'clock under a blazing sun, but after a few minutes' rowing a slight breeze sprang up and induced our men to hoist a sail. This pleasantly varied the manner of our progress, but it did not last long: the breeze died away, and once more the men took to their oars and rowed us over the glassy waters. Another attempt at sailing proved successful, but I noticed that the men were careful to hold the sail-rope loose and kept a steady look-out ahead. The cause of their caution soon became apparent. In the far distance the clouds were gathering, and there were signs of rain, and every moment we crept nearer and nearer to the shadowy veil which was spreading across the fjord. It was plain that we were going straight into the heart of a storm, and although the surface of the water was still calm, and the sky above our heads was brilliantly blue, and the mountains on either hand were bathed in sunlight, we prepared for a bit of bad weather.

As we put on our macintoshes the men took in their sail, and, seizing the oars, pulled with a will. For we were about to cross the branch fjord which we had passed in the morning, and it was from this quarter that the storm was emerging. We could see it stealing along in a solid body of mist, which suddenly was split across by a flash of forked lightning, and then there was a boom of thunder which rolled away in repeated echoes among the mountains. We now arrived at the mouth of the branch fjord, and soon were in the very teeth of the storm. The sea by this time was lashed into angry waves, which, however, our sturdy little boat rode buoyantly, and now the rain came down upon us in torrents—and such rain! It descended like steel wire, and beat the water with a shrill, hissing sound which almost stifled the voice of the thunder that burst over us at intervals. The men rowed hard through the raging waves and the cross wind from the side fjord in their endeavour to gain the shelter of the land. When this, after a fierce struggle, was reached at last, we found ourselves in smooth water, with the storm still raging

D

to our right, and the rest of the passage was comparatively easy. By the time we arrived at Sand the storm had rolled away, and all was bright and sunny around us. It was but a taste of rough weather on the fjords, and as such was an interesting experience, but it sufficiently realised the dangers of these uncertain waters, and warned us that they were not to be sailed without ample precaution.

The charge made for the day's trip was a characteristic example of the cheapness of locomotion in Norway. For the use of a boat for an entire day, that is, from ten in the morning till six in the evening, and the services of two rowers who had pulled us twenty-eight miles, we had to pay only six *kroner*, or six shillings and eightpence. Naturally we gave the men what they evidently regarded as a liberal *drikkepenge* or *pourboire*, which they well deserved, considering the extra labour they had gone through in the storm. The man who received the money took off his hat and offered me his hand, a graceful and invariable custom which all Norwegian boatmen and drivers observe after their 'job' has been completed. I shook hands heartily with the good fellow, and we parted mutually satisfied. After our long and partly rough voyage we thought we had done enough for the day, so we abandoned our intention to drive at once through the Suldal to Osen or Oset, and spent another pleasant evening at Sand.

CHAPTER VI.

THE SULDAL.

It would no doubt have been desirable to get on to Oset that day, as the steamer was to start thence on the Suldal lake at the early hour of nine the next morning, and it was a drive of some two hours and a half to the place of embarkation. But the delay only involved the necessity of starting very early, and as it turned out a brilliantly fine morning the journey was all the more delightful. And now we had to gain our first experience of one of those vehicles which are peculiar to Norway.

Of these there are three classes : the *carriole* or *karriol*, a little two-wheeled gig shaped like a boot, which accommodates only one traveller while the driver sits behind him ; the *stolkjærre* (pronounced *stolcherer*), which has places for two travellers ; and the *trille*, more rarely used, with four wheels, for four persons, and drawn by two horses. My companion and I naturally chose a *stolkjærre* as being a more sociable mode of conveyance, and having the further advantage of being cheaper, as two persons travel by it for a fare and a half. Our first *stolkjærre* was not a favourable specimen of its class, being old and rickety, and exhibiting a capacity for jolting and bumping which could hardly be excelled. I think the *portier* at the hotel might have got us a better trap, and it was due to our inexperience that we did not demand one. However, we thought we were getting the usual thing, and made the best of it.

Our *skydsgut* (pronounced *shusgut*), or driver, was a lad of about sixteen, a bright lively fellow who drove carefully and well, and did his best to make himself agreeable. He spoke a little—a very little—English, and took every possible opportunity of airing his accomplishment. But the results were not altogether satisfactory, for his efforts to make himself intelligible were by no means successful. However, after vain attempts by driver and passengers to understand each other, every conversation wound up with an emphatic 'Ya-as' on the part of the former, which signified that he, at any rate, was perfectly satisfied. Thus our youthful *skydsgut* showed himself extremely anxious that his 'fares' should be made aware of any feature of the journey likely to be specially interesting to persons of their nationality. Places, for instance, occupied by Britons would be eagerly pointed out by him with such a remark as, 'Englishman house, dar — Mr. Schmid — jabber — jabber — ya, Englishman.' Not quite understanding all he said, I would say, 'I beg your pardon?' Then the *skydsgut* would repeat his information with a little

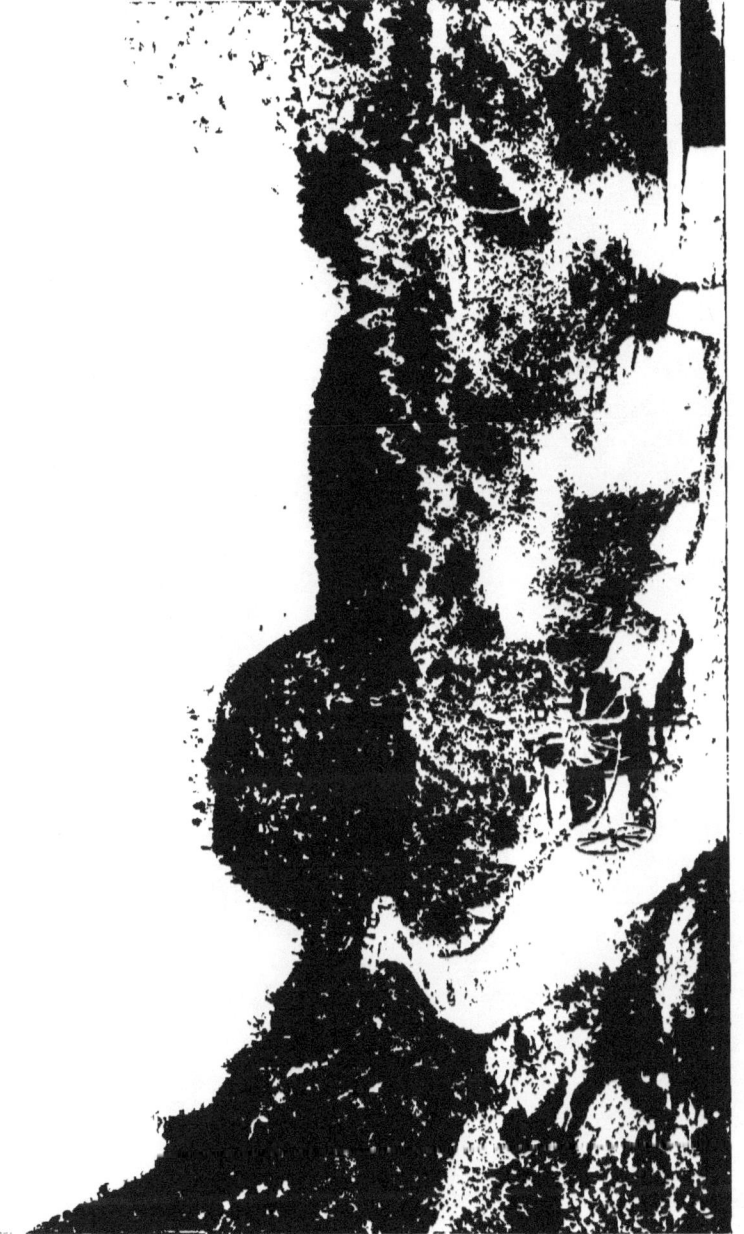

IN THE SULDAL.
(Page 51.)

more Norsk thrown into it. 'Jabber, jabber, jabber—Englishman house—Mr. Schmid—jabber, jabber, jabber.' 'Oh, thank you,' I would reply, giving it up in despair, whereupon he would exclaim, 'Ya-as,' as having settled everything.

The care and skill with which Norwegians of all ages and classes handle their horses have been noted by many travellers ere now, and I can bear testimony to the truth of their observations. The horses themselves, pretty little beasts of the cob class, always look very plump and sleek and well-groomed, and are generally of a peculiar fawn or dove colour though sometimes brown or bay. They are wonderfully docile and sure-footed, very rarely shying or stumbling, and are capital trotters on a good level road. But the *skydsgut*, as a rule, does not force their pace; he is, in fact, disposed to drive slowly rather than fast, and in ascending hills takes it very easy indeed, while making up for it in descending. The whip is little used, and often the driver has none, though he sometimes finds it desirable to provide himself with one on the way, by cutting a switch by the roadside and pruning it as he goes. He encourages his horse to make progress by uttering an indescribable sound, something between a groan and a grunt, while the invariable signal for pulling up is a guttural 'bur-r-r,' which the animal instantly obeys.

There are exceptions, however, to every rule, and I am bound to say that some of the *skydsguts* are both unskilled and reckless drivers. You do not often come across one of this class, but when you do it would be well to warn him for your own sake, and report him for the benefit of future travellers. I have sometimes checked a Jehu of this sort by exclaiming now and then, '*Ikke saa hurtig*,'— 'not so fast,' while if this caution has to be too often repeated it is desirable to make a complaint in the *dagbog* of the next station you come to. Accidents are very rare, but they do happen occasionally, and to be thrown out of a car driven at full speed down a steep road, and perhaps on the brink of a precipice, is not a pleasant prospect to contemplate.

The horses are changed at fixed stages called *skydstations*, from ten to fifteen miles apart. These are under the strictest Government supervision, and a *dagbog* or day-book is kept at all of them, in which the traveller is expected to record his name, the place from which he started, his next destination, the number of horses he has used, and any complaints or remarks he may have to make. This is intended as a check on the postmaster, who has to render an account of the business he has done, the *dagbog* being periodically inspected by Government officials. English travellers, I am sorry to say, too often neglect this useful rule, and sometimes scribble nonsense in the book, or irrelevant information. Thus we occasionally found such entries as these :—
'Name ?—John Smith. Where from ?—London.

Next destination ?—Banker. Number of horses used ?—Forty-five last birthday,' and so on.

The *skydstations* are subsidised by the State, and one class of them, known as 'fast stations,' are obliged to keep a certain number of horses and vehicles ready ; while others, called *tilsigelse*, or 'slow stations,' are only required to supply such means of carriage as they can procure at the time. As a rule, there is little difficulty in getting horses and cars at any of these places, but in the busy season it is sometimes necessary to give notice beforehand of the traveller's requirements, if he does not wish to incur a long detention. One great advantage of the station system is that the traveller need never be at a loss to know what he has to pay. The prices per kilomètre are absolutely fixed, and what is more, the tariff is rigidly enforced. It is easy to ascertain at each station what is the fare to the next ; and the best way to avoid disputes or mistakes, not to speak of imposition, which is very rare in this honest country, is to get the station-master to write down the fare for you, and show it to the *skydsgut* when the period arrives for settling up with him.

The driver is always satisfied with a very moderate 'tip' for himself. The inhabitants tell you that you ought not to give him anything at all, as his pay is included in the fare ; but if this is too much for your conscience, and especially if he happens to have driven you particularly well, and made himself generally pleasant, you will reward him very liberally indeed with the equivalent of sixpence for a whole day's journey. And the cost of travelling by road is moderate enough. It does not average more than about twopence-halfpenny or threepence a mile for each traveller, so that you often find you have spent no more than six or seven shillings on your day's driving.

Starting, as I have said, shortly after 6 A.M., under a brilliant morning sun, we were jolted through the one street of Sand in our rather rickety *stolkjærre*, and, once clear of the village, took a sudden turn to the left and found ourselves in the Suldal. A splendid river traverses the valley and goes roaring and boiling in mighty cataracts of foam to the fjord, and the road keeps alongside of it for several miles. The valley is somewhat wide at first, but exceedingly picturesque, being flanked on either side by noble mountains, and richly clothed with birch, pine and fir. The road is very well made, and in a more comfortable vehicle than that which carried us must be pleasant to travel on. As it was, we proceeded slowly at the outset—the *skydsguts* never drive quickly for the first few miles—and this enabled us the better to survey the charming landscape around us. I was struck at once by the close resemblance of the scene to the beautiful Haslithal, on the road from Meyringen to the Grimsel, and the likeness increased rather than diminished as we went on.

Presently the valley contracted, or rather we were shut in by a large mass of rock which rose to our left in its midst, and for a while hid the river from sight. But soon we emerged from the ravine thus formed and entered more open country, and at last approached a huge shoulder of mountain that seemed to cross our path, but gave entrance through a turning to a new scene. Another bend of the road showed us a silver gleam of water in the distance, and there was no need for our *skydsgut* to point to it with his switch and exclaim 'Suldalsvand.' We guessed of course that it was the lake upon which we were to embark, and in a few minutes we were on its shores.

There are very few houses at Oset, which stands at the lake-head, and two of them are small hotels. A little steamer, the *Suldal*, lay alongside the pier, and we had plenty of time to board her. We wondered how such a vessel could have been got to such an out of the way place, but were told by the genial Captain Kolheustvedt, that she was made at Christiania and brought to Oset in pieces, and put together there. We had only about half a dozen fellow-passengers, chiefly natives of the peasant class, and felt surprised that such a beautiful route as we were making should be so little used.

For it is difficult to describe the magnificence of the Suldal lake without being suspected of exaggeration. I thought the scenery of Norway must be grand indeed that was to surpass this imposing combination of mountain and lake, and indeed I rarely saw anything finer anywhere else. The rocks here rise to the height of at least two thousand feet on each side straight out of the water, and the lake twists and turns among them, revealing a new and beautiful picture in every reach. The finest point is the famous Portal or Gate—for famous it is, at any rate, among the Norwegians. Two perpendicular masses of granite, which seem at first almost to be united, so narrow is the cleft between them, rise on either hand, towering above us to a tremendous height. The passage, on being neared, becomes wider than it first appeared, but still is only a hundred feet or so in breadth, and on being passed it seems to close behind us, admitting us to a wider reach of the lake. A rocky island stands here in the centre, and the shores are gaunt and almost barren, save for the thin pastures that we see on the banks. A few huts or *sæters* present themselves to view here and there, but there are no other signs of human habitation. We stop off one or two of these 'villages,' if they can be so called, and two or three of the peasants put off in boats to come on board. In one case we take in a young woman with a baby and a box, and elsewhere, at the foot of a waterfall, where we touch the shore—the water is so deep— we land an old man, by means of skilful gymnastics on his part, with a capacious copper stewpan, which he is taking home. Where that home may be we

SULDAL LAKE—THE PORTAL.
(Page 57.)

know not, but ere we lose sight of him we see him clambering up a steep mountain-path with the precious pan on his back, and showing an agility quite wonderful for one of his years.

At Waage—a collection of scattered huts at the foot of a rough road—we take on board a party of young ladies, Norwegians, as neatly dressed as though they were going to church. They seem to have come down the path which leads over the mountain to the head of the Hylen fjord, the mouth of which we had seen at Sand. At a later stage of our journey, when we had taken once more to the road, these natty damsels suddenly stopped their car in the midst of a wild and desolate valley, then alighted, and dismissing their vehicle, ran up the mountain-side and mysteriously disappeared. It was a strange proceeding, for which we were utterly at a loss to account, as there was no sign of any human habitation within several miles of the spot.

From Waage we start again, and passing more ranges of rock, which seem to be inhabited by myriads of wild-fowl, we are confronted with what appears to be the most impenetrable mass of mountain that we have yet seen. Our vessel makes straight for it, and we know that it must have an opening somewhere, but for the life of us we cannot discover how we are to get through it. We make wild guesses as to this point and that, and at last decide that we are to penetrate through the very opposite corner to that which, at length, we actually traverse. We seem almost about to run into the rock, when a sharp turn of the wheel changes our course, and we find ourselves abreast of a strip of the shore, which shows an opening at the further end. Into this we steal, and sure enough there is plenty of room for us round the corner, and a wide stretch of water on the other side. And now Næsflaten appears in sight with its hotels and landing-stage, and here we are to alight, although the steamer goes some miles further up the lake.

CHAPTER VII.

THROUGH THE BRATLANDSDAL TO BREIFOND.

Næs is as common a local name in Norway as Sand or Vik. There are scores of them all over the country by the fjord or lake side. Næs, in fact, is synonymous with our Ness or Nose, and signifies a point of land on the shore. It is often compounded with some other name, as in the cases of Aandalsnæs, Veblungsnæs, and so forth. Næs in Suldal, as Næsflaten is usually called, lies in a perfect basin of mountains, and its surroundings are magnificent. The tourists seemed at last to have found their way thither, as there were several at the hotel where we stopped for refreshment. This was a new building by the lake side, but there is another and larger one further along the road, and indeed on every hand there are signs that Næs is being prepared to accommodate a much greater number of visitors than it has hitherto attracted. It must indeed be a lovely spot for a short stay, as it is evident at a glance that there are many opportunities for a delightful ramble in the neighbourhood. However, we had spent so much time at Sand that we could not afford to linger even in beautiful Næs. It was now nearly noon, and we decided to push on in the direction of the Hardanger country.

We were more fortunate in our choice of a *stolkjærre* this time, and were provided with a really sumptuous car with plush velvet cushions and excellent springs, and a handsome little horse. We were the more lucky in this respect, as there was a considerable demand for vehicles, and some of our fellow-travellers were not so well provided as ourselves. So we started in our comfortable trap up the hill over which the road passes from Næs, and approached one of those great mountain barriers which we had so often found in our path before. These mysterious gateways are always more or less fascinating on account of the surprises they give you when you have once passed their portals. But in this case we certainly had the greatest and most agreeable surprise that we had yet experienced.

We had but just entered the inevitable opening in the mountain mass when suddenly the Bratlandsdal burst upon us. And what, it may be asked, is the Bratlandsdal? Even those not unfamiliar with Norwegian scenery have confessed that they never heard of it. The fact is not surprising, for this gem of gems among the beauties of Norway is very little known. The Bratlandsdal is, then, a valley of great extent and surpassing loveliness, which winds for many miles on the way to the Hardanger. It has been open to carriage traffic

IN THE BRATLANDSDAL
(Page 62)

only within the last two years, for hitherto it could not be traversed except on horseback or foot over a rugged bridle-road. But the Government, sensible of its splendid opportunities as a tourist route, had the enterprise to cut a road through this fine valley.

Though the Bratlandsdal is everywhere beautiful, it is only in its first section and for a stretch of about a mile or so that it can be called wonderful. And the tremendous ravine which forms its gateway indeed deserves to be ranked among the chief marvels of Norway. As soon as we had passed that sudden opening in the rocks of which I have spoken, we found ourselves between two high walls shooting up to an altitude of some hundreds of feet, but presenting a passage so narrow that it was easy to throw a stone from the road and strike with it the opposite rock. Between this very narrow cleft rushed a river, whose waters, enormous in volume, were confined in so close a space that they were lashed into vast clouds of foam as they sped along. Their colour was of the deepest emerald with exquisite opalescent tints like the hues of an ice cave. Here and there they flowed through cavities only a few inches in width, and now and then they took leaps in magnificent cascades. And the walls of rock which rose above them on either hand were not gaunt and bare, but clothed with verdure to the very summit. In every cleft, and on every ledge, grew plants and small trees, forming natural hanging gardens of exquisite beauty. The well-made road crept along one side of the ravine, high above the roaring torrent, and we could see that it had been cut through the solid rock. Before it was made there could hardly have been foothold for a goat between the mountain-side and the river. Indeed, a little further along we found that the road had been continued under even greater difficulties. For here it was so excavated that the rock hung over our heads like a canopy. A few steps further and we came to a tunnel, for here it was necessary to cut through the rock for several yards. The tunnel forms a curious rugged grotto, the effects of the light at either end being very singular, and beyond it there are several places where the rock overhangs the road again, in one place presenting the outline of a gigantic nose.

The making of this rock-cut road must have been a work of great difficulty. In fact, it is said that the workmen had to be suspended by ropes from the top of the mountain in order to drill the sides for the necessary blasting operations. I am indebted to Mr. T. W. Barth, the Director-in-chief of the Department of Posts at Christiania, for some interesting information respecting the works, which he was kind enough to procure for me from the Department of Public Works.

From these particulars I draw two suggestive inferences. In the first place, the work has been done with remarkable celerity, and next, its cost has been surprisingly small. It will be seen from the figures

TUNNEL IN BRATLANDSDAL.
(Page 65.)

I am about to quote that the road was made at the rate of something under a mile a year, but this seems very fair progress when it is remembered that during the winter months, from October to March, there are only a very few hours of daylight in Norway. Again, I shall presently show that, if this be an example of Norwegian management, the Norsemen possess a capacity for keeping within their estimates, which many another nation might do well to emulate.

But to come to the facts. The road was commenced in 1879, and was not entirely completed until the spring of 1891, so that I was among the first travellers who traversed it. The entire length of the highway is 22 kilomètres, 162 mètres, of which 5 kilomètres, 951 mètres, lie in the *Amt*, or county, of Stavanger, and 16 kilomètres, 211 mètres in South Bergenhus—that is nearly 15 English miles. About one-half of this distance comprises the Bratlandsdal, the remainder lying for the most part along the shore of the Röldal lake. The Bratlandsdal extends from within a short distance of Næs to the village of Botten, and it is naturally in the first mile or so of this section that the most difficult part of the work is found. Some of the statistics with which I have been supplied are curious. Thus I am told that 50,385 cubic mètres of rock were 'mined out,' while 35,542 cubic mètres of masonry and stone work were used. The blasting operations consumed 7070 kilogrammes of dynamite, and 670 kegs of gunpowder. There were 52,700 metres of 'match' used, 51,700 caps, and 1430 electrical fuses, while the number of shots fired was 53,130.

The difficulty of the work will further be appreciated when it is stated that from Botten to Næs there is a rise of ground to the height of 300 metres, necessitating gradients of from 1 in 12 to 1 in 30. I may add that the breadth of the road varies in different places from 2·5 to 3·75 metres. The whole work was executed by the Government, and the accuracy with which its cost was calculated, is quite remarkable. The amount granted was 352,100 *kroner*, and the actual expenditure 352,780, so that the estimate was exceeded by only 680 *kroner*. Thus this excellent and valuable road, some of which, we have seen, was executed under the greatest difficulties, only cost about £20,000, or something like £1300 a mile. Yet, considering how cheap everything is in Norway, the labourers seem to have been fairly well paid, for I am told that the average earnings of the men employed on the works was 2 *kroner*, 18 *öre*, or about half-a-crown a day. The number of work days paid for was 122,063, so that about two-thirds of the entire cost must have gone in wages.

On the occasion of my first visit to the Bratlandsdal I drove through the valley with a companion, and therefore was unable thoroughly to appreciate the most wonderful part of it. It was a mere glimpse that we obtained in the very short time that we were in this majestic and lovely ravine, although the way was uphill and the pace comparatively slow. Future travellers must by all means avoid this mistake, and sending on their cars, *walk* from Næs to that point where the great chasm terminates. The distance is not much more than a mile, and the road, as I have said, is perfect. The most delicate lady could do this short stroll without the slightest fatigue. Moreover, it is a scene to be lingered over, for nothing like it will be witnessed in any other part of the country. I would advise any one starting from Næs to instruct his *skydsgut* to wait for him at the end of the pass, and to 'do' this surpassingly beautiful bit of the valley very leisurely indeed. For the sketcher it abounds in fine points, but it is difficult to photograph, owing to the narrowness of the ravine and the height of its walls. The accompanying illustrations give some idea of its beauty and grandeur, but it is impossible to realise these to the eye through the agency of the camera.

There is another reason why we should have done well to walk rather than drive through the Bratlandsdal. This journey developed a peculiarity of road-travelling in Norway which is not a little inconvenient. We did not suffer from it in our journey from Sand to Oset, for the reason that there were no other travellers going our way. But several *carrioles* and *stolkjærres* started at the same time from Næs, and formed a long procession through the valley. So closely did they march together that the nose of one horse all but touched the back of the next car, and in this order was the whole journey performed. This arrangement might appear a sociable one, as at any rate it enabled the *skydsguts* to get down and walk and chat together, but to the passengers it had the disadvantage of travelling in a crowd, and destroying the charm due to the solitude and quiet of the scenes around them. I found that this was no exceptional occurrence, but a regular practice. The *skydsguts* declare that they are not responsible for it, but that the horses like to keep together for the sake of company—which, of course, is very pretty and nice of the horses, but, apart from the other considerations I have mentioned, is not pleasant for the travellers on a dry breezy day : for to journey for miles through the clouds of dust thrown up by a dozen vehicles in front of you is not agreeable. We endured this infliction as best we could on the present occasion, but we were wiser and less forbearing in future, and, acting under the advice of more experienced tourists, insisted on our driver hanging back a little, and letting the other cars go forward. Even this device did not succeed at first, for we found our little horse putting on the pace of his own accord, and in a few minutes overtaking his nearest neighbour. So we had to order a very considerable detention to enable the next car to have a good start of us, and this plan was successful at last.

On my return to Norway in 1891 I traversed the Bratlandsdal from the opposite direction, that is from Röldal, and arranged to walk through the last section of the road. It is hard to say from which point the ravine is best approached. It is a glorious wind up for the day's journey to the Suldal; but, on the other hand, the startling suddenness with which you plunge into it from the Næs end gives the pleasing sensation of a surprise, though possibly I may have deprived my readers of this source of pleasurable excitement. However, approach it as he may, no traveller, I am sure, will be disappointed with this unique gem of Norwegian scenery.

The exit from this part of the Bratlandsdal is as sudden as the entrance thereto. A mass of rock seems to block up the glen, but the road winds round it in an abrupt curve, and the traveller finds himself in a wider but still very beautiful part of the valley. It is just round this corner that it would be advisable to have the cars kept in waiting, and hence there is nothing in the valley which need detain the tourist. Not but what the scenery is still very fine. The Bratlandsdal throughout its whole length is richly fertile, abounding in fine trees of many different kinds, and wealthy in ferns and wildflowers, while the outlines of the mountain-ranges are picturesque in form, and the valley is again and again shut in by huge barriers which open to present a new scene beyond. Thus you pass from one section to another until you reach the point where the river merges in a dark lake, the Lonevand, lying at the foot of a singular mass of glacier-polished rock. A little further on is the scattered group of blackened cottages which forms the village of Botten, and here the Bratlandsdal ends.

Nothing very noticeable came in sight during the remainder of that day's journey. The scenery, as I have said, grew less interesting after we had emerged from the Bratlandsdal, and indeed its comparative tameness afforded a welcome rest for the eye and mind, which had been dazzled and almost wearied by a succession of such scenes as the Suldal, the Suldal lake, and the Bratlandsdal had presented. It is a mistake to seek too much enjoyment of this kind in one day, and, besides, that perpetual craning of the neck to look up at lofty mountains, and endeavour to avoid missing any particularly picturesque bit, is very fatiguing. So we resolved to go no further than the next stage we should reach, although we were to arrive quite early in the afternoon.

That destination was Haare or Horre, situated on the Röldal lake, where, at an altitude of more than a thousand feet above the sea-level, stands the Breifond Hotel, a sanatorium much advertised and recommended. This establishment is capacious and clean, though rather new and raw in appearance; but, no doubt, before long it will be a very nice place. This, I believe, was its first season, and things had not yet got into shape. The attendants were very civil girls, who looked charming in their Hardanger costumes, the first we had seen.

There is a fine wild view from the terrace on which Breifond stands. The dark Röldal lake lies at the foot of ranges of gloomy mountains almost bare of trees, and in the plain, at its head, are scattered a number of isolated huts, cottages, and farm-houses, while small, bony cattle browse in the meadows. The scene reminded me of similar ones in Connemara, and there was an air of weird desolation about the country which was less pleasing than the picturesque solitudes I had previously surveyed. Röldal, it struck me, might have been the scene of some dismal tragedy like the massacre of Glencoe, though, I believe, there is nothing terrible in its history. The walk to the village of Röldal, which we took after supper, was, however, a pleasant one, and the repose of the whole place was welcome after our long day's journey.

Many of the cottages about here are very prettily adorned. Their roofs are thatched, and the dust and mould they accumulate upon their surfaces give growth to wild-flowers, and even small shrubs and trees. Some of these roofs are completely carpeted all over with wild pansies, presenting beautiful masses of blue and yellow in the light of the sun. I noticed the same pretty sight in many other parts of Norway. Elsewhere corn and grass grow on the cottage roofs, and are regularly reaped by the inmates.

Breifond is, perhaps, as proud of its 'wooden walls' as England used to be, and certainly these are very much in evidence. It smells all over of the new pine—not, to my taste, an unpleasant odour—but there is nothing to relieve the bareness of the walls or floors—no papering, no carpets, no curtains. The bedrooms seemed to me like those of an hospital or a barrack; but this implies, of course, that they were perfectly clean and neat. I slept well enough in one of them, and rose the next morning refreshed, and ready to enjoy the luxury of a pipe after breakfast under the ample verandah before the hotel, which commands a fine view of the lake. My companion and I had ordered a *stolkjærre* to be reserved for us, so I could afford to amuse myself by looking on while our fellow-travellers took their departure, some of these going off in large and apparently comfortable four-wheeled *trilles* drawn by two horses, and others in two-wheeled cars.

CHAPTER VIII.

A DRIVE TO THE HARDANGER.

We started at 10 A.M., the weather being still as bright and sunny as before. Breifond and Haare, as I have said, stand at an elevation of more than a thousand feet above the sea, but the mountain road behind them rises to a much greater height. The Horrabrækker, as it is called, is well made, and ascends very gradually in snake-like bends almost as sharp as those of the Furka Pass. Although we took our seats in the *stolkjærre* at starting, we soon perceived that a walk over the grass would be more agreeable, while relieving the little slow-creeping horse of the bulk of his burden. So we alighted and pushed on, taking here and there a short cut across the windings of the road, which, as we looked back, lay like a coiled ribbon upon the ground behind us. Finer views of the lake and valley we had left were developed, of course, as we ascended, but the scene around us was of the most savage and desolate character. Hardly a tree was in sight; the mountain-side was boggy and barren, and strewn with stones and boulders, and to right and left rose mighty crags, grey and cold even in the sunshine. It was not a beautiful scene, but it was one that had a certain air of gloomy grandeur, and was thus full of romantic charm. Not a human being or habitation did we pass during our long walk, and we enjoyed all the advantage of having allowed preceding travellers to get well on ahead.

After a time my companion and I took different paths, always keeping the road well in sight, and I greatly enjoyed the solitude of this wild ramble. Snow in more or less large patches had been visible from below, and some of these I gradually approached, and at last reached. They lay scattered in hollows of the valley, and presently I came upon huge mounds of snow which had evidently not long before been cleared away from the road and lay piled up in heaps on either side. They formed hard granulated masses, and were but slowly melting even under the hot sun that beat upon them. In due course I found myself on a level part of the road, and perceived that I had reached the summit of the Horrabrækker, which there attains a height of some 3400 feet above the sea. So I seated myself by the roadside and awaited the arrival of my fellow-traveller and our car.

Remounting the *stolkjærre* we now commenced the downward journey, and soon found ourselves in a deep, narrow ravine, as savage as the scene we had just left, but more picturesque. Far below us we saw the beginnings of the river which we were

THE HORRABRÆKKER, NEAR RÖLDAL.
(Page 73.)

to skirt all the way to the Hardanger, and which increased in volume at almost every step as it was joined by the torrents that descended from the mountains, sometimes in really fine cascades. The valley, too, became more thickly wooded as we progressed, and the distant views gained in beauty by contrast with the green foreground. Here we passed two or three fosses, or waterfalls, of more than usual magnitude. All of them descended from the opposite side of the valley, and some of them were of sufficient importance to have names of their own. The Espelandsfos, from its picturesque surroundings, and the great body of water it discharges, appeared to be the finest of these, but there were several of almost equal beauty.

And now, after a journey of about four hours, we came to Seljestad, a village situated on the slope of the road, and having two neat little inns, at one of which we stayed to dine and change horses. We had a nice dinner, and were waited on by a bright, cheerful young woman, who spoke German, a rare accomplishment among the trading folk in Norway. Then we resumed our journey, and once more were gratified with the sight of a really magnificent scene.

Within a mile or two of Seljestad we may be said to enter the valley which belongs to the Hardanger district. This, clothed thickly with forest of fir, pine, alder, and birch, and presenting combinations of wood and rock of surpassing loveliness, is hardly to be exceeded by any scene of its kind in Norway.

From the higher ground, too, one gets a view of the wonderful Folgefond, that vast field of snow and ice which spreads over the table-land upon the summits of the mountains that overhang the Hardanger. It was a mere glimpse that we obtained of the great frozen plateau, but the spectacle of this brilliant white fringe above the grey and the green greatly enhanced the beauty of the landscape. Down, down in many windings, the road twisted and turned, through the woods and above the roaring river, till it reached ground level enough to allow it to pursue a tolerably straight course.

And now we came upon quite the finest waterfall we had yet seen. Immediately to our right, and in the depths of a dark ravine, fell the splendid Laatefos (pronounced Lotefos). We could see its spray rising in volumes of cloud, and sailing across the road long before we reached it; and when it came fully in sight we stopped the car to survey it at leisure. The fall descends from a great height in one leap, and then spreads over the rocks beneath, breaking up into separate cascades, widening in their area as they approach the channel which carries the waters away to the river below. It is a sight worth dwelling upon, a spot that one would wish to linger over for many an hour. It is a favourite drive to this place from Odde, and there is a small hotel here for those who wish to spend some time in this delightful region. The Laatefos is not one of the greatest

THE LAATEFOS.
(Page 76.)

waterfalls of Norway, but it is one of the most beautiful, and its convenient situation by the very roadside will be regarded as an advantage by those who do not care to take the trouble of penetrating long miles into the heart of the mountains and scrambling along the brink of terrific precipices in order to see Norway's grandest fosses.

Ever lovely is the valley still as we get nearer and nearer to Odde. Soon we come to a fine lake, the Sandvensvand, which the road skirts all the way. Across it we presently perceive the gap, at the further end of which descends one of the many glaciers from the Folgefond, the Buarbræ. It seems but a short distance away, and we wonder to find such a mass of ice on so low a level. But as I had an opportunity of examining the Buarbræ more closely on a subsequent occasion, I will say no more about it at present. At the end of the Sandvensvand there is a hilly barrier of no great height, crested with woods, and over this the road passes. Soon we are at its summit, and now for the first time the great and famous Hardanger fjord bursts into sight.

Properly speaking, it is not the Hardanger, but a branch of it bearing the local name of the Sör fjord. However, it is really a continuation of the Hardanger, and Odde is the most distant point of that mighty arm of the sea, the second in magnitude in Norway, which, joining the ocean at Bergen, winds for some eighty or ninety miles through the heart of the country, throwing off many branches in different directions, and constituting a very maze or labyrinth of waters, whose depth in many places almost equals the heights of the mountains above them.

I do not profess in these pages to go into questions of physical geography. For those who desire to study the economy of glaciers and volcanoes, and ascertain how the coast of Norway came to be thus rent and riven; how the stormy ocean found these quiet resting-places in the heart of the mountains, and all the other marvellous secrets of Nature's work in Norway—are there not a multitude of easily accessible treatises and handbooks that will tell the wondrous story far better than I can? I know it is the habit of those who write books of travel to pillage freely the works of their scientific predecessors, and bring down the information thus gleaned to what they regard as the level of the intelligence of their readers. But it is not my purpose to write an 'instructive' book about Norway. I have nothing to tell my readers on the subjects of geology, history, legend, or archæology; I only profess to give them some *impressions de voyage*, hoping to recall familiar scenes to those who have already travelled in Norway, and to throw out some useful hints to those who have that pleasure yet to come.

Still, no one who surveys the Hardanger for the first time, reflecting that he is standing at a point so far from the open sea, and that the sea yet lies at his feet, can fail to be impressed by the wonder and the strangeness of the situation. There is no parallel or likeness to it in any other part of Europe, and herein consists the peculiar charm and romance of Nature in Norway. The scenery cannot be compared with that of Switzerland and the Tyrol: its character is absolutely unique. An old friend, unhappily deceased, the late accomplished journalist, Edward Spender, has described the general characteristics of Norwegian scenery in language at once so eloquent and so true that I cannot do better than quote his words:—

'There are,' he writes, 'fine mountains in Switzerland, but there is nowhere else such a combination of mountain and ocean; nowhere else in Europe does the snow-clad peak rise directly out of the sea; nowhere else will the traveller find that most distinguishing feature of Norway, the Fjord, guarded at its entrance by a breakwater of islands; winding inland through forest-clad hills where the silver birch gleams amidst the sombre pines, and at whose feet lie the greenest of green pastures, dotted with quaint houses; forcing its way further still through the ever-narrowing gorges, down whose sides plunge, at one leap, countless torrents fed from the great ice-fields overhead. Nowhere else in Europe is there such a country of waterfalls as this, . . . cataracts of tremendous volume and force, far away up among the mountains, requiring perhaps a whole day's journey to reach them. Above all, nowhere are there such sunsets as in the country of which we are speaking. The memory of one night in Norway makes one feel how powerless language is to describe the splendour of that evening glory of carmine and orange and indigo, which floods not only the heavens, but the sea, and makes the waves beneath our keel a "flash of living fire." Language cannot paint that wonderful mystic light, so unspeakably soft and tender, which travels round the northern horizon from west to east, so that one cannot tell where night ends or day begins.'

CHAPTER IX.

ODDE AND ITS 'LIONS.'

Odde, which now comes in sight between us and the fjord, has a picturesque appearance, surrounded by a frame of wood and rock. At the further end of a stretch of meadows there is a cluster of neat wooden houses, and a church spire rising from the midst of them, and beyond are the dark waters of the fjord, with what looks like an island in the middle, but is really a promontory or peninsula connected with the left shore, while the lake-like water is overshadowed by great mountain spurs, whose summits are fringed with patches of snow, and whose sides are thinly clothed with woods of pine and fir.

It is a beautiful spot, much resorted to by visitors, and may be regarded as the Interlaken of Norway. Here, in fact, we were entering what is recognised as the regular tourist track, and many of the scenes I have hereafter to describe will doubtless be familiar to most readers who have visited Western Norway. Odde is generally approached from Bergen —a long voyage by steamer, which can be accomplished, by the vessels that do not stop at many stations, in about thirteen hours. This route, no doubt, is well worth travelling. In fact, it is impossible to form an adequate idea of the grandeur of the Hardanger without seeing the scenery of the whole fjord—that which lies between Odde and Eide being not nearly so fine as much of the country between Eide and Bergen. But one cannot do everything, and according to my present plan it will be necessary to reserve what may be called the Bergen side of the Hardanger for a future occasion. By starting at once from Bergen the traveller misses the magnificent scenery between Stavanger and Odde, and, besides, has to go all the way back again as far as Eide if he is bound for the north. Beyond all question Odde is best approached by the Stavanger and Suldal route.

There is one first-class hotel at Odde, the Hardanger, admirably managed, and several smaller ones, all of which are homely and comfortable. I chose Præstegaarde's, which has a charming lookout on the fjord. When I visited Odde again I put up at the more luxurious Hardanger. Indeed this hotel is so much frequented by British travellers that the proprietor is said to be, in the busy season, by no means desirous of entertaining his own countrymen. In the height of the summer Odde is sometimes inconveniently crowded, but I was fortunate not to find it so.

It was Sunday, and there was a considerable influx of people from the neighbouring villages all attired

ODDE AND THE SORFJORD.

in their best, and thus we had a good display of the pretty Hardanger costume. Only the women, however, showed anything characteristic in their attire, being dressed in gowns of dark blue or black, with white chemisettes crossed by gaily-coloured bodices embroidered with bead-work, and with bands of coloured cloth passing over the shoulders and down to the waist-belt, while on their heads they bore white caps folded in different shapes, some broad and some narrow at the top, and both with long lappets. A number of them thus attired formed picturesque groups, whether sitting by the roadside or promenading the one main thoroughfare of the village.

There are a few shops at Odde, but all were closed; yet there was a brightness and gaiety in the life of the place, contrasting pleasantly with the Sunday dulness to which we Britons are accustomed at home. And here let me say a word on the subject of Sunday in Norway, which I hope may be found suggestive and instructive. There is perhaps no more sincerely and fervently religious people to be found in Europe than the Norwegians. They are strict Protestants, as a rule, of the Lutheran Church, and are exemplary in their attendance at public worship and in the study of their faith. Confirmation is regarded in Norway as a peculiarly important rite, and indeed it is often held as a *sine qua non* that any applicant for a situation in domestic service should have been confirmed. The Norwegians not only go to church, but are most devout in their behaviour there, and in the more out of the way parts of the country will travel long miles by sea and land to reach their favourite place of worship. But no such thing is known in the land as that sour, narrow Sabbatarianism which we find in England and Scotland. The Norwegian thinks it no harm to amuse himself and be cheerful on the Sabbath Day, and do any necessary work that may be called for. We had been in doubt at first whether it would be possible to continue our journey on that Sunday, but were at once assured there would be no difficulty in the matter. Vehicles were let for hire just the same as usual, and the *skydsgut* recognised the sanctity of the day only by appearing rather better dressed than at other times.

On the following morning the few shops of Odde were opened. There are not many of them, but they include two or three of some pretensions, established for the purpose of tempting the tourist to purchase and carry away with him souvenirs of the country. And in the matter of ingenious knick-knacks, and more useful commodities representative of the produce and industry of the land, Norway is not less prolific than Switzerland. It must indeed in justice be said that the articles offered for sale to the foreigner are by no means rubbish, and in general are well worth the not extravagant prices charged for them. There are thousands of different sorts of pretty and curious objects carved in wood, and the national pocket-knife, which has a character of its own, has always a handle or sheath, also elaborately and tastefully carved. Then there are the costume dolls of all sizes and prices, some got up as Norwegian brides in their showy paraphernalia, and toys representing *carrioles* and *stolkjærres*, sledges, *sæters* and *staburs*. The Norwegian jewellery, both of the ancient and modern imitation sort, is very pretty and characteristic, especially the double brooches, with their quaint pendants, and these are made of the silver which abounds in the country. More serviceable presents are to be found in the splendid skins of bear, wolf, fox, seal, lynx, wildcat, and other native animals, while the supply of photographs of beautiful scenes in Norway is fairly bewildering in its quantity and diversity. At every principal station in Norway a variety shop of this sort is to be found, and it must fairly be admitted that in no country in Europe is the tourist more legitimately tempted to spend money on beautiful or curious things. Those who desire to carry away such souvenirs of Norway would do well to spread their purchases over several different places, so as to give each a fair share of custom, for I speak from experience when I say that I never found a more honest set of dealers than the Norwegian shopkeepers. As a rule, all prices are marked on the articles, and it is very rarely indeed that a smaller sum than that originally asked is accepted anywhere.

Most people spend at least two or three days at Odde, as it is a good centre for excursions. The favourite drive to Seljestad we had already done in the opposite direction, but there are two expeditions from Odde to be made, one of which at least is among the most notable in Norway. This is a visit to the Skjæggedal (pronounced Stcheggedal) foss, a waterfall of such stupendous dimensions that it is said to make almost as imposing an impression on the mind of the spectator as Niagara itself. Whether it merits this comparison is a question to be decided by those who have seen both falls, but it seems to be pretty generally conceded that the Skjæggedal foss is quite the finest in Norway, and therefore in Europe. But a visit to these great waterfalls is no easy matter. All those of the first magnitude lie far away up in the heart of the mountains, and in every case a long and fatiguing day's journey is necessary to get at them. Whether the spectacle is worth the trouble that must be taken by those who wish to enjoy it is a question for the traveller to consider. But every one who wishes to see the Skjæggedal, the Vöring, the Vetti, and the Rjukan fosses must bear in mind that he has in every case a very rough scramble before him, and that a considerable part of it, and that the most difficult, has to be done on foot.

The expedition to the Skjæggedal foss begins with a trip by boat to a place called Tyssedal, to the right of the fjord from Odde. There the passengers land, and thence they have to climb up the mountain-side and then down by a rough path till they come to the Skjæggedal farm. It is a long and laborious ascent and descent, occupying three or four hours, and in parts slippery rocks have to be traversed, though the difficulty and danger of these places have been diminished by the provision of planks or logs, which give a better foothold to the pedestrian. From the farm you are ferried across the small Vetlevand, and thence there is a short walk to the Ringedal lake, where a boat awaits you, and in this you are rowed for nearly two hours, till you come to the great gorge, in which the fall is found. The greatest leap of the water, which descends in vast volume, and clears, in its impetuous bound, the ledge of rocks from which several other cascades overflow, has been variously estimated at from four to seven hundred feet. It reaches at last a lower plateau, whence it rebounds in great clouds of spray, and from that point it falls over another precipice, and finally plunges into the bed of the river, to rush on further in foaming torrents to the lake below. The gloomy surroundings of the foss, as well as the stupendous character of the fall itself, render the Skjæggedal the most imposing sight of its kind in Norway. It has also a neighbour, called the Tyssestrængene, a twin fall which descends in two parallel streaks. It is very fine, and can be easily reached in the same expedition. The journey to the Skjæggedal and back occupies the whole day of about twelve hours, and is rather hard work.

The other 'lion' of the Odde district is the Buarbræ, of which I have already made mention. It is a charming trip to this place, and, unlike the visit to the Skjæggedal, is unattended with difficulty or fatigue. There is a little steam-launch on the Sandvens lake, which keeps plying backwards and forwards to Buar incessantly all day long, whether it has passengers or not. I was much surprised at the restless activity of this tiny craft, which takes so much trouble to do so little, for the run across the lake occupies only ten minutes, and I wondered it did not at least vary the monotony of its proceedings by making a tour round the lake. I could not discover, however, any solution of the mystery of its energy, which certainly seemed to be sadly wasted. On the occasion of my visit to the Buar valley I was the sole passenger both going and returning, and as the double fare was only a *krone*, I am afraid I could hardly have paid for the coal consumed on the voyage.

The village of Buar consists of a small group of farm-houses and cottages, through which you have to pass to the road up the valley. As there were two or three different paths, I accosted one of the inhabitants, a peasant-girl, who was standing at the door of a cottage, engaged in knitting. I had not spoken, and only made a sign with my hand, by way of asking her to show me which turning I was to take. She immediately pointed to the path to my right, and then I saw that she was blind. I suppose she must have recognised me as a stranger and a traveller by my step. The people of Buar, indeed, are used to visitors, and have not always been so ready to oblige them as this poor blind girl was in my case. In fact, in this same village, so I afterwards learned, an attempt at imposition was made some time ago, a trifling toll being demanded from visitors for the privilege of passing through the place. This, it appears, was quite illegal, and a complaint being made about it to the *Lendsman*, or chief constable, of the locality, it was promptly put a stop to. The beauties of nature in Norway are always exhibited strictly on the 'no fees' system, except in one or two instances, where expensive approaches have been made to some of the waterfalls, and small tolls are levied to cover the cost.

The Buar is a very pretty narrow valley, traversed by a magnificent stream, which falls in many places in splendid cascades. It is richly timbered, and appears shorter than it really is. The glacier faces you as you enter the glen, and is nearly always in sight, growing, of course, more imposing in appearance as you approach it. But the distance to this outflow of the great Folgefond is longer than it seems, though not so long after all. The walk by the river-side and through the lovely woods is a delightful ramble, though the path here and there is rather rough. The stream is crossed at several points by rustic bridges, and from these there are charming views of the lake on the one hand and the glacier on the other. As you near the latter, a very fine fall comes tumbling down from the mountains, and makes a noble cataract in the river itself; then you pass through a gate into a fertile meadow and find yourself at the foot of a hill, at the summit of which is perched a refreshment house.

It is as great a mystery as the movements of the steam-launch why nothing more substantial is supplied at this restaurant than bread and butter, cheese and eggs, beer, aerated waters, and milk. Surely there could be hardly a pleasanter spot for a picnic party than this, and the good folks who keep the restaurant might find it to their profit to provide visitors, of whom a large number must often come from Odde, with a more liberal meal. But so it is in Norway: although the people generally show themselves intelligently sensible to the advantages of attracting tourists, yet here and there they display a curious lack of enterprise.

The Buarbræ is a handsome bit of glacier, but is not of very vast dimensions, and is not likely to impress greatly those who have seen larger masses of the frozen rivers and seas of ice elsewhere. Its advantage is that it is so easily accessible, and as a specimen of the wonders of the Folgefond it is decidedly interesting. It stands a massive barrier,

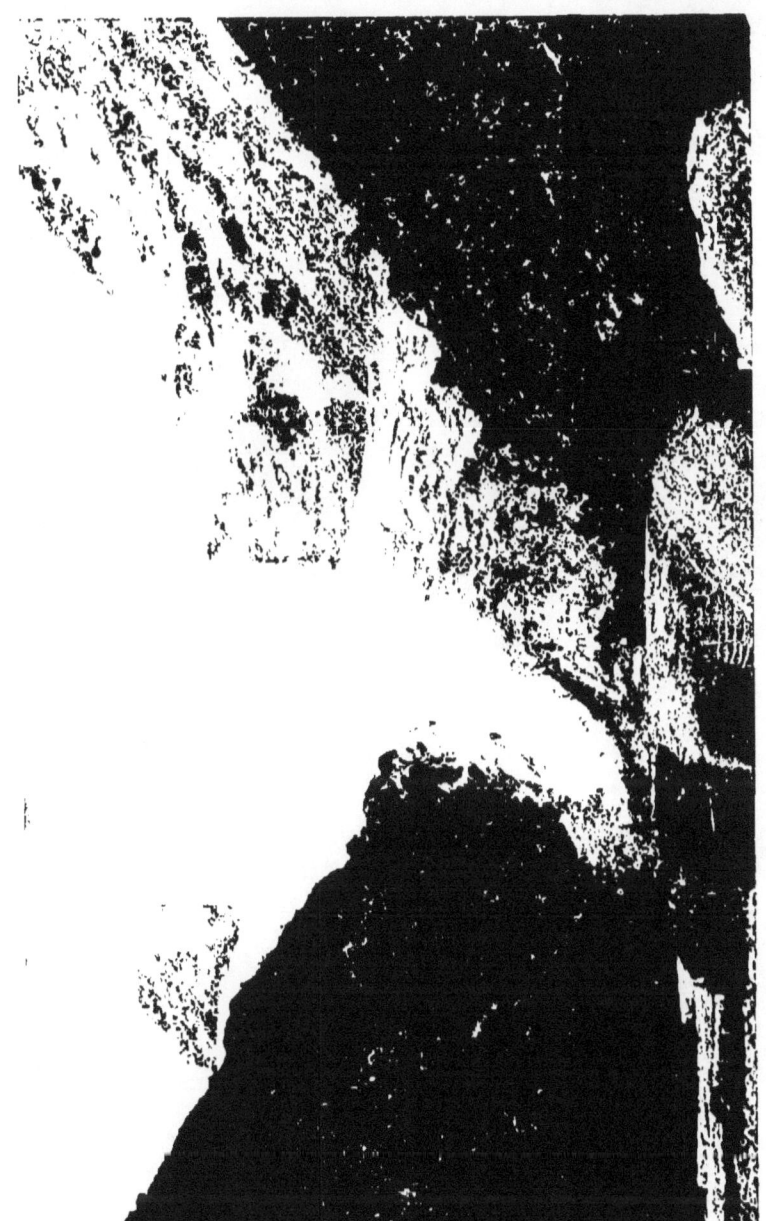

BUARBRÆ.

affording a delicious but dangerous coolness on a hot day, blocking up the head of the valley, and allows good opportunities for a scramble up its side, though it is necessary to be careful in performing such feats, as great lumps of the glacier sometimes break loose. There are wonderful ice-caves to be found in its front, especially that deep blue tunnel through which the river flows. The glacier itself is slowly descending into the valley, and has advanced many feet of late years, destroying several habitations and much pasture-land. Active travellers, used to mountaineering, make the Buarbræ a starting-point for excursions on the Folgefond, which spreads its snows far and wide above it.

I spent some time at the glacier, and in the valley on my way back, as the latter especially is a delightful lounge, and I found it very pleasant to lie on the grass and among the ferns under the shade of a tree, watching the leaping waters of the river, and listening to their roar. The Buar, too, is full of song-birds, and altogether a more delicious place for spending a lazy summer afternoon could hardly be imagined.

CHAPTER X.

SLEDGING ACROSS THE FOLGEFOND.

WHILE visiting Odde the more able-bodied and enterprising of the tourists that assemble there would do well to undertake an expedition more interesting even than the journey to the Skjæggedalsfos. The guide-books tell us that it is practicable to cross the Folgefond in sledges provided for that purpose by the Norwegian Tourist Club, but they do not vouchsafe much information on the subject. Yet it is very desirable to know how this expedition is to be performed, as it is not quite so easy as it may look. The sledging is the most enjoyable but the briefest portion of the journey, and there is a good deal of rough work to be done before the undertaking can be accomplished.

The usual starting place for this journey is Sundal on the Mauranger fjord, a branch of the Hardanger, at which the steamers plying between Bergen and Odde touch twice a week each way, viz., on Sundays and Fridays from Bergen, and on Mondays and Saturdays from Odde, arriving there from either place about 1 or 1.30 p.m. But it is necessary to make the start from Sundal as there is no means of getting across the Folgefond from Odde except on foot. For the sledges are kept on the Sundal side, and unless you happen to hear at Odde, from news brought by the steamer, that travellers are crossing, and you hit the right moment when the sledges have arrived, these vehicles are not available. Perhaps some day the popularity of the route may induce the Tourist Club to station sledges on the Odde side, thereby enabling the traveller to cross to Sundal without having to return to Odde.

Meanwhile, as I have said, if you wish to cross the Folgefond in these carriages you must first get to Sundal by steamer. It is a beautiful voyage both from Bergen and Odde, in which the grandest portions of the Hardanger are seen, and the scenery, as the Maurauger is approached, perhaps displays the most picturesque grouping of high mountains on the great fjord. I myself reached Sundal from Bergen, to which I had proceeded from Stavanger, on my way from Telemarken and the Suldal during my second visit to Norway. But, to bring the journey within the compass of the route I am now describing, the start must be made from Odde. The steamer leaves at 6 a.m., and the voyage to Sundal occupies seven or eight hours.

Thus you arrive at Sundal at dinner time, and a fairly satisfactory meal is to be obtained at a neat little hotel there by the fjord side. But do not depend upon Sundal for provisions for the Folgefond expedition. The party of which I was one, found the supplies furnished to us at that place by no means satisfactory. They consisted mainly of meat and cheese sandwiches, the bread of which was of the coarser sort, together with such comestibles as smoked salmon and tinned viands, good enough no doubt when you can get nothing else, but not to be put up with when all the larders of civilised Odde are at command. My advice, therefore, is to take an abundant supply of good food from Odde, for it will be needed before the journey is over.

The next point to be considered is the choice of a guide, as a guide is absolutely necessary. I had happened to meet on board the boat a German gentleman who had made the passage of the Folgefond, and kindly volunteered some useful information with regard to it. Among the rest he told me that we should find at Sundal or at Gjerde, not far off, a guide duly accredited and recommended by the Tourist Club, and by name Godtskalk. He was a capital fellow, said the German, and the best man to employ. It might be necessary to go and seek him at his home, Gjerde, a village at the head of the Mauranger fjord, and if so we should have to take a boat to that place. As luck would have it, Mr. Godtskalk happened to be on the quay at Sundal looking out for a job. He could not speak English, but he produced a little book containing his testimonials and the *cachet* of the Tourist Club, which of course constituted ample credentials.

They tell you that the journey from Sundal across the mountains to Odde can be done in ten or eleven hours. Probably very active mountaineers may do it in that or less time, but ordinary travellers may reckon that it will take them quite twelve hours to make the passage if they do it all at once. But such a course is, I think, not at all desirable. Remember, in the first place, that you do not arrive at Sundal till 1 or 1.30 p.m. You must then have dinner. This will occupy at least an hour, so that, with other preparations, the start cannot be made much before 3 p.m. When the sun is shining this is the hottest part of the day, and a very stiff climb is before you. In any case, if you start at 3 o'clock you cannot get to Odde till the same hour the next morning, and therefore you would have to cross the snow-field in darkness or semi-darkness. There is an alternative in remaining at Sundal for the night, and starting early the next morning. It is a beautiful place, and the afternoon might be well spent on the fjord or in a trip to the Bondhus glacier, if you are equal to the labour of such an excursion with the Folgefond to follow.

I cannot help thinking, however, that the best plan is that which we adopted. About half-way on the route there is a hut, with sleeping accommodation, provided by the Tourist Club, and we decided to break the journey and pass the night there. By taking this course, we were enabled to start in the cool of the evening and rest before resuming our travels. Having carried out this plan and found it in every way successful, I recommend it to others. So much preliminary information is necessary, and I will now proceed to describe how I crossed the great snow-field.

I had joined a party collected in a very haphazard manner. We were all strangers to one another till we formed the common plan afterwards carried out. I happened to mention my design to a fellow-traveller on board the boat from Bergen. He offered to go with me, and I assured him that I should be glad of his company. Then he in his turn spoke of our intended journey to a third, who asked and received permission to join us. A fourth was picked up in the same way, and the most valuable member of the party was a young Norwegian, a Christiania student, to whose useful services as interpreter we were much indebted. Geographically considered, we were a very mixed and representative band, as one hailed from London, another from Newcastle, the third was from Bristol, the fourth from Edinburgh, while the fifth was, so to speak, 'on his native heath,' and a more congenial set of comrades could hardly be found; at any rate, such was my view of the company I was in.

'Nansen' was the hero of the expedition. No, not Nansen the great Arctic explorer, but the ingenuous youth from Christiania, whom one of us playfully nicknamed after the famous traveller. He was so called on account of his daringly adventurous disposition. 'Nansen' was for ever wandering from the right path and getting himself into difficulties. He was always ahead of everybody else, and when he was so everybody was anxious. But, as I have said, 'Nansen' was very useful, besides being a gay, light-hearted young fellow who kept us amused all the way, for, speaking English fairly well, he acted as our mouthpiece when the guide had to be communicated with.

Godtskalk himself was a fine fellow. Tall, with broad shoulders and strong limbs, with an open, honest face and rugged ruddy beard, he was quite a model mountain guide in appearance, while his carefulness, his patience, and his readiness of resource completed his character in that capacity.

At 7 p.m. we were ready to start, and we began our journey with a short trip by boat to the head of the fjord. There we landed at Gjerde, a cluster of dark pine-wood cottages, in one of which we rested while our guide completed his preparations. We mounted a ladder-like staircase to an upper room containing a bed or two and some gaudily-painted cabinets, and were refreshed with real Norwegian peasants' beer, drinking it from a wooden bowl, the outer rim of which bore the inscription, 'En skaal for Folgefonden. Godtskalk Andersen, 1891.' This vessel, in fact, was the property of our honest guide, who had provided it in order that his patrons might drink the health of the mighty giant whose territories they were about to invade. The liquor it contained was doubtless as honest as himself, but, unhappily, we were not educated up to its virtues. It was very wholesome, I am sure, but it was also very brown and very thick, and had a sort of sweet-sour flavour which could only be appreciated by those to the manner born.

There seemed to be a good deal to do before we could fairly get on the march, for our guide made many mysterious disappearances and held many incomprehensible conferences with his fellow-villagers. But at last Godtskalk was ready, and so were the two lads, his sons, who were going to carry our traps and wraps, while their father burdened himself with the provisions. The good folks of Gjerde gathered about in groups, looking grave and stolid as the Norwegian peasants always do, but evidently regarding the expedition as an object of no ordinary interest. As we passed, they signified a quietly civil farewell, the men lifting their hats, but there was none of that noisy demonstration of leave-taking which one is accustomed to elsewhere. Even the village boys had not a cheer in them.

Once clear of the village, our route lay through a few fields traversed by a roaring torrent, which, as we proceeded, broke over the rocks in fine cascades. Then we entered a wood and, on emerging, found ourselves in full view of a really magnificent waterfall, the Sondefos, tumbling from a great height and throwing up clouds of spray through which it was evident we should have to pass, for a wooden bridge spanned the torrent at this point, and the rebound of the foss threw up an ascending shower right across it. The more careful of the party put on their waterproofs, while the others prepared to rush through the watery veil, but a slight wetting on so warm a day was refreshing rather than otherwise.

We were now in the centre of a tremendous amphitheatre, the walls of which rose before us and on either side almost perpendicularly to a height of some two or three thousand feet. How these terrific precipices were to be climbed it was impossible for the moment to foresee, but our guide soon showed us the way, and, rough and rugged as the path was, it presented no difficulty. The ascent, however, was very steep, and frequent stoppages for rest were found necessary. All the way the great waterfall was kept in view, presenting an increasingly grand appearance as we ascended. Its height in one leap could not be less than five hundred feet. Presently we reached more level ground, and looked down upon the dark gorge through which we had passed to the spot where the Mauranger fjord lay green and gleaming in the distance. Before us rose another tier of precipices, and again it was impossible to tell by what path we should advance. Assuredly a guide was necessary in such a place, as the track was very faintly indicated and easily lost.

It was here that 'Nansen' distinguished himself. He was always ahead, as I have said before, but now he was out of sight. We had reached a sort of plateau and could see the land around for many acres, but no 'Nansen' was visible. The guide paused and looked about him, but with no result. Presently he raised a shrill cry, but there was no response. Then he took counsel with his lads, and from the direction in which they turned their gaze it was evident that they suspected that the intrepid 'Nansen' had gone wrong—that he had, in fact, climbed those huge perpendicular walls in front of us and disappeared. Shout after shout was raised, and, at last, an answer was heard; and then, to our unbounded astonishment, there we saw, on the very brink of the highest precipice, standing a mere tiny dark speck out against the sky, a moving figure. It was 'Nansen,' perched up at an altitude of a thousand feet above our heads in a place where he had no business to be at all. There was more shouting and signalling between our guides and the lost explorer. Then one of the lads was sent after him, and as he did not return, Godtskalk motioned to us to be seated, and made off up the mountain in search of the missing ones. It was an unwelcome detention, as it was growing late and the sun was declining, so as we sprawled upon the grass we all cursed 'Nansen' very heartily and vowed to give him a piece of our joint minds when we should get him back. But anger was lost in laughter when, at last, we saw the erratic Norseman come bounding down the mountain-side, waving his arms and shouting, with comical irrelevance, 'Rule Britannia!' The gay-hearted young fellow had added an unnecessary thousand feet to his day's climbing, but he seemed to think nothing of it, and he apologised for his truancy with such charming frankness that it was impossible to be angry with him.

Once more *en route*, we marched along the mountain-side under what may be termed a screen of rock, at the further end of which it was plain that we should have to make a bend to the right. Sure enough, after a short walk we suddenly came to a turning, and, this being rounded, we found ourselves on a novel and rather startling scene. We had reached the head of that mighty waterfall, the Sondefos, beside which we had been so long climbing, and at our feet the waters that supplied it roared and rushed in enormous volume, emerging from a lake which we descried not far distant, and which received the waters of another and smaller fall. This raging torrent crossed our path, and it was not without some hesitation that we contemplated the task of traversing it. There were but a few slippery rocks to give us passage to the middle of the stream, and thence there was a plank bridge to the other side. One by one we stepped across with care, for a slip of the foot must have been death, as no one once in that boiling flood could have been saved. In an instant he must have been drawn into the great waterfall and dashed to pieces in the gulf five hundred feet below.

But Godtskalk was very careful and handed us across in safety. Then we traversed the plank bridge and reached the other side. There was, however, but little foothold here—only a few inches of ground between the wall of rock beyond and the roaring stream. We crept along this narrow path and soon reached more open ground. It was all over in a very few minutes, but it was certainly the 'nastiest' bit in the day's march, and rendered the more formidable by the growing dusk. A halt was now called, for we were by the lake side, and it was necessary to traverse this piece of water by boat. It was to find this boat that our guide and the enterprising 'Nansen' now left us, and I believe they had to wade up to their knees along the margin of the lake to seek the boat. It was not long before they returned, and then the whole party embarked. After a short row we reached the point of landing, and there we saw before us a wild, desolate valley, strewn with huge boulders, and not far off, to our great satisfaction, the bourne of our day's journey, the Tourist Hut.

It is a small, plain wooden building standing in a sheltered corner of the valley, and divided into two rooms, one of which contains two large beds and the other a single very long one. The former is generally used by travellers, the latter by the guides, but there is no difference in the character of their fittings. A plain wooden table and a few chairs constitute their sole furniture, besides the beds; there are hooks on the walls to hang things on, and a stove for cooking and warmth. A few necessaries are left for the use of travellers, such as plates, knives, and forks, towels, and so forth, and some slender supplies of tinned meats are also provided for those who need them, it being understood that visitors shall assess themselves for the victuals they consume and leave the money with the guides. There is something roughly graceful in this careless hospitality, and I hope that no one ever takes unfair advantage of it. Not many people seem to have visited the hut as yet. A few names are scribbled on the pine-wood walls, and here and there some traveller, desiring to be remembered, has attached his visiting card to the planks with a pin.

We were a merry party and enjoyed our impromptu supper, eaten off table-cloths of newspaper, with the grog and beer we had brought with us drunk out of tumblers and cups which we had to use in turn. 'Nansen' was in high spirits, and, in spite of his delinquencies, in high favour. He sang songs and proposed toasts, and took with the greatest good humour our attempts to bewilder him with English colloquialisms and slang. It was not till past one in the morning that we thought of 'turning in,' and then the dim light of early dawn, differing little from the gleam of twilight which had preceded it, stole in through the one window of the hut. We slept more or less well, and awoke at six o'clock on a dull grey morning which promised ill for the remainder of our expedition. The guide, in fact, did not like the look of the weather at all. Watery clouds were driving over the mountains, a soft south-west wind was blowing, and it seemed quite on the cards that we should have to cross the snow field in mist and rain. However, we were prepared to make the best of it, and at eight o'clock started once more to finish our climb.

For we had by no means yet got to the highest point. There was still a good thousand feet to ascend, and we could see from a distance that the road before us, if it might be called one at all, was steep and rugged. It was indeed rather stiff work this creeping up bare rocks, like mounting the steps of a ladder, and an occasional plateau came as a welcome change and relief. On one of these level bits we presently observed two men and a boy with two horses, which had been brought up from Sundal to draw the sledges. But we were not to avail ourselves of their services just yet. One of the animals had cast a shoe and had to be re-shod, so we took a rest while the operation was being performed. And then there was more climbing. The horses preceded us, and it was wonderful to see how the sure-footed little beasts managed to scramble up the steep slippery rocks without a stumble. We had now got to the snow, and several broad patches of it had to be crossed. It was rather heavy work, but the surface was tolerably hard and crisp, thanks to the absence of sun, for it was still cloudy and cool. These snow patches alternated with stretches of rough scrub and rock, but after a while we came to a point where the great snow-field appeared to begin in earnest. Still we had to tramp it over the frozen surface, and here and there the harder and more slippery ground told that the glacier was beneath our feet. It was all safe enough, for the crevasses are only to be found at the borders of the fjeld, though once the adventurous 'Nansen,' who could not be persuaded to follow the guide, and was always finding out short cuts for himself, was seen making straight for a mass of snow overhanging a great black gulf, into which he must have been precipitated if he had reached it. We called him back and scolded him well for his rashness, but he took our rating with his usual good nature and promised not to 'do it again.'

As the oldest, and perhaps not the most active of the party, I was pressed to take advantage of the aid of one of the horses and ride the rest of the way to the point where the sledges were stationed. I was, indeed, not reluctant to get this lift, and so mounted the quiet little steed without a saddle, while the others trudged behind on foot. Thus with my guide I was the first to reach the sledges, which lay, about half-a-dozen in number, under the shelter of a cluster of rocks which rose like islands in the midst of the great sea of ice and snow.

They were light in build and constructed entirely of wood, runners and all, and each had a seat for two with a plank behind for the driver.

As soon as our party were together the horses were harnessed to the sleighs and all was ready for the start. Four only took seats, as the enterprising 'Nansen' preferred to walk with the guides. And now we were off. Our progress at first was slow, for we had still to ascend, and the snow slopes were steep. But at last we reached the highest point and were told that we were standing at an altitude of 5200 feet above the sea. So far we had been singularly fortunate in the weather. That threatened mist and rain had not overtaken us. The sky was still cloudy, but the atmosphere was clear, and we were enabled to survey in all its splendour the glorious and wonderful scene around us. We were at the summit of the Folgefond, which stretched for mile upon mile on every side in one broad sheet of spotless snow. There were vast plains of snow and hills and domes of snow, grand and awe-inspiring in their spaciousness, and under that peculiar solemn silence which holds the air in a snow-bound country when the winds are at rest. And round the margin of this great white ocean rose a border of dark rugged mountain tops of every shape and outline that such ranges present. We could see nothing of the fjords, but knew that they lay quietly sleeping at our feet, deep down there at the bottom of those dark valleys which encircled the fjeld on every side. Between us and the ranges to the south lay the Sör branch of the Hardanger, with little Odde, as yet unseen, at its head. And straight across this invisible gulf we presently descried the dark ravine of the Skjæggedal, and caught a glimpse of the gloomy Ringedalsvand beyond, while two long twin milky streaks descending to the lake were recognised at once as the Tyssestrængene which is seen in the expedition to the Skjæggedalsfos. Immediately above the ravine the curious square top of the Haarteigen mountain rises, while far away to the left we survey many of the giant peaks of the Hardanger proper.

After a short pause at the highest point of the Folgefond we begin to descend. And now, at last, we understand what sledging really means. The horses start off at a gallop, and we spin along over the crisp snow with a rapidity and smoothness which constitute the very perfection of locomotion. The ground is fairly hard, but the horses' hoofs pelt us with little snow-balls now and then, and the wind sings in our ears as we speed onward. If only one could always travel in this way! Such, no doubt, is the aspiration of every member of the party. But alas! this rapid, exhilarating motion is too delightful to last; not that the little horses are tired, but there are more hills to mount and the pace has to be slackened. However, we are soon off again at a gallop, and time, as well as the sledge, flies. We have a good hour and a half of sleighing over the snow, but the journey has been all too brief. At last we reach a steep declivity, and here the men stop and request us to alight. They might have taken us a little further, but at this moment we perceive some figures in the distance climbing the slope from the direction of Odde. They prove to be two plucky Swedish ladies, with a guide, who have ascended from Odde with the intention of proceeding on foot to the Buarbræ. What splendid mountaineers women are when they once take to climbing! The two Swedes have had a stiff pull up to this height of nearly 5000 feet, yet they have 'not turned a hair.' They seem as fresh and unconcerned as though they had been only taking a ramble by the fjord side below. None the less do they seem glad enough to get the benefit of our sledges, for our journey on runners is now over and Godtskalk is naturally pleased to have a return fare at least part of the way back.

We settle up with him, and find that the cost of the expedition, like everything else in Norway, is surprisingly cheap. The total being reckoned up and divided, we find that the whole expense for guides, sledges, horses, provisions on the road, etc., is not more than fifteen shillings a head. I need hardly say that there is a cordial handshaking all round as we part with honest Godtskalk and his boys, but not before we sign a testimonial in his book recording our satisfaction with his guidance. Then he starts off with the Swedish ladies, and we commence the descent to Odde.

We have with us one of the men who came up with the horses from Sundal, and an excellent companion he proves. Down the slopes we slip and run at racing speed, for it is quite safe to do so, as there are no crevasses to dread. 'Nansen' is in wild spirits. He has run after the sledges all the way from the summit, and now he actually waltzes down the snow slopes with our new guide. In a very few minutes we are off the snow and are stumbling among rocks and stones and scanty herbage some hundreds of feet below the highest point of the Folgefond. The descent is very steep, much more than the rise from Sundal, though I fancy it must be rather easier to mount. We have been wonderfully lucky in our weather. It was cloudy and cool all the way across the fjeld, and only as we enter on the downward path does the sun break out and begin to soften the snow. But we have little more snow to trudge through, and before long arrive on solid ground. Going down a mountain is usually harder work than going up, and we found the descent to Odde a particularly arduous task. The sun, as I have said, had come out, and the afternoon became intensely hot, the paths, such as they were, were very rugged, and the scene before us somewhat monotonous. In a very short time we caught sight of the Sör fjord and Odde, and the view underwent some development, but very little change, till we reached the foot of the mountain. The pleasantest part of the walk was that which followed the course of the fine Tokheimsfos from its head to the fjord level, the view of it about half way up or down being strikingly picturesque. But by the time we arrived at the bottom of the mountain side we were all pretty well 'done up,' and I am afraid somewhat justified the whispered sarcasm, which, I believe, one hardy Norseman passed to a friend, that 'Englishmen can't walk.'

Anyhow, we were very glad to get to Tokheim and enjoy a rest as well as the famous beer and cherries of the place. Tokheim beer is beer indeed, a very different brew alike from the muddy native sort we tried at Gjerde, and the thin, though agreeable lager, which is the usual *öl* of the country. It has strength and body, and foams temptingly in the glass or tankard. I wonder that it is not more generally supplied at the hotels.

From Tokheim it is but some two miles or so to Odde either by land or water. Having had enough of the road, though there is a fair path to the head of the fjord, we preferred to seek our destination by boat, and in the beautiful twilight of this lovely summer evening we rowed to Odde and the Hardanger hotel. We did not arrive until about 10 p.m., but we had taken our journey leisurely, making long and frequent halts to survey the landscape, for what is the use of hurrying when the object of an expedition is simple enjoyment?

CHAPTER XI.

ON THE HARDANGER.

ON the third day of my first visit to Odde I left its pleasant shores to commence a voyage on the Hardanger, as I shall continue to call it, though here its name is the Sör fjord. A steamer arrives every day from Bergen late in the evening, and this or another usually departs early the next morning. Of these steamers there are two classes, the fast and the slow. The former stops at very few stations, and reaches Bergen in about thirteen or fourteen hours, while the other calls at a large number of villages and other places on the fjord, and does not get to the great seaport for about twenty hours. On the morning I had selected for my departure the slow boat was running. I intended to go as far as Eide, a distance of some thirty miles, and would have reached that place in about three hours if I had gone by the *Lyderhorn*. I was fortunate, however, in finding myself a passenger by the *Hordaland*, although, or rather I should say because, it takes three times as long on its journey as its sister vessel. For what could be more delightful in such perfect weather as we were then enjoying than this leisurely trip on the most beautiful of the greater fjords, with its frequent stoppages enabling one to obtain fair views of the principal points of interest on the way, and its visits to those offspring fjords with their narrow waters and bolder mountain-scenes which intersect the main water throughout its course?

Nor indeed had I reason to regret this more protracted voyage. The *Hordaland* is a fine large steamer, fitted up with every possible convenience and comfort. It started from Odde at 7 A.M., but one only had, as it were, to step out of one's bedroom into the vessel where in about an hour's time an excellent and abundant breakfast was provided. To smoke my pipe after this good meal, on the deck in the sunshine, and in one of the many cosy nooks to be found in every part of the vessel, while the beautiful fjord scenery glided by like a panorama—this was indeed perfect enjoyment. Now and then we touched at some village where there was an evidently comfortable hotel tempting the traveller to step out and stay there, and explore the lovely glens with which the mountain-sides were riven; but this was a luxury only to be enjoyed by those who had more time at their disposal than I had, and notwithstanding my aversion to 'rushing' I felt it was necessary to 'get on,' if I were to see as much of Western Norway as I desired.

At Grimo, a pretty little village, near the end of the Sör fjord, we had a long stoppage for a purpose that formed an interesting and amusing incident of our voyage. On arriving there we found the quay the scene of a lively and picturesque gathering. A crowd of peasants of all ages and both sexes, many of the women in costume, had come down from the hills with their cows and calves in order to ship their animals on board the steamer, and have them conveyed to 'pastures new' in another part of the country. It was indeed an animated spectacle. There were strong men struggling with scared and quarrelsome beasts; old women endeavouring to bring to reason that most unreasonable of creatures, the youthful and wayward calf; and boys everywhere helping their elders to prevent the animals from tumbling over the quay into the water. The shouts of the drovers, the lowing of the cattle, and the constant movement of the crowd, gave this scene on the little quay the appearance of a fair in the smallest possible compass, which would have made an excellent subject for a Landseer or an Ansdell.

The arrival of the steamer soon began to reduce this miniature chaos to something like order. In a very few minutes the hatches on the foredeck were opened, and revealed to us on the bridge the empty hold swept and cleaned and ready to receive the living cargo. A donkey-engine was set to work in connection with a crane, from which depended a chain attached to a broad canvas belt. This apparatus was put to use with no loss of time. One after another the cattle were driven to the quay-side;

in a moment the belt was slipped under the beast's belly and made fast; then the donkey-engine was set in motion, and up went the cow or calf with a slight struggle of alarm at its unwonted position, though in an instant it became quiet enough. Then the crane was swung round, and down went the beast into the hold, where it was unceremoniously pushed into its place. This operation was repeated again and again with admirable dexterity and despatch. The animals were handled with firmness and vigour, but evidently with the most tender care, so that no accident occurred, and after a while the hold was filled, and the hatches fastened down. There were still many beasts to be shipped, and these were packed neatly on the fore-deck till the quay was cleared, and the peasants, having got rid of their charges, dispersed, with the exception of a few who came on board to look after the animals. They were not going far, and the price per head for the carriage of each beast was, I understood, a mere trifle, not more than a few *öre*.

Within a few miles of Grimo we came to Utne—a very favourite place of resort, as was suggested by its snug, comfortable aspect. Its situation is beautiful as it stands at the junction of three arms of the Hardanger, the views of which must be very fine from any of the higher ground above the village. Utne seemed distinctly a place to stay at for any one who has time for a short sojourn. We merely touched at the landing-stage for a few minutes, and then went on. The views of the fjord, or fjords, for three great avenues of water and mountain are visible at once, are here very grand, presenting, in fact, the finest bit of scenery I had witnessed during the voyage. We now took the route to the right, passing, as we did so, the opening of another branch fjord leading to Ulvik, which we were afterwards to visit. Our present course took us up the water-alley, if I may so call it, which ends at Vik, and there forks off again into the beautiful Simodal.

There are any number of Viks in Norway, and as Næs corresponds with our Ness, so Vik is, I believe, the counterpart of that which we call a 'wick' or 'wich,' as in Chiswick and Sandwich. It signifies, in fact, a creek or indentation of the land on any water; and I understand that the familiar name of 'viking' is really derived from this local word as that of a class of seafarers who came from the *viks*. Thus they ought properly to be called 'vikings' with the first 'i' short, as in 'trick,' and not long as in 'like,' according to the ordinary pronunciation. There was, in fact, nothing royal about these daring pirates, and to give the viking the imposing equivalent of 'sea king' is altogether a mistake. They were simply vikings, because they lived in the *viks*.

The cattle we had taken on board at Grimo had here reached their destination, and the process of landing them was performed as quickly and cleverly as was that of taking them on board, and by the same means. The beasts were pretty little animals, not much larger than Alderneys, generally of a sort of fawn colour, with a white stripe along the ridge of the back. They seemed in rather poor condition; their blade-bones being particularly prominent. This would, of course, be due to their insufficient sustenance during the long winter among the scanty herbage of their home. In the more fertile pastures around Vik they would, no doubt, pick up again, and there they were to be left for the summer months.

The process of unloading them, however expeditious, would naturally be a somewhat lengthy one, for there were more than a hundred head on board, and the captain of the *Hordaland* considerately gave the passengers notice of this fact, suggesting that if any of them cared to take a short trip into the country there would be plenty of time to do so. Some of us hesitated at the idea of quitting the steamer in view of the risk of being left behind; but the captain said there need be no fear of that, as he was going for a drive himself. So most of us landed, and were at once surrounded by a crowd of *skydsguts* all anxious for the honour and profit of conveying us. As this was not a regular station journey there was a little bargaining at first, for some of the good fellows wanted rather more for the trip than they had a right to demand. But there was nothing at all offensive in their mode of haggling. They simply asked so much for the drive, and on being offered half the sum, quietly waited to ascertain the state of the market, and then usually gave in and accepted the reduced terms. I shared a *stolkjærre* with another traveller, and we had a short but very pleasant drive up a lovely valley by the margin of a lake in the direction of Sæbo. If time had permitted, a stay of a day or two at Vik might have been desirable, as there is some very fine scenery in the neighbourhood, and not far off is the Vöringfos, which is generally regarded as Norway's second grandest waterfall. It is merely necessary to mention the fact in this place, as the Vöringfos has, like the Skjæggedal, a world-wide fame, and any guide-book will give full particulars about it and the way to see it.

As our captain headed the procession of cars up the Sæbo valley and back again, we ran no risk of missing the steamer, and boarded her just before dinner-time. *Middagsmad* was as satisfactory as *frokost* had been, and when we went on deck we found that we were steaming up the narrow fjord that leads to Ulvik. We lost nothing of the scenery by going below for our meal, as we had to retrace our steps and return as far as Utne in order to pursue our course westwards. Here we entered the main road, so to speak, of the Hardanger, which is of considerable width, and can be seen stretching far into the distance for many miles. By following this great waterway we should have arrived at last, after many turnings and twistings northward and southward, at Bergen, and it is by this route in the reverse direction that the tourist generally proceeds to Odde. The scenery on the way is extremely fine, more so even than that of the Sör fjord. Much of it will be seen by those who go from Odde to Sundal in order to cross the Folgefond, but travellers who have time to spare will do well to make the whole voyage to Bergen and back. They will find that it amply repays them.

The ordinary conventional tourist sometimes complains that the Hardanger is monotonous: and doubtless for those who crave for some new scenic sensation every few miles or hours the pictures presented to their view are wanting in variety. But to persons gifted with anything like artistic taste and imagination these fjord voyages have a very peculiar and subtle charm, and are no more monotonous than the passage across the open sea. The mountains on either hand—grey, bare, and rugged, or clothed with forest and tipped with snow—may be all very much alike in themselves, but as you glide among them their forms and outlines are ever changing, constantly presenting some new and beautiful combination, and varying in their aspect under different conditions of atmosphere and the alternations of light and shade. I saw the Hardanger under brilliant sunshine and an almost unclouded sky, but I can well imagine that its rugged ranges must appear even grander still in more unsettled weather. I had abundant opportunities of seeing the fjords elsewhere under other conditions, and consider that I was fortunate in being able to contrast their appearance in cloud and mist with that of the Hardanger in the full glory of the summer sunlight.

CHAPTER XII.

FROM EIDE TO VOSSEVANGEN.

A VERY narrow arm of the fjord, called Graven, led to our destination, Eide, which we reached at about 4 P.M., nine hours after our departure from Odde. It had been a delightful voyage, just three times as long as that by the 'fast' boat would have been, and for this privilege we had nothing extra to pay, as the fares by both boats are the same. In fine weather, therefore, I would advise all future travellers to choose the 'slow' steamer in making their way from Odde. Eide is another tempting stopping-place, for it has a central position in the midst of beautiful scenery, and, I believe, offers excellent accommodation, as well as good sport for the angler. It has also the further advantage of being a telegraph station, and you do not find many places in Norway whence you can despatch a message by wire. In this respect it presents a curious contrast to Switzerland, where you can telegraph from any little hamlet to another, and from the foot of a mountain to the top.

Some tourists, no doubt, find this inconvenient, and in the same way they miss the postal facilities they enjoy elsewhere, for the post in Norway is a somewhat fitful institution. In many places there is a despatch and delivery only two or three times a week, and it is very difficult indeed to get news of your friends at home unless you have made quite sure of your route, and can give notice long in advance of your future destination. This, however, is not always practicable. No matter how carefully you may plan your movements, changes and modifications are often inevitable, and you find it necessary to omit some place you intended to visit, and bend your steps in quite a different direction. Perhaps the best way to get letters is to have them addressed to you at Bergen, to the care of the ever courteous and obliging Mr. Bennett, the tourists' agent, who willingly takes charge of travellers' letters without fee, keeps a register of them, and undertakes to forward them to any part of the country. Thus, if you are making any stay at a telegraph station, or are pretty sure to be stopping at some other point of the route ahead, all you have to do is to 'wire' to Bennett's for your correspondence, and it will be forwarded as promptly as circumstances will permit. I myself telegraphed from Eide and got my letters the next day at Vossevangen, which is in railway communication with Bergen.

It was, in fact, for Vossevangen that I was bound when quitting Eide with my companion in a very decent *stolkjærre*. There is no greater charm of travel in Norway than this sandwiching, so to speak, of the journeys with the voyages. It lends a delightful variety to the tour, not only by presenting scenes of different character to the eye, but by giving change of exercise to the limbs. After lounging or sitting about the deck of a steamer all day, a drive or a walk is all the more pleasant the next, and then after exploring the valleys on wheels or on foot, it is agreeable to get on board again and glide in and out among the sombre, silent fjords. So, after our long voyage upon the grey Hardanger, we were glad to plunge at once, as we did as soon as we had passed the last house in Eide, into an exquisitely wooded valley, wide enough to hold a broad and gleaming lake, the Gravensvand, round which the road winds on one side upon the very narrow strip left to it, at the foot of precipitous crags. The lake being passed, the road ascends and skirts one of those many impetuous and translucent rivers which abound in Norway.

There is nothing savage or gloomy, though much that is grand, in this drive from Eide to Vossevangen. The country is green and fertile, thick forests of pine and fir give contrast to the grey rocks, and the rising road affords charming prospects of the landscape. The most beautiful part of this journey is at Skerve, where there is a very handsome foss. It is seen to perfection from the road, which winds in zigzags up a steep hill, keeping it in view all the way. I walked up this hill and did not hurry over it, as the scene was too lovely to be hastily passed by. At the summit we found the views more extensive; the woods, no longer confined to narrow valleys, spread over a vast stretch of hill and dale. There were also some pretty river scenes, especially at one or two points, where we came upon several of those quaint old sawmills, which form such a picturesque feature in the Norwegian landscape. They are often to be found at the foot of a waterfall, by which, in fact, the wheel is worked. They are queer, tumble-down sheds, blackened and battered, and patched up, and the rickety troughs that supply them with the motive-power which works the machinery cross the stream in no unsightly form. It is hither that the fir-trunks from the forest are brought to be sawn into logs and planks, and the operation is as much in harmony with the scene around as the pretty spectacle of the mill itself. No one surely will begrudge the good Norsk folk the use of their fosses for industrial purposes when they pay for the privilege with such welcome tributes to the artistic sense? Less picturesque are the long wires which are stretched tightly from the tops of the mountains to the valleys below, and the appearance of which in many places puzzles the traveller, until he is told that they are used for conveying bundles of grass and litter, gathered on the heights, to the farms beneath. We never saw any of these aerial lines put in operation, as I believe they are not worked at the time of the year when I was travelling.

But of another peculiar agricultural arrangement we had many examples on this road; I refer to the fences or hurdles set up by the side of every meadow for the purpose of drying the hay. The grass is never stacked as in England, but hung over these wooden rails. I am not learned enough in farming affairs to say whether this is a good plan or not, but it certainly seems to have much to recommend it, as it stands to reason that hay must dry much more quickly, and keep dry better, in any but very wet weather, in being thus hung up, than when piled in heaps on the ground. Yet another noticeable feature of the wayside are the inscriptions on boards or stones, giving a name and some mysterious figures and numbers. These are the landmarks denoting the length of road which every farmer has to keep in repair, in lieu of being taxed for the maintenance of the highway.

A bold mountain, the Lönchorje, confronts us as we get near Vossevangen. It is thickly sprinkled with snow, and is 4490 feet in height, while Graasiden, on the opposite side of the Voss valley, stands 4150 feet high. These lend a certain dignity to the surroundings of the village, the situation of which, moreover, on the shores of the Vands lake, is very pleasant. Otherwise I cannot say that Vossevangen, though an important station on the tourist track, is one of the most picturesque places I had seen. It is comfortable rather than beautiful, and is provided with several decent shops, and three or

VOSSEVANGEN.
(Page 124.)

four good hotels, of which Fleischer's is among the most deservedly noted in Norway. It is a fine building, constructed, of course, of wood, and one of the best specimens of Norwegian hotel architecture. The *spise-sal* is of noble dimensions, handsomely and tastefully decorated, and opens on to a long sheltered gallery commanding a full view of the lake. The house replaces one burnt down a few years ago, and its landlord has the reputation of being one of the most enterprising and popular of his class. Large as Fleischer's is, it is often full, for Vossevangen is a great place of resort, not only for tourists, but for Bergen folk on Sundays and holidays.

It was on the occasion of my second visit that I lodged at Fleischer's. In 1890 I had been recommended to put up at Dykesten's, and chose it for my brief sojourn. It is one of those good old-fashioned country inns, where the people are very obliging and thoroughly honest, the sort of place where you can 'feel at home,' though they do not offer all the luxuries provided at the bigger hotels. At Dykesten's I found everything quite satisfactory —a genial landlord, an affable young woman who acted as head waitress and spoke English perfectly, and a very civil and obliging *portier*, to whom I was indebted for several special services. Dykesten has two houses on opposite sides of the road, but I chose the 'dépendance,' as I could have a fine large bedroom there, with a charming look-out on the garden and the lake, while the hotel proper, where we took our meals, has a more confined situation. It presents this peculiarity, that it has a shop attached to it, kept by the landlord, where you can buy almost anything in the 'dry goods' line. The garden I spoke of above is a pretty, wild bit of ground,— it is surprising that the Norwegians seem to be utterly indifferent to the charms and advantages of horticulture,—but it has something like a lawn, where you can play at sea-quoits, such as are provided on board ship.

Vossevangen is one of the very few places in Western Norway served by a railway, and a remarkable line runs between it and Bergen, having no fewer than fifty-four tunnels on its course of sixty-seven miles. Many of these are little more than mere arches cut through the rock, but the making of the line has been a triumph of engineering, and is an example of difficulties which lovers of the beautiful, of Wordsworth's way of thinking, must hope will be found insuperable elsewhere. Railways would, in a certain sense, be the ruin of Norway, and happily, excepting this small line from Bergen to Vossevangen, there are none in the country which I traversed. I did not make any excursion on this line, as it was not part of my plan to visit Bergen just then. Still, a short run to one of the stations and back would be an interesting trip from Vossevangen, as the railway is well worth seeing. Of course the excursion could be just as well made from the other terminus, and reserved for the end of the tour at Bergen. Trains run twice a day each way, morning and evening, and the single journey occupies four hours. As on many other railways in Norway, there is no first-class—all trains are second and third—an odder incongruity even than the 'no second' on some of our lines.

It was at Vossevangen that I discovered the disadvantage of knowing nothing of the language of the country in which I was travelling. Nearly everywhere else I had always found somebody who could speak English, at any rate a little—at the hotels, on the steamers, in shops, and even in the streets and on the country roads. But now and again you come in contact with some native absolutely ignorant of the Anglo-Saxon tongue, and that, too, occasionally at an important juncture when a word or two of Norsk would be invaluable. So I advise every one who visits Norway hereafter not to depend exclusively on the 'English spoken' there, but to get up, at any rate, a few useful words or sentences from Bennett's *Phrase Book*, which is one of the best of its kind, as it is constructed on an excellent plan, giving a vocabulary of words, together with sentences in connection with them.

I wanted a small supply of some effervescing powder, which is always a good thing to carry about with one—almost any sort will do, and I am not going to advertise anybody's magic 'salt' or infallible 'saline' by mentioning it in particular—so I went to the Vossevangen 'apothek,' and endeavoured to make my wishes known. But the 'apothek,' or his assistant, knew no English, and after he had offered me tooth-brushes, hair-combs, lip-salve, lozenges, and half a dozen other unnecessaries, I really thought I should have to give it up. At last, however, the right idea dawned upon his mind, and to my great delight he suddenly suggested 'Magnesia-citrat!' The very thing! Our good old friend the sparkling, refreshing, and cooling citrate of magnesia would do as well as anything, and better than most. So I gladly purchased a bottle of 'magnesia-citrat,' and carried it off in triumph.

'Magnesia-citrat'—citrate of magnesia. Dear me! I thought, how like after all are the two languages! It would not be so difficult, perhaps, to get up a little Norsk if this was a sample of it. So I took home my bottle, and resolved to make a beginning by endeavouring to translate the directions on the label. 'Magnesia-citrat,' I found, was otherwise described as 'Engelsk bruspulver.' That was plain enough—*Engelsk*, English ; *pulver*, powder ; and as for *brus*, that might mean anything effervescing or fizzing. Next came the directions. '*Dette Præparat*'—Yes, 'this preparation'—I was really getting on capitally, and I advanced with confidence. 'Der er sammenset'—hum! ha!— that looked like something about a 'summersault' or 'summer salt,' but it couldn't mean that ; so I skipped a few words, and thought I might pick up the meaning by the aid of one or two that I recognised. There was *stoffe*—stuff, no doubt—and *vand*, which I knew to be water as well as lake—and *drik*, which is drink. But I could not connect these scattered nouns with the intermediate verbs, and at last I came to '*anbefalelsesværdig*,' and then I gave it up in despair! However, I had got my citrate of magnesia, and very pleasant I found it afterwards to mix in my collapsible cup with the cool water of the fosses by the roadside. Nevertheless a little Norsk will not do the traveller in Norway any harm.

I saw a funeral at Vossevangen. The landlord of one of the hotels, by name Johnsen, had died at the age of forty, under very sad circumstances, leaving a large family. The funeral was of the simplest kind. The coffin, covered with a profusion of flowers, was borne on a low cart or trolly, drawn by one black horse, and followed by about twenty mourners on foot. As it passed through the village, the people turned out in considerable numbers to see it go by. We thought the body was to be interred in the burial-ground of the much-restored old thirteenth-century church, which stands in the middle of the village, but as the procession passed on, and its destination was a somewhat distant cemetery, and as, moreover, it was a very hot day, we did not follow it. There was nothing particularly noticeable about the proceedings, except that, as a mark of respect, the proprietors of the hotels on the route strewed fir-twigs and juniper-leaves on the road before their doors, and these distributed a faint and pleasant fragrance throughout the village.

We spent the rest of the evening and a great part of the next day at Vossevangen, as there are many nice walks in the neighbourhood, especially one through a wood to the lake side. Here, too, we saw a little costume, for the women of the Voss country have a dress of their own which slightly differs from that worn in the Hardanger district, being without the ornamental piece which goes across the breast, but preserving the coloured bands from the shoulder to the waist. On high days and holidays, however, I believe they wear more elaborate decorations.

CHAPTER XIII.

STALHEIM.

We started in the afternoon for Stalheim, and had a very pleasant drive. The valleys traversed in this route are wide, presenting fine prospects of wood and water, for on the way several lakes are passed. The first of these is the Tvindesvand, and at Tvinde itself there is a rather handsome waterfall. The next station is Vinje, also a pretty place; and further on you come to Opheim with another lake. Several small villages are also dotted about this valley, and altogether the district appears more populous than most others of its kind. Those picturesque old sawmills, of which I have previously spoken, are frequently seen, and here too there are many *staburs*, or storehouses, which also look well in the landscape. The trout-fishing all along this valley is said to be particularly good. A gentleman whom I met at Tvinde told me that he had had capital sport, and I had ocular proof that there were fish to be caught by seeing a couple of country lads armed with very rough tackle whipping out trout after trout, not very large, it is true, but with enviable rapidity. This was in one of the rivers, but there were also two or three fishing parties on the lake. At a place called Morkdalsond, about two kilomètres distant from Vinje, and easily reached by carriage, I heard that an English tourist had lately caught twenty trout of from one and a half to two pounds.

Along the course of this valley there is a series of hotels at convenient stages, and most of them, I believe, of recent construction. They are very prettily built with those elegant frontages, arabesque in character, which seem to be a favourite form of ornament in Norway. Not having put up at any of these hostelries, and having only visited one or two of them for the purpose of temporary refreshment, I cannot say much about them from personal experience, but their appearance is in every case decidedly prepossessing, and all seem to bear a good name. Comfortable quarters would no doubt be found in any of them, whether at Tvinde, Vinje, or Opheim. And it is very desirable to bear the fact in mind that in such districts it is possible to break one's journey under stress of circumstances. I had travelled so far in the most perfect of weather, but a drive in an open car through such an exposed country as that which lies between Vossevangen and Stalheim, under heavy rain, is an experience which some people, and especially ladies, would probably wish to terminate at the earliest possible stage. Apart from that, however, no one could go far wrong in spending a day, or part of one, in this beautiful

NÆRÖDALEN.
Page 156.

valley, but, of course, if the traveller is pressed for time he had better push on to Stalheim.

The road through the valley is tolerably level most of the way, but near Opheim it gradually ascends. Thence there are very fine views looking backward, and the bulky form of the Lönehorje—at least, that, I think, is the mountain which we keep in view all the way—with its patchy fields of snow mottling its crests, assumed more majestic proportions. Then as we approached Stalheim we alighted at the rather stiff bit of road that brought us to the end of our day's journey, and walked up the hill.

Stalheim is situated on very high ground, some 1200 feet in fact above the sea, and in view of two beautiful valleys—that which we had just left and the famous Nærödal. This last is one of the 'big things' of Norway, and every traveller is expected to go into raptures about it. There can be no question that it is magnificent, but greatly as I object, as a rule, to making invidious comparisons between one fine bit of scenery and another, I certainly do not think it equal in beauty to the Bratlandsdal. Still, as I have said, it is very grand. It is so straight that from Stalheim you can look down it almost to its furthest extremity, a distance of about eight miles. It is extremely narrow, and is flanked by mountains from three to five thousand feet high, and projecting into the valley in a series of well-defined spurs, most conspicuous among them being the famous Jordalsnut with its peak shaped like a dome. The view of the Nærödal, as seen from Stalheim, resembles not a little that of Lauterbrunnen from Mürren.

Stalheim ranks as a village and station, but it is a 'place,' as the Americans would say, chiefly in virtue of its hotel. The Stalheim hotel is, to all intents and purposes, Stalheim, and there alone you can get whatever has to be got in the locality. It is a large building erected on the site of a smaller one by its proprietor during the winter of 1890-1. For those who like a lively place of abode, a longer or shorter stay at Stalheim is to be recommended. It may, perhaps, be too lively for some people; a little too much like the conventional Continental hotel with its cosmopolitan company of the most mixed character, and the constant bustle and confusion arising from arrivals and departures at all hours of the day. Stalheim is hardly the place in which to seek quiet and repose, and those who prefer more peaceful, if less pretentious, quarters would do well to put up for the night in one of the many comfortable hotels between Vossevangen and Stalheim, and merely visit the latter for their midday meal *en route* for Gudvangen.

It would be a great mistake, however, to hurry through so lovely a spot as the Nærödal, the beauties of which deserve leisurely inspection, and to be appreciated must be seen under different conditions of weather and atmosphere. I saw them under both cloud and sunshine, now looking bright and smiling, now dark and frowning, and in both aspects this great gorge was equally striking, though, perhaps, it appears at its best in the evening when the mountains put on a robe of purple haze, and their summits are touched with gold by the declining sun, while the depths of the valley lie in shadow. The Nærödal also should be seen from different points of view, not only from the bit of rising ground or hillock in front of the hotel, but from the winding road below, whence the two grand waterfalls, the Stalheimsfos and the Sivlefos, unseen from above, are visible, and especially from the path along the ridge of the mountains to the left of the hotel.

It was while exploring this last-named track that I entered upon an adventure little expected, but fruitful of a very curious experience.

I had set out shortly after breakfast with a companion for a stroll along this ridge, and we walked together as far as the point where a branch valley intersects the Nærödal at the foot of the Jordalsnut. Here my friend and I parted, as he was anxious to get back to dinner, and I was tempted by the beauty of this new valley to wander a little further. Besides, I thought I could return by another route, as the map indicated a path over the mountains to a road parallel with that which I was about to traverse. Such short cuts in Norway, however, look more easy upon paper than they prove in reality.

The valley, branching from the Nærödal, and

called, I think, Naalene, was indeed very fine, being exceedingly narrow, richly clothed with foliage, and watered by a boiling torrent, while the rough path which I had to follow wound up and down along the mountain-side, and afforded beautiful views at every step. At the end of the ravine the river took one great leap below, and thence it broadened with the land between the mountains, and I saw before me a wide extent of barren open country rolling away into the unknown.

Being still anxious to find the by-path over the mountains indicated on my map, I pushed on, and at last found myself in a very wild country indeed. I had inquired at a farmhouse whether I could get to Stalheim that way, and, being answered in the affirmative, I was encouraged to proceed; but for some miles no other habitation appeared in sight, and I did not meet a living soul. At last, however, I caught sight of a lad on horseback, and I followed him to a cluster of *sæters*, where I managed to obtain some rough refreshment, consisting of *fladbrod*, or oatcake, and a sort of cream cheese, together with plenty of good fresh milk. Here, too, I secured a guide, who conducted me to the river-side, and took me across the stream on horseback to the foot of the path which he said led to Stalheim.

This path, rough as it was, seemed so plain, and the dip in the mountain range towards which it climbed appeared so low, that I thought I should have no difficulty in getting over the pass alone, and I therefore dismissed my conductor. A little further on there was a lonely *sæter*, occupied by a woman, who gave me some milk and assured me that I was on the right track. But this same track gradually became fainter and fainter, and was at last lost in bogs and brushwood, and then I found before me a series of snow patches, which proved to be more serious obstacles to progress than they appeared from below. For they lay upon the steep hill-side, and their surface, exposed all day to the heat of a fierce sun, was soft, and afforded but uncertain foothold. Moreover, I had come provided with no better alpenstock than an umbrella, and had no nails to my boots. So it was toilsome work getting over these slippery *arêtes*, and, after I had traversed about half-a-dozen of them, I found myself near the top of the pass, and with a snow-field of unknown extent stretching in front of me.

The sun was now setting, and I was very hungry, having tasted no food since morning, except the very rough meal I had obtained at the *sæter*. Under these circumstances, I thought it would not be prudent to attempt to cross the snow-field, which for aught I knew might be two or three miles in width, and perhaps end in precipices. So, although it is always disagreeable to 'go back,' I determined to return down the mountain and get what lodging I could at a *sæter*, for to reach Stalheim that night by the road I had come was out of the question. The particular *sæter* I had in view as a possible resting-place was that one about half-way down the mountain where the woman had given me some milk. I soon came to the hut, and was there once more hospitably received by the good woman who occupied it. These *sæters* are not permanent residences, but are only inhabited in the summer by people who have cattle and pasture, and their owners are not always so poor as the accommodation which these hovels provide, but are often well-to-do peasants. The woman who dwelt in this particular *sæter* was, as I afterwards ascertained, the wife of a respectable farmer, who owned a considerable quantity of land and cattle, and had been a member of the Storthing or Parliament.

My hostess was attired in a neat, plain, peasant's dress, was apparently about thirty years of age, and had a comely but weather-bronzed countenance, while her manner was marked by that quiet, grave good-nature which is so characteristic of all Norwegians. She admitted me and gave me a meal, such as it was, of more *fladbrod* and milk, together with some soft, stodgy bread that turned to paste in the mouth, and a particularly detestable sort of pancake like a disk of leather. She could not speak a word of English, nor I of Norsk, so that it was not without difficulty that I could get her to understand that I wished to have a night's lodging in her hut. However, I at last conveyed by signs that I should feel obliged if she would give me accommodation, and when she at last grasped my meaning she pointed to her own couch and insisted upon giving it up to me. Then she discreetly retired, leaving me to my repose. I had but little sleep, and was glad when, at half-past four in the morning, I saw my hostess moving about, and I was enabled to quit my couch. Soon afterwards we had breakfast of the same unsatisfactory kind as our last night's supper, and I hoped to start at once so as to arrive at Stalheim before they could miss me at the hotel. But I was not to get away so quickly. It will be remembered that a river lay between me and the path I had to follow, and there was no horse this time to carry me across the stream. So I managed to make the woman understand that she must show me where I could pass the river, and she promised to do so, but in her turn gave me to understand that she must milk her cows first.

This somewhat tedious process, which she forthwith commenced, went on for two mortal hours, till, greatly to my satisfaction, the last cow was milked, and the good woman signified that she was ready to accompany me. It was but a short walk, and if only we could have commanded language enough to make each other understand, I might have ascertained long before, that, but a few hundred yards down the river, I should find a plank by which I could cross it. So at this simple bridge I took leave of my kind hostess, after having had some difficulty in inducing her to accept a couple of *kroner* in payment of my night's lodging. She uttered some words, which obviously meant that she wished me a safe journey, and to which I replied with the universally understood 'adieu,' and the ever useful *mange tak*, and indispensable handshake.

I had of course to retrace my steps by the road I had traversed on the previous day, but it was a longer journey than I had thought it to be, and it was not till noon that I found myself at my destination. Here I was received with much satisfaction, as the people at the hotel had begun to get uneasy about me, and were about to send out a search party to look for me. However, after a bath, a nap, and a good dinner, I felt none the worse for my little adventure.

CHAPTER XIV.

GUDVANGEN.

I DID not stay long at Stalheim after this. In the course of that same afternoon I hired a *carriole*—my first, for hitherto I had travelled by road only in *stolkjærres*—and was driven through the Nærödal to Gudvangen. The distance, as I have said before, was only some eight miles, and I walked the first stage of it, comprised in the wonderful *klev*, or zig-zag road, that leads from Stalheim to the level of the valley. This winding way has, I believe, sixteen distinct bends, and at every turning commands a fine view, first of one and then of the other of the two splendid waterfalls, the Stalheimsfos and the Sivlefos. The former takes the longer leap of the two, falling from the gap whence it emerges, without a break, to the bottom; but the latter is more picturesque, as it bounds from rock to rock in a succession of foaming cascades.

The Nærödal is magnificent from every point of view, but a drive through its depths is necessary for a full appreciation of its grandeur. The tremendous mountains tower above your head on both sides, with their king, the bold Jordalsnut wearing his singular oval crown, in their midst, and the narrowness of the valley, nowhere more than a few hundred yards in width, gives an awful sublimity to the scene. Nor does that scene become at all tamer as you advance; on the contrary, it grows grander still as the sight of the lofty and precipitous mountains is at last rendered yet more imposing by their combination in the picture with the deep, dark waters of the fjord that lies at their feet. For when about a a quarter of a mile from Gudvangen I caught a glimpse of the arm of the sea, which is called the Nærö, or narrow fjord, and is a branch of the great Sogne fjord, the most extensive in Norway, its remotest point being over a hundred miles distant from the ocean.

Gudvangen lies within a few yards of the head of the fjord, and on the bank of the river that flows through the Nærödal. It is a small village of a few houses, including two hotels, Hansen's and Holland's. These hostelries are much less pretentious in character than the showy establishment at Stalheim, but they are both, I believe, good old-fashioned country inns, and, at any rate, I found Mr. Hansen's to answer that description.

Mr. Hansen is the station-master at Gudvangen, and I hope he will not be offended, should he ever read these lines, if I call him a 'character.' He is

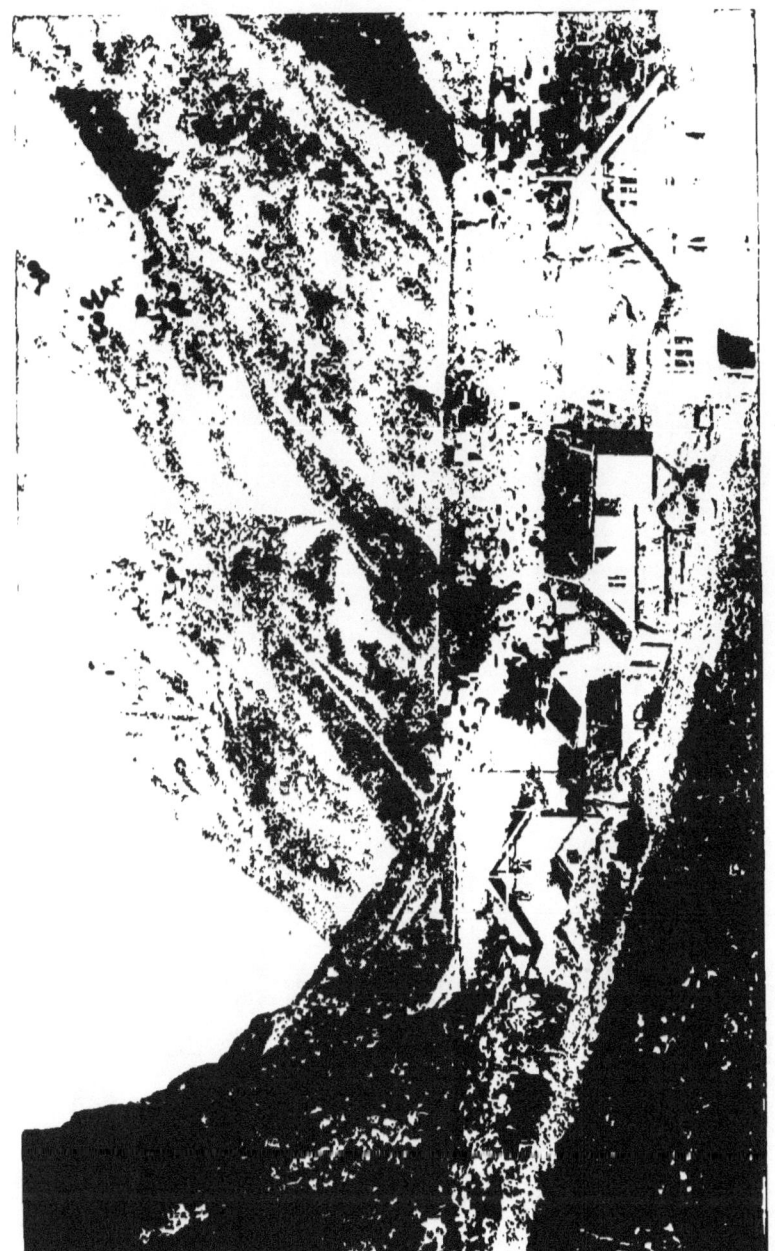

GUDVANGEN.
(Pag. 141.)

a most worthy and estimable person, and a landlord of the old school rather than the new. That is to say, he is conservative rather than progressive, and is content to jog along on the good old lines which have been the law of landlords in Norway from time immemorial. Mr. Hansen is of the 'slow and sure' class. It seems to take a long time with him to absorb a new idea, or to get rid of an old one. As he sits under the shadow of the balcony before his hotel, and below the level of the road, on his favourite bench, smoking his pipe,—a position in which he is usually to be found,—he appears to be the very embodiment of the Immutable. Nothing disturbs him; nothing excites him; nothing surprises him; he takes life easily, and lets the world go by. If you told him there had been an earthquake at Stalheim, he would probably reply, 'Just so,' and go on smoking his pipe. If you were to propose that he should pull down his hotel and build a new one, he would, no doubt, respond that it might be done—he would think about it. He accepts, in fact, every proposition as feasible, and looks upon action only as a possibility of the distant future.

Yet he is a shrewd and intelligent man, and does things excellently if you will only let him do them in his own way. The telephone is the one great trouble of Mr. Hansen's life. He is its slave, and he hates it. He talks English very well; but to chat with British travellers is one thing, and to speak their tongue through a telephone is quite another. The difficulties connected with strange names, and such unpronounceable words as 'this' and 'that' are almost too much for Mr. Hansen, and make him unhappy. I discovered this for myself when, on arriving at Gudvangen, I wished to despatch a message to England. It would be Mr. Hansen's business to telephone it to Stalheim, whence it would be wired to its address.

'Ah!' cried the good station-master, surveying my message with a doleful air, and shaking his head, 'dat is too long.'

It contained only some twenty or thirty words, and I explained that I could not possibly shorten it. But, no; he said again with a sigh, 'dat is too long'; and, once more, when I represented that, being willing to pay for the transmission, I had a right to send what I pleased, he sadly murmured, 'It is too long.' However, in the end he did manage to get off this lengthy message, and it duly arrived without mistakes.

Another example of good Mr. Hansen's peculiarities is characteristic. The Empress Eugénie was just then making a tour among the fjords, and I had heard at Stalheim that she was to land at Gudvangen, from the steam-yacht *Victoria*, on the morning of the day after my arrival, and drive through the Nærödal and back. I remarked casually to Mr. Hansen, as we sat together smoking in the porch, that the Empress was to arrive on the morrow.

'No,' replied the station-master, very quietly, 'not to-morrow—next veek.'

I then assured him that my information was correct, for had not an agent gone to Bergen to make arrangements for the Empress's reception, and was not the *Victoria* due the next day ?—No, Mr. Hansen would not have it so.

'The *Victoria* come to-morrow. Ya!' he said; 'but not the Empress—she come next veek.'

So I let the matter drop, as it was not worth arguing. Sure enough, the next morning the *Victoria* duly arrived with the Empress on board, and I saw her land and drive off to Stalheim. I could not help triumphing over Mr. Hansen in a mild way.

'There,' I said. 'You see the Empress has come after all!'

'Ya!' replied the station-master stolidly, 'the Empress has come;' and that was all he had to say on the subject.

Yet I am not quite sure whether there was not some underlying motive for the worthy landlord's seeming apathy. I was told that on a recent occasion he had been rather shabbily treated by a party of yachting tourists, who had in like manner landed at Gudvangen. They had, so it was said, telegraphed to him that they intended to stop and lunch at his hotel, and he had provided a meal for the whole party—a tolerably large one. Nevertheless, on arriving at Gudvangen, they, for some reason or

K

other, changed their minds, and, instead of staying and refreshing themselves there, went on direct to Stalheim, leaving poor Mr. Hansen to eat his dinner for twenty, or whatever the number was, or otherwise dispose of it. If this story were true, and I repeat it as it was related to me, the indifference of Mr. Hansen to the arrival of the *Victoria* and its distinguished and undistinguished passengers would not be very surprising after all, but only a little example of Norwegian independence. If you treat these good folks rudely or inconsiderately, they do not openly resent it; they simply leave you to shift for yourself.

Hansen's hotel, notwithstanding the old-fashioned ways of its worthy landlord, is still one of the cosiest and most comfortable in Norway, and the living there is as good as in any place of its class. Its situation is really magnificent, midway between two of the finest valley and fjord scenes in Norway, while, as a centre of tourist traffic, through which travellers in large numbers are always going and coming, by car from one direction and by steamer from the other, it is as lively a place as Flüelen, on the Lake of Lucerne, with which it has not a little in common.

I cannot, however, include among the chief attractions of Gudvangen that strangely exaggerated marvel, the mountain-torrent which is said to be the highest waterfall in Europe. This is the Kilfos, and it is plainly seen from the village, descending down the side of a lofty precipice that overhangs the river which flows through the Nærödal into the fjord. It is reputed to have an unbroken leap of 2000 feet, but its uninterrupted downward course was certainly not more than one-fourth of that length when I saw it. Even this was a very thin spurt of water, which at last dispersed in fine spray. Possibly under certain conditions it may present a bolder appearance, as when the snows above are melting rapidly; but there are many other falls in this very neighbourhood, not to speak of those to be seen elsewhere, which far surpass the Kilfos both in length of leap and volume of water.

There is, however, nothing else that is disappointing in or about Gudvangen. One of the pleasantest and easiest excursions in its neighbourhood is the beautiful walk or drive that can be taken by the margin of the Nærö fjord to Bakke. The distance is only three and a half miles, for the road ends perforce at the village last-named, where the mountains rise sheer out of the water, leaving not an inch of space for even a path. There are few villages in Norway so picturesque as Bakke, for it is much more compactly built than most others of its kind; it is intersected by a rushing torrent, which works a sawmill, and has a neat little church, with a bold spire, by the fjord side. From any point of view Bakke and its surroundings would present a tempting subject for the landscape-painter, but it is best seen at the distance of about a quarter of a mile on the Gudvangen side, with its noble background of precipitous and snow-topped mountains, which cross each other in the perspective, and completely shut in this reach of the fjord. In fact, I regard the view of Bakke as one of the very finest scenes in Norway.

I spent an entire day in this beautiful region. Indeed, it could hardly be possible to find a spot more suitable for a summer ramble. The many waterfalls which descend from an enormous height close at hand, and go rushing in roaring torrents under the road to the fjord, invite you to sit at their feet and watch them as they sink in fold upon fold from rock to rock; while at every elevation of the road, which often passes through shady woods, and hugs the shore from end to end of the walk, there is some new and beautiful combination of mountain and water to be noticed and admired. You must take your lunch with you, as there is no hotel at Bakke, but it is very pleasant to picnic by the fjord-side, as I did, on the summit of a little cluster of rocks, close by the church, which commands the grandest view of this almost incomparable scene.

Gudvangen, indeed, ought not to be hurriedly passed over by those who wish thoroughly to enjoy the most characteristic beauties of Norwegian scenery.

CHAPTER XV.

ON THE SOGNE FJORD.

A FIRST-CLASS steamer arrives nearly every day at Gudvangen, and starts at the convenient hour of 3 or 4 P.M. for a long voyage on the Sogne fjord. In the vessel called the *Alden*, which is at least equal, in the comfort of its accommodation and the excellence of its living, to the *Hordaland*, in which I made the tour of the Hardanger, I took my departure.

I had seen much of the beauty of the Nærö fjord in my walk to Bakke, and saw it again from the steamer. But the views on passing the village are even finer still. Narrow waters flanked by stately mountains are no doubt to be seen in many places elsewhere, but nowhere do the heights group themselves in such picturesque combinations as in the few miles between Bakke and the Sogne. There are many who regard this as the very finest fjord scenery in Norway, more beautiful than anything on the Hardanger, more imposing even than the mighty Geiranger itself. I will not venture to decide upon the relative claims of these lordly spots. I will only say that, in my opinion, there is nothing in all Norway to exceed in magnificence the Nærö fjord.

The weather by this time had undergone a change. I had walked the day before to Bakke amidst alternate showers and sunshine; but now the sky was overcast and bad weather seemed threatened. Yet it proved not so bad after all, and was indeed just the best sort of weather for seeing the Sogne fjord. Sunshine, I should think, would make the scenery of those stately waters look almost tame, but under cloud, and with the mist spread in long white strips across the mountains, or gathering in fleecy volumes about their summits, the Sogne really seemed to deserve its reputation as the most savagely grand of the fjords.

When the Nærö fjord is once passed, the waters take the name of the Aurlands fjord, which crosses the Nærö at right angles and bends away to the right deep into the country, and to the left in the direction of the Sogne. The stately grandeur of the mountain scenery is well maintained, but at the mouth of the fjord the space between the shores widens considerably, and the traveller is no longer tempted to imagine that he is steaming on some great river or lake, but really on the inland sea. For the water here can be disagreeably rough for those who are not good sailors, and I can well understand what I was told, that they are sometimes swept by terrific storms, the force of which is increased rather than diminished by confinement between the mountain-

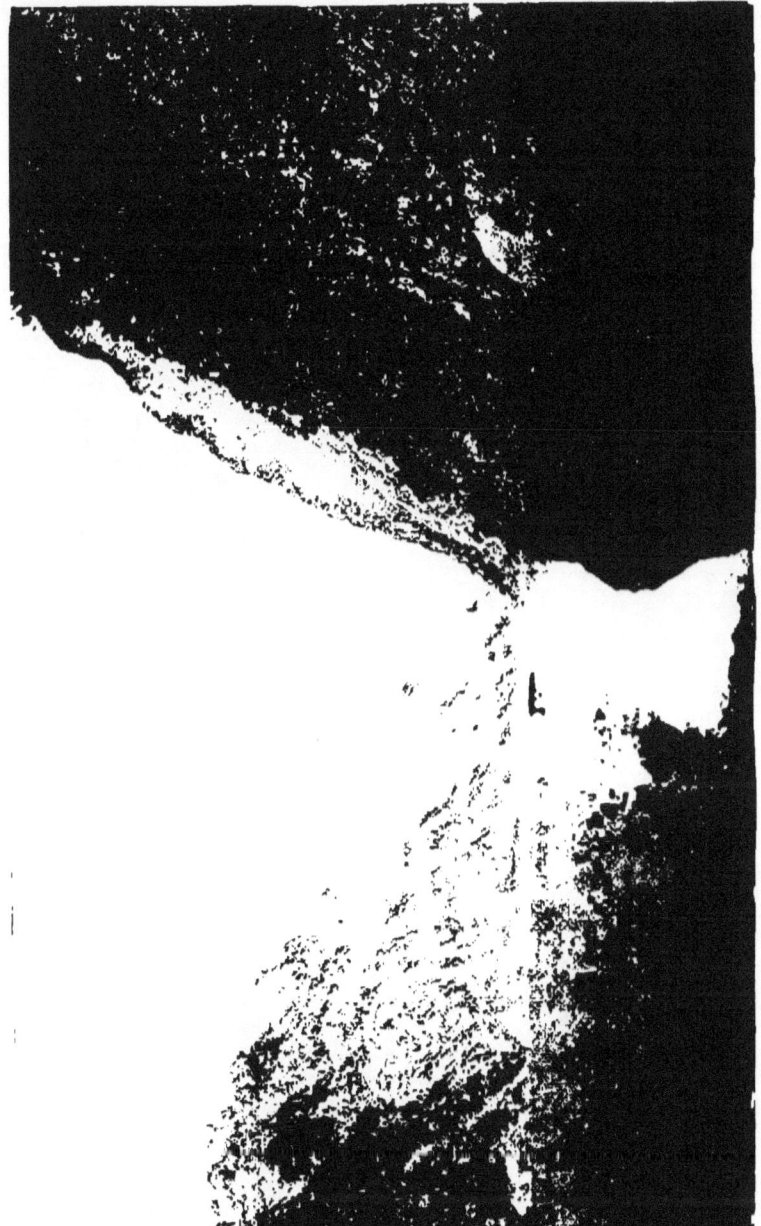

THE NÆROFJORD.

ranges. When I traversed the fjord there was cloud, but little wind, and the surface was calm enough. So we had a very tranquil voyage to Lærdalsören, which we reached about seven o'clock in the evening, and there the steamer was moored for the night.

Lærdal, as the place is more briefly called, is an important station, and large enough to be regarded as a small town rather than a village. It occupies a very central position, being about half-way between the extreme points of interest usually visited by tourists in Western Norway. It is easily accessible from every direction, as good roads lead to it as well as the great waterway on which it stands; or rather, I should say, that Lærdal does not exactly stand on the fjord, for the village lies a good mile from the landing-place, where cars are found ready in large numbers to convey passengers from the steamer to the hotels. But it is a very pleasant walk to the village, and indeed through it and beyond it. Once well advanced up the valley you find yourself in the midst of a vast basin, for it is a wide plain completely surrounded by lofty mountains. Lærdal at once strikes you as a comfortable and lively place, provided with ample accommodation, and I understand that many people make a long sojourn here.

There are several excursions to be taken from Lærdal, and the favourite one is a journey of some twenty miles to the famous and quaint old church of Borgund, with its pagoda-like roof, an edifice so frequently described that I need say no more about it here, especially as I had not time to go and see it. But distinctly an expedition to Borgund is a 'thing to be done,' as well as one to Marifjæren, where the scenery is said to be magnificent.

Within reach, though I cannot say within easy reach, of Lærdal is also the famous Vettisfos, one of the bigger waterfalls of Norway, with a sheer, unbroken descent of 1000 feet. But it is a long and troublesome journey to get to it—by boat to Aardal, and then a very stiff climb up mountains to the height of some 5000 feet. The path, it is true, passes through exquisitely beautiful scenery, but those who have seen the fall confess themselves a little disappointed with it, and declare the very rough work necessary for getting to it hardly worth the trouble. I suppose it is only to be seen to advantage when the snows are rapidly melting. Be this as it may, I left the Vettisfos unvisited.

You cannot indeed do everything, and my plans did not admit of a long stay at Lærdal. Still, after supper at Lindström's excellent hotel, I took as pleasant a walk as the rain, which now fell in a disagreeable drizzle, permitted in the environs of the village, passing a new and extremely handsome church, with double spires, built of wood, and some farm-houses embowered among really fine trees—a sight you do not often see in Norway—and getting as far as the broad and noble river Læra, which sweeps majestically through the valley to the fjord.

LÆRDALSÖREN.
(Page 151.)

The *Alden* was to start from Lærdal at three o'clock in the morning, but there was no need to sit up all night or sleep at an hotel in order to join the vessel at that early hour, for excellent and comfortable berths are provided on board, as on an ocean-going steamer. So I 'turned in' at my usual bed-time, and awoke to find the *Alden* well on her voyage.

It is a very fine trip, and is made, as I have said, on broad and stately waters, flanked on either side by great mountain-ranges. Several charming places are passed by the way. One of the most beautiful of these is Balholm, a place greatly resorted to by tourists not in a hurry. The sight of it, with its lovely background of wood, and the many delightful walks it must offer, was very tempting, but I could not afford the time to land.

I marked it out, however, as distinctly a place to make some stay at, and on the occasion of my second visit I proceeded direct from Gudvangen to Balholm in a steamer, which does not touch at Lærdal. It leaves Gudvangen four times a week at convenient hours, ranging between noon and 5 P.M., and after landing passengers at Balholm, goes up the Fjærland fjord to Mundal, which it reaches in two hours, returning immediately. It is not a bad plan to get out at Mundal, where there is a new and excellent hotel, and spend a day in exploring the very fine Suphelle and Bojum glaciers, offshoots of the Jostedalsbræ, which are famous for the beauty and purity of their ice, comparatively unsoiled as it is by the *débris* of *moraines*. Active climbers will do well to scramble up the Bojum to the top of the Skjeidesnipa mountain, 4725 feet, and descend by the Suphelle, an expedition worth the trouble and unattended by much difficulty. In any case, a trip up the Fjærland fjord should on no account be omitted during a visit to Balholm. The scenery on the way is not particularly remarkable till the glaciers come in sight, but then it is very fine indeed, on account of the beautiful colour of the ice and the stately manner in which it seems to descend almost to the level of the fjord. There are also some very pretty branches off the Fjærland, but these are best visited by boat from Balholm.

An unfortunate mishap took place in connection with this trip up the Fjærland fjord. Two young men who had been introduced to me in London, and for whom I had planned out a route, accompanied me on board the steamer from Gudvangen, and had decided to get out at Mundal with the intention of crossing the mountain from one glacier to the other. They were eager to do a bit of climbing over the snow and ice before their return, and I told them they could not have a better chance than they would find here, so I left them enjoying the anticipation of their projected adventure, and, being myself content with my trip up the fjord, returned by the steamer to Balholm.

The two youths went to the Mundal hotel and

BALHOLM.
(Page 153.)

engaged a guide to take them over the mountain. Unfortunately also, as it turned out, they decided also to hire a trap for the purpose of driving the short distance to the foot of the Bojumsbræ. They did not do this 'to save their legs,' but, as they expressed it, 'to see what a *stolkjærre* was like,' for they were on a walking tour, and had not yet used a vehicle in Norway. It was by a strange fatality that under these circumstances they should have met with an accident almost as soon as they had begun to take to the road on wheels. They were driven by a steady and experienced man from the hotel, but even the best of the *skydsguts* often drive too fast and without sufficient heed to the possible obstacles in their path. In the present case the party had not left Mundal half-an-hour when, spinning round a corner at a sharp bend of the road, one of the wheels of the car came in contact with a large stone; the vehicle was suddenly tilted on one side, and the two young travellers were shot out with great violence into the road. Both were hurt, one in the arm, the other being rather badly cut about the face. Luckily there was at this moment an English yacht lying in the fjord, and still more fortunately, the yachting party happened to be on the same road as my two friends, while, best of all, one of them was a surgeon. The injured youths were therefore promptly and skilfully attended to, but they had to remain several days at Mundal before they were in a fit state to travel.

It was not until long afterwards that I heard of the accident, when I was on my way back to Bergen, and it was too late for me to go to their assistance. Not, indeed, that this was needed, as they had every care and attention at Mundal, and the worthy landlord there was said to seem almost heartbroken by the mishap. He at once reported it to Bennett's, whose local agent he was, stating the circumstances with unimpeachable accuracy. Accidents of this kind, or indeed of any kind, are extremely rare in Norway, but they do happen sometimes, and travellers cannot be too particular in making their *skydsguts* drive them with care, and in reporting the conduct of those who drive recklessly.

Little anticipating the fate in store for my young friends, I parted with them on the quay at Mundal, and returning to Balholm took up my quarters there for the night. There is a noted hotel here called Kviknes', which is very popular and greatly resorted to, but it is sometimes over-crowded. I was recommended to go to a new hotel, the Balestrand, only just opened, and indeed hardly finished, and I cannot speak too gratefully of the manner in which I was treated there. It has quite as pleasant a lookout as its older neighbour, and possesses the advantage of a long pier, which is an agreeable lounge. The landlord is a capital fellow, though, unfortunately, he does not speak English, but he had, when I was there, the services of one of the brightest and most intelligent waiting-maids—

Anna Himry, for she really deserves that her name should be mentioned — whom it was my fortune to meet in all Norway. She has been in America, and speaks English perfectly, and is one of the most obliging girls that ever made a visitor comfortable. The landlord of the Balestrand got up a 'spring dance' specially for my amusement, and took part in it himself. This dance demands much agility and rapidity of movement. The partners set to one another and waltz, and the men, taking the women by the hands, twirl their arms over their heads and make them spin round every now and then. This figure is, as a rule, executed with much grace and dexterity, and it is especially noticeable that the men, though often big heavy fellows, have a singularly light step. The Norwegians, indeed, are exceptionally good dancers, for in the winter, in many places, dancing forms almost their only amusement.

It is agreeable to have such good quarters in so charming a spot, for Balholm is beyond doubt one of the most attractive resting places in the country. It is beautifully situated on the margin of the Sogne, here several miles broad, and across these wide waters a grand range of mountains is seen. Balholm, moreover, is a more than usually picturesque village, the houses being pretty, and the foliage more rich and varied than you find elsewhere. It has also a famous 'lion' in the grave of Frithjof, whose Saga, sung by Tegner, is one of the most romantic of Norse poems. Everybody, of course, goes to see Frithjof's grave, often, I fear, without the slightest idea as to who Frithjof was. It is a mound of earth surmounted by a Runic cross, and commands the most picturesque view in the neighbourhood. Balholm is a quiet place, but it is capable of great development. While very much prettier than Lærdal, it shares with that noted centre the advantage of being situated just about half-way between what may be called the two sections, northern and southern, of the 'grand' Norwegian tour. Those who have travelled from Stavanger to the Sogne, and who feel the want of a little rest, could not do better than seek such repose at Balholm before proceeding further, while, of course, it will be equally desirable and convenient to tarry here awhile on the way from the north.

One great advantage that Balholm offers lies in the fact that it is not only a pleasant place in itself, but is within such easy reach of so many other pleasant places. Not here, as elsewhere on the fjords, do you sometimes find yourself stranded, unable to get away for some days. Not a day passes without the arrival and departure of more than one steamer, and as the place grows, it is probable that the facilities for getting about will be still further increased. Already there are two local steamers carrying on an active rivalry, but starting and arriving with somewhat embarrassing fitfulness. When I was at Balholm an unfortunate traveller was warned that he must get up at six o'clock to catch a certain boat at seven. The unhappy man was disturbed at his breakfast by the news that the steamer was just going to start, and then having half-choked himself, he was informed that the captain had altered his mind and did not intend to depart till 8.30. Then there was a further respite till I think 11 A.M., and meanwhile the vessel did actually get off about 10.30. I am not sure whether I am quite right about the hours, but the vacillations of the steamboat captain were much as I have described them.

All this no doubt will be altered when Balholm takes the place it ought to occupy as a pleasure resort. At present it is comparatively virgin ground for the tourist who is not in a hurry. Its air is fresh and bracing, there are possibilities not yet realised of delightful walks by paths not yet cut among the hills and woods, and many a delicious backwater on a grand scale among the minor fjords to loaf about in a boat and fish for sea-trout and whiting. I hope no big speculator will seize upon Balholm one of these days and turn it into a noisy watering-place, with grand hotels, casinos, bands, and concert-halls, but the opportunities it offers in virtue of its fine and accessible situation are, I admit, tempting.

CHAPTER XVI.

VADHEIM TO THE JÖLSTERVAND.

THE stations on the Sogne stand at wide intervals, and all else along the shore is barren, desolate, and grand. Here and there you catch sight of a little village, which looks exactly like a box of child's toys, of the most old-fashioned and conventional sort, scattered anyhow, as by a child, on the shore. For the walls are white, with little dark dots representing the windows and door, and there is a bright strip of red roof above, while the little church with its sharp spire, and also with white walls and red roof, completes the toy idea. There can be no doubt that this quaint resemblance is due to the fact that these simple playthings were modelled 'from the life.'

In the course of the Sogne voyage the steamer runs up a branch called the Arne fjord, which is not seen of course in the night, but is visible when the boat starts early from Balholm. The fjord itself is of much the same character as many that we see elsewhere, but at the head of it is one of the most picturesque villages to be encountered on the trip.

It stands before you, piled up the hill in tier upon tier, the houses being capped with red roofs, and the whole crowned by a commanding church with a black roof and spire, while the scene is backed by a grand mass of mountain, down the side of which a fine waterfall descends. There is a warehouse in the foreground, and on the first floor of this building stood three little maidens in red, and on the second three more in blue, each group in a row. The whole scene would have made a pretty picture. Two other small fjords fork from the Arne, and the junction of their waters forms a very striking combination.

The route from Balholm to Bergen is indeed full of points of interest which are missed in the voyage by the direct steamer from Lærdal. The local boats take you into a number of pretty inlets, where you catch interesting glimpses of the life of the people. Gjvindvik, for instance, is a lovely spot, where the waters are extremely narrow, the mountains stand high, and the shores are richly wooded, while the scattered houses with their ruddy roofs, and the boats of the peasants flitting to and fro, lend great animation to the scene. Here and there, too, in these comparatively busy waters, you come across many of those great timber barges with their wide square-cut main-sails and top-sails, apparently fitted to catch nothing but a good stern wind, which I believe are peculiar to Norway, and are as picturesque as a Norfolk wherry or a Dutch *trekschuit*.

But these objects I saw in my second tour, and are off the route I am now describing.

My next destination was Vadheim. It is situated at the end of a narrow arm of the Sogne, which the steamer enters before pursuing her voyage to Bergen. But I had no intention of stopping at Vadheim, and I rather hesitate to say why. It is very rarely indeed in Norway that you are warned not to put up at some particular place, but the reasons for passing Vadheim by were so cogent, and were reiterated by so many people, that I could not but be guided by them. When I arrived at Vadheim I found that I had not been misinformed, and I got away from the place as soon as possible. Future travellers may easily ascertain on the road thither why Vadheim is not recommended as a resting-place, though it is pretty and healthy enough in itself. But no doubt one of these days the general objection to it will be removed. Meanwhile, let the reader take my advice and, hiring a *carriole* or *stolkjærre*, push on for Sande.

It is a lovely drive to Sande, as the scenery in many respects differs from that seen elsewhere. There are grand mountain-gorges to be traversed, especially at either end of the route, but the most noticeable characteristic of the landscape is its striking resemblance to some parts of Devonshire on the borders of Dartmoor. This likeness is most conspicuous when Sande itself is reached. The village stands in the midst of a richly wooded

ROAD NEAR VADHEIM.

valley, watered by a broad babbling river, the Gula, not unlike some parts of the Dart. The scene, indeed, in its soft beauty, affords a very pleasant relief after the sombre grandeur of the Sogne, and it is these bold contrasts that render travel in Norway so delightful. One day's journey differs so widely from the last as to lend all the best charm of variety to the tour.

Sivertsen's hotel at Sande is one of the best of the old-fashioned class, and there is no more attentive landlord than its host to be found in Norway. He was rather 'full' when I arrived—that is, of course, full of visitors—and offered at first to put me up at his 'dépendance,' which stands on a hill some little way off. But I preferred to lodge in the hotel if possible, and he told me that I could have a room if I did not mind sleeping at the top of the house. I said I was not particular, as long as I had not to go out of doors, so he gave me quarters in a sort of garret with a low sloping roof, which might have been rather embarrassing to a taller man than myself. However, I was comfortable enough there, and after all it was only for one night.

I spent the rest of the evening sauntering along the river-side, and the weather had now turned out fine again. I noticed several people fishing in the stream, but nobody seemed to be catching anything. Two young Englishmen who had gone further up or down the river had been more fortunate, and brought in several dozen trout between them, but the fish were very small, none weighing more than half a pound, and most of them only a few ounces.

And here let me say a word about fishing in Norway. There is a prevalent popular delusion on this subject which I may as well correct. About two-thirds of the people of my acquaintance to whom, on my return home, I imparted the fact that I had been spending my holiday in Norway, asked me at once, 'Did you do any fishing?' Some persons seem to think that you cannot go to Norway without fishing, and that if you do fish there you must have good sport. There could not be a greater mistake. In the first place, salmon-fishing in Norway is a very serious business, and is by no means accessible to every stray tourist. All the salmon-rivers are leased, and at very high rents, chiefly to wealthy foreigners, for the most part Englishmen, and to cast a fly into them, without poaching of course, is a very expensive privilege, and only to be obtained gratis by those fortunate persons who happen to be well acquainted with some proprietor of a river, or part of one, and is allowed by him to angle in his waters.

Trout-fishing, no doubt, is easily obtained—more easily than the trout themselves. You can get it almost anywhere either by leave or without, by payment of a small fee, or none at all. But trout of any size or in large quantity are not to be caught, as a rule, on the ordinary tourist track. You must go to places often very much out of the way to get

SANDE.
(Page 162.)

at fine heavy fish, weighing not ounces, but pounds. The best and biggest are caught in lakes and tarns far up among the mountains or in remote rivers, and it is undeniable that very good sport indeed is to be obtained if you know well how to cast your fly, and have the right flies to cast, and do not mind taking a good deal of trouble. I met one young gentleman on the road who had had very good sport, and had taken trout of several pounds' weight, but he was evidently an experienced hand, and had wandered some distance off the ordinary road. Those who are content with milder sport, and with trout of moderate size, may as well strap up a fly-rod with their umbrella, and try their luck where they get a chance. But, as a rule, you must come to Norway either to fish or to see the country. You cannot very well do both in a mere holiday tour.[1]

I had another charming drive from Sande the next day in cloudy, but otherwise fine, weather. My route still continued northward, and passed through scenery not less beautiful than that which I had enjoyed on the way from Vadheim to Sande. In the course of this journey I skirted several fine lakes, including the noble Langelandsvand, but I do not remember any other point of the route that calls for special notice. I fear to weary my readers by going into raptures over every pretty bit of landscape that pleased me at the time. It is enough to mention anything particularly striking when I

[1] See also page 322.

come to it. The scenery on the road was all more or less beautiful, and indeed in travelling in this country you become so satiated with fine views that you grow fastidious, and are apt to depreciate scenes which anywhere else would be thought wonderful. It is the quiet enjoyment of wandering day after day among such lovely country that to my taste constitutes the chief charm of travel in Norway, but if you record every thing you witnessed you will speedily come to be regarded as a bore.

There was one feature of the journey in this part of the country which, however, I must mention. Elsewhere in Norway the roads are excellent: level and well-made where the land is flat, and cleverly wound about in zigzags where hills have to be climbed. Oddly enough the Norwegians rarely make a cutting or build up an embankment; they go over the surface of the land, and where they find a difficulty they 'dodge' it, often in the most ingenious way. But I had now come to a part of the country where road-making had been carried on in a very uncompromising fashion. I had reached, in fact, the region of what I may call the 'switchback' road, if I may apply to it the term so familiarly associated with an engine of amusement and suffering that has lately become popular in connection with some of our exhibitions. 'Switchback' is, indeed, the only name to give to the abrupt and frequent ups and downs of the roads I traversed on the way from

FÖRDE (SÖNDFJORD.)
(Pag. 16)

Sande to Förde. Every few minutes you are crawling up a hill; the next you are rattling down one, until your journey is very much like what it would be on a tempest-tossed ocean if the waves were solid. 'Up we go and down we go' might be the cry all the way for miles upon miles.

Förde, where I stayed to dine, is a very charming place indeed, and is one of those chosen for a prolonged residence. It stands in the midst of a wide fertile valley abounding in pretty views of all kinds. The brother of Mr. Sivertsen, of Sande, has a hotel here, and judging from the *table d'hôte*, at which I dined, and the general appearance of the house, which is delightfully situated near the river, it must be a most comfortable one to stay at. Förde lies at the head of a comparatively short fjord bearing its name, by which you can steam to the open sea, and go either south to Bergen or north to Molde. My road lay round the head of this fjord, and through pretty but somewhat wilder country to Nedre Vasenden.

Here there is a fine lake, the Jölstervand, some fourteen miles long, and steam-launches ply on it two or three times a day each way. These severally belong to the hotels at Fuglehaug (the Stanley), and at Skei (pronounced Stehei), a little further along the lake. There is great jealousy and rivalry between the proprietors of these hostelries, so it is advisable not to ask the captain of one steamer to put you down at the hotel which owns the other vessel, as he will probably decline to do so. But as a matter of fact, I believe, one hotel is as good as the other for a short stay, though the Stanley has the higher reputation. As a matter of fact, the steamer that was about to start when I arrived at Nedre Vasenden belonged to the Skei establishment, so I went on there.

While waiting to start I noticed a group of peasant women in a sort of costume which I had not seen elsewhere. It consisted of a dark blue gown, and a curious peaked cap, round in front and terminating in a point at the back. It was not so showy as the Hardanger and Voss dresses, but quaint and picturesque.

The Jölster lake is overshadowed on one side by the mountains which form a border of the vast tableland covered by the Jostedalsbræ, the most gigantic glacier in Europe, which spreads over an area of about five hundred square miles, and is said to throw off more than twenty branches into the valleys around it. We got a few glimpses of this tremendous ice-field as we passed, but you cannot see much of these great frozen plains without ascending mountains, as, unlike the snow-peaks of the Alps, they lie flat and above the line of sight. For the hardy pedestrian, well accustomed to mountaineering, a ramble over the Jostedal must be an experience after his own heart. It can be traversed without any great difficulty from point to point in many places, but guides are often necessary. While

JÖLSTERSVAND.
(Page 167.

I was at Skei two young gentlemen, who had come across the glacier, presented themselves at the hotel at two o'clock in the morning. This early visit, of which, of course, nothing would be thought in Switzerland, obtained for the travellers a somewhat grumbling reception, for Norwegian hotel-keepers are not accustomed to be knocked up in the middle of the night.

It is a pleasant run of some two hours in the steamer to Skei, for the lake is much longer than it looks from Nedre Vasenden. What seems to be its boundary is only the shoulder of a mountain that cuts across it, but affords a passage to the further and larger part of the lake when you turn the corner.

From a village off which we stopped a boat put out laden with girls and boys, who came on board to be conveyed to Skei, where they were to be prepared for confirmation, a rite to which great importance is attached in Norway, as I believe I have observed elsewhere. Very nice, well-behaved youngsters were these children. They were all neatly dressed; most of the boys wearing caps of fine grey bearskin, very light, but warm and soft to the touch. The children were promptly stowed away below, and I amused myself by looking down at them from the upper deck. The girls were sitting demurely side by side, and the boys wandering about as boys are wont to do everywhere. They were all very quiet, so I thought I would try to get up a little excitement among them.

Having read somewhere that sugar is scarce and dear in Norway, and sweetmeats a rarity, I had brought with me from England a bag of lollipops for the enjoyment of any children I might chance to meet. I found that I had not been misinformed as to the scarcity of sweetmeats in Norway, and I need hardly say that my small gifts were keenly appreciated wherever I distributed them. It was often amusing to see the wonder and delight of the little ones at receiving a bit of 'rock' or candy. They generally, however, accepted it very gravely and quietly, the girls acknowledging it with a curtsey, and the boys with a doffing of the hat, and both with a '*mange tak*' and shake of the hand. I now treated the lads and lasses below deck to a scramble, and instantly these quiet youngsters threw off their national gravity, and struggled for the dainties I threw down among them as vigorously as any boys or girls elsewhere. It was benevolence, if I may call it so, well bestowed, and doubtless these youngsters would go home with kindly recollections of the Englishman they had met on board the steamer.

CHAPTER XVII.

BY MOLDESTAD TO THE NORD FJORD.

It had been a pleasant voyage on the Jölster lake, but a very cold one. The afternoon had been cloudy, and though there was little wind the air was keen. I may say that at all times, even in the height of summer, it is apt to be more or less chilly in Norway when the sun is not actually shining, and those are unwise who come to this country unprovided with warm wraps. You do not want anything very heavy, but an overcoat or cloak is indispensable. I had neither, and suffered slightly from my want of precaution. I had never found it so cold in any other part of Norway as it was on board the lake boat. Doubtless this was due to the fact that we were so near the great ice-field of the Jostedal. Be it as it may, I caught a chill and arrived at Skei in by no means good condition. I mention this fact partly to warn future travellers against the imprudence of travelling in Norway without sufficiently warm clothing, and partly for another reason which will presently be apparent.

The hotel at Skei is beautifully situated at the head of the lake, and you can see from its front windows the other hotel, the Stanley, to the right of the lake, a few miles off. The quarters assigned me were very comfortable, and the good lady who managed the hotel was one of the most obliging hostesses I had ever met. Being unwell, I was treated with remarkable kindness, and I desire to call attention to one fact which hitherto had been unexampled in my experience. I sat down to supper and ordered tea. A cup of that beverage was placed before me, and I was also provided with hot fish and other comestibles. But I had lost my appetite and was unable to eat or drink, and so retired to my room before supper was over. *Now that meal was not charged for in my bill*, and, as I found on asking for an explanation, had been intentionally omitted. In what other part of the Continent, or, for the matter of that, the world, would such scrupulous honesty have been displayed?

Nor was this an exceptional instance of Norwegian conscientiousness. The next day I went on to Egge, but by the time I arrived there I had not recovered my appetite. I sat down to dinner, but played a very poor knife and fork, once more rising from the table before the meal was finished. *Again no charge was made.* I pointed out to the landlord's representative that my dinner did not figure in the bill, and his simple reply was, 'No, sir; you did not eat much!' It was indeed astonishing; but I was told that it was thoroughly characteristic of the habits of this wonderfully honourable people.

In connection with this same indisposition of mine, I may mention another little incident curiously illustrative of Norwegian ways. I must premise by saying that the licensing laws in Norway are extraordinarily stringent, and those who talk here about the restriction of the liquor traffic, whether by way of objection or approval, have probably but a faint idea of the limitation put upon the sale of intoxicants in that country. In neither town nor village is there such a thing to be seen as a house devoted to the sale of drink—no public-houses or beershops of any kind whatever. The sale of spirits is permitted at hotels and refreshment places in large towns like Stavanger and Bergen, but not after 8 P.M., or 5 P.M. on Saturdays, while at all country hotels it is absolutely prohibited. To many travellers of course this is a great hardship, but they have to put up with it. There is a way no doubt of obtaining a 'nip' of brandy and the like, but it is an irregularity not very often risked. The landlord, or his representative, if you seem a person to be trusted, and you make a very pressing demand or feasible excuse for a dram, will say that he cannot sell it you, but would not mind 'making you a present of it,' though you must be careful not to 'tell.' In this way you may sometimes, but by no means always, get your drop of strong drink. It was thus that I induced the attendant at Egge to supply me with a little brandy which in this case was really a necessary. I could not find that the natives complained much, if at all, of the very strict temperance laws of their country, and was informed that since these were enacted there had been hardly any drunkenness in Norway. Possibly the people have become resigned to this state of things, because the only spirits they ever distil consist of a detestable liquid called *akvavit*, with a taste of carraway or aniseed, one sip of which was enough for me. Future travellers who cannot do without their 'drop of comfort' will do well to take it with them.

Thanks to the gratuitous brandy and other remedies, I soon shook off my little indisposition, or at any rate felt well enough to start once more on my travels. I was now bound for the district traversed by the Nord fjord and its offshoots; and this country may be reached from the Jölsterdal by either of two routes, the old or the new. You can proceed by the old road to the lake Bredhjem, and go by boat to Reed (pronounced Red), and drive thence to Moldestad; or you may take the new road which runs direct to the last-named place, and avoids the lake altogether.

As the weather was bad, I chose the latter and easier route, but they say the former is more picturesque. The new road was pretty enough, or rather it would have appeared so if it had not been such a bad day—the first I had had in Norway. And to make the position more unpleasant I had before me the stiffest bit of travelling I had yet experienced. A new and excellent road, as I have said, leads to Moldestad, but from that point, over the mountain which has to be crossed to reach the fjord, there is what is said to be the steepest highway in Europe. It is certainly very rough, and the *skydsguts* frequently request their passengers to walk it. I myself, though by no means in good walking condition, could not find it in my heart to make the little horse drag me up such a hill, so I performed the journey for the most part on foot. In fine weather it is only a rather rough climb, but under a drizzling rain such as fell during my march, it is not at all agreeable. There are grand views looking backward, too, as you ascend, but these were partially obliterated by the clouds that hung about the mountains. So I was not sorry when I got to the top of this rugged hill road, and could reconcile it to my sense of humanity to re-enter the *carriole*. That it must be a fearful pass to traverse in the winter, is suggested by the presence of a long series of tall poles like telegraph posts which skirt the road for the purpose of marking the course of the highway when the snows lie thick on the ground. A long wild barren ridge forms the summit of the pass, and then a splendid road descends in easy windings, through thick forest, to Utvik and the Nord fjord.

Utvik is the usual sort of place of its kind, for I found these fjord villages all very much alike—a few wooden houses and a hotel or two, but nothing noticeable about them except the scenery with which they are surrounded. Nor was there at first sight anything very novel in the aspect of the Nord fjord. In its general features it resembles the Sogne rather than the Hardanger, the waters being broad and the mountains rocky and bare.

It is customary to cross from Utvik to Faleide in a rowing boat. The distance is some seven miles, and the passage generally occupies about two hours. On this occasion the water was very rough, and I am not sure whether the boatmen would have ventured to take me over; certainly I doubt whether I should have cared to cross just then. But I had been singularly lucky hitherto in catching steamers when I wanted them, and I was equally fortunate now, as a steam-launch was to start for Faleide an hour or so after my arrival. It was called the *Gordon*, and ran once or twice a day between Faleide and Utvik.

I was not the only passenger, as soon after I arrived I was overtaken by a party consisting of three young ladies and one gentleman. Two of the former were Dutch and one English, while their male friend was a Norwegian. They were all on a walking-tour, provided with knapsacks—and a very merry party they were as well as a plucky one. The ladies had marched over that terrible Moldestad hill in spite of the wretched weather, and had walked a distance of some twenty miles from Skei, yet they did not seem in the least degree fatigued, and chatted and laughed among themselves with a vivacity that

FALEIDE.
(Page 176.)

was very amusing. They spoke sometimes in Dutch, sometimes in Norsk, and sometimes in English, and all three languages seemed the same to them. They were good 'sailors,' too, and were in no way disconcerted by the tossing of the waves over which the little *Gordon* bounded like a cork. A drizzling rain was still falling, but we were quite snug in the *Gordon's* little cabin, and had a lively passage in every sense.

Faleide is a place of great resort for tourists in Norway. As at Stalheim and Odde, 'everybody' goes there. Its situation by the fjord side is very pleasant, and the accommodation of Tenden's, its principal hotel, is excellent. This house, I believe, is to be extended, as it is often overcrowded in the season. The principal attraction of Faleide no doubt lies in its surroundings, for it can be made the base of a great many interesting excursions, most of which, however, involve a rather long trip across the fjord. For this purpose the steam-launch *Gordon* is frequently used. The steamer, it appears, is the property of the landlord of the *Gordon* hotel at Reed, but oddly enough the people of the hotel at Faleide seem to repudiate it, for on being asked when it is going to start they tell you that they know nothing about it. However, it is only a step to the quay, and full information can be had on board, though, strange to say, no notice is put up anywhere acquainting strangers as to the movements, or even the existence, of the little vessel. This is

M

one of the eccentricities of Norwegian life, of which I have given an example or two elsewhere. One would surely expect to see, in a place so much frequented as Faleide, a regular recognised ferry service.

I have no particular fault to find with Faleide, and admit that for the regular conventional tourist, it is quite the proper place to go to. Still I am not sure whether I might not have done better to take the advice given me by an experienced traveller of my own way of thinking as regards places to stop at, who recommended me to go to Olden or Loen on the other side of the fjord. There is excellent accommodation at both, as well as at Visnæs, at the head of the fjord, and all these spots are more conveniently situated than Faleide for excursions to the many magnificent scenes to be viewed in the neighbourhood.

The finest and most easily accessible of these are to be found on the Loen and Opstrynd lakes, which are among the most beautiful in Norway, presenting views of glaciers and snow-fields much more extensive than are to be obtained from the Jölstervand. The lakes can be reached by *carriole* or other conveyance, and there are always boats ready for a trip on the waters. Of Opstrynd I cannot speak from personal experience, though photographs of its scenery show it to be of exquisite beauty. But the Loen lake, which I visited, must be almost equally fine, especially in better weather than I was favoured with.

LOEN LAKE.
(Page 178.)

There is a great deal more to see in this district for those who have time to devote to it, and a good climber would do well to mount some height or other, and there are many which are not difficult to ascend, for the purpose of surveying the incomparable ice and snow-fields of the Jostedal. I should have done more in this interesting region if the weather had been finer, but it is not pleasant to make excursions on lakes in an open boat under a persistent drizzle, and with thick mists hanging about the mountains. So, very reluctantly, I quitted the Nord fjord, leaving many of its most interesting scenes unvisited.

CHAPTER XVIII.

HELLESYLT AND THE GEIRANGER.

When I left Falcide the sky was cloudy, but there was no rain. I started early, for I had a long drive before me, as the destination I had selected for the day was Hellesylt, distant about thirty miles. While making preparations for my departure I felt put to shame by the sight of the three plucky young ladies I had met at Utvik packing and buckling on their knapsacks, with the view of walking the road over which I intended to drive. I had made many a pedestrian tour at home and abroad in bygone years, and no one is more sensible to the delights of a journey on foot than I am. Its careless freedom, the health and strength it gives you, and last, but not least, its cheapness, are advantages to be obtained by no other mode of travel. And Norway, let me say, is in every way suitable for a walking-tour. It has capital roads, none the worse, indeed all the better, as old pedestrians will admit, for being hilly, and is well supplied with hotels and resting-places. It is even practicable for very skilful and experienced cyclists; at any rate, I met several young men here and there, who had brought with them, and were using, both bicycles and tricycles. But Norway is such a vast country, and its picturesque scenery is scattered over so wide a space of ground, that it is impossible to see more than a comparatively small portion of it, if your time is limited, and you trust only to 'Shanks' mare.'

This must be my apology, if apology be needed, for making what some may regard as a rather lazy tour, using somebody else's wheels instead of my own legs. I must confess that I envied those plucky damsels and other pedestrians whom I met on the road, and felt more than once strongly disposed to send my light baggage forward, and go on the tramp with them. As it was, it afforded me great pleasure to comply with their request that I would take their knapsacks and some of their wraps with me in my *carriole*, which I was able to do, as my own luggage was very light. I rendered them the same little service later on, after we had reached Hellesylt. And here is a hint to future pedestrians, which they will find useful. They will often find some traveller who is driving able and willing to take their knapsack for them, and the *skydsguts* and postmasters make no objection to this arrangement.

I started early for Hellesylt, and was fortunate in securing a tolerably good *carriole* at any rate for the first stage. But when about half-way to my destination I had to change both horses and vehicle. At the station, Indre Haugen, they had no *carrioles*, but gave me a *stolkjærre*. This was a pretty good one, but I was accompanied by the biggest and heaviest *skydsgut* that had yet driven me; and this young giant, who sat by my side, so greatly outweighed me that all the rest of the way I found myself seated on a slope, which was not a comfortable position.

The first few miles of the journey passed through very pretty country. Immediately on quitting Faleide the road mounts a hill, through thick pine woods, revealing here and there wide views of the fjord. After a while you lose sight of it, and plunge into a deep narrow valley, and on emerging from this the scenery becomes rather less interesting, though still bold and imposing. The first station on the road is Kjos, a small village at one extremity of the great Horningdal lake, which is about twenty miles long.

I arrived here about noon, and had been at the hotel scarcely half an hour, when I was surprised to see the three lady-walkers and their companion come in. They must have marched well to have thus almost overtaken me in my *carriole*, and I complimented them on their activity. They scarcely indeed seemed to require a rest, but they proposed to vary the method of their journey by proceeding by boat to the next station, Grodaas, which lies at the northern corner of the head of the lake, we being, at Kjos, at the southern angle. The two points are connected, of course, by road, but obviously the more pleasant route would be by water, for the

KJOS ON HORNINGDAL LAKE.
(Page 1-2.)

scenery of the Horningdalsvand is very fine, and can best be seen from the lake. So, as I readily obtained permission to join the party, we engaged a large boat, with two rowers, and set out on our little water-excursion. The distance is not great, but it is stiff rowing in these heavy boats, and our progress was slow. After a time one of the young Dutchwomen took a pair of oars and rowed as vigorously and steadily as the two strong men behind her.

Our course lay at the foot of a gigantic mass of rock towering many hundred feet above our heads, and round this we gradually crept, till at a bend of the shore Grodaas appeared in sight. There we landed, after a trip of about an hour and a half, arriving in time for dinner.

The price I had to pay for this pleasant little voyage was, perhaps, the very smallest in my record of travelling expenses. We were a party of five, and my proportion was, therefore, one-fifth. Will it be believed that the charge for a boat for an hour and a half, with two rowers, not counting the lady, came to only 30 *öre* : that is about fourpence a head ? It is a fact nevertheless.

There are two hotels at Grodaas, both pleasantly situated on the very margin of the lake, and having balconies commanding splendid views of it. We chose Raftevold's, and chose wisely, as we afterwards learned. It is a long-established house, and a perfect type of that old-fashioned country inn, which some people prefer to any other class. The landlord's daughter, who speaks English fluently, waits on the guests, and it is evident, from the inscriptions you see in her many books which are lying about the room, that she is a popular person besides being a young lady of superior education.

The advertisement-cards of Raftevold's tell you that an ancient bride's costume is to be seen at the hotel, and, I need hardly say, that we—more especially the ladies of our party—were eager to inspect this curiosity. At our request Miss Raftevold duly produced it, and exhibited its splendours before our admiring eyes. Very gorgeous indeed were these bridal trappings. They consisted of bands and belts, and a skirt of various bright-coloured stuffs, profusely garnished with silver and silver-gilt ornaments and embroidery, and with these was worn a large and gaudily decorated crown, the elaborate finery of which almost defies description. In this barbaric splendour the brides of the family had been wedded for many generations—in fact the same costume had been in use at intervals during a space of nearly two hundred years.

Having dined well, we travellers set forth again, the pedestrians resuming their march, and I mounting my *carriole*. The road ascends for some distance from Grodaas presenting beautiful prospects of the Horningdalsvand, which is in some respects not a little like our Ullswater. After it disappears from view the landscape becomes very bleak and barren, several small lakes are passed and you enter as wild and desolate a track of country as any seen elsewhere. But there are some remarkable mountains here and there, the most noticeable of which is the Horningdalsrok, shaped like a cone, and having a peak of singular sharpness. The road is very rough in some places, but a new one is in course of construction along the bottom of the valley. This is seen in its fragmentary condition from the higher ground, and when you descend to its level you frequently join and cross it. Here and there it is practicable for driving, and it will make a fine highway for this much-travelled district when it is finished.

The stations passed on the way are Indre Haugen and Kjelstadli, but they are very poor places with scanty accommodation for travellers. Both are, however, provided with a few beds, and are available for lodging in an emergency. They are of a class common enough in the interior and more out-of-the-way parts of the country, but no one would think of stopping at them if he could help it. It was for this reason that I was making so long a journey, for indeed there is no spot worth staying at between Grodaas and Hellesylt.

Within a few miles of the last-named place a side valley opens to the left. This is the Nebbedal, and it leads to the Hjörund fjord, which I subsequently visited. At this point the scenery greatly improves, and so does the road. We are now on the descent to Hellesylt, and our way lies through a splendid ravine resembling in character some of the finer glens of North Wales. The mountain-sides are thickly clothed with fir and birch, and far below one of those grand torrents, which are among the chief glories of Norway, foams and roars on its way to the fjord. The road winds very gradually down the valley-side, and near the mouth of the glen it crosses a bridge, both above and below which there are magnificent cascades. From this point the descent is steeper, and the highway doubles on itself repeatedly to obtain a more gradual incline.

My *skydsgut*, the gigantic person I picked up at Haugen, now makes up for lost time, as our progress till we reached this valley had been very slow, and he spins down the road to Hellesylt at a fine pace! But that the little horses are so sure-footed, and the cars, as a rule, so well looked after in the matter of springs, axles, and the like, this headlong descent might be thought somewhat risky. However, the *skydsgut* seems to know what he is about, and with one dashing sweep round the last angle of the road he lands me safely at the door of the Hellesylt hotel.

This is a very comfortable house, and has the advantage of a functionary called the 'interpreter,' a highly intelligent young man who speaks excellent English, and makes himself generally agreeable and useful. He is brim full of local information of every kind, is able to tell you when the steamboats leave not only Hellesylt, but distant places, and what are the best walks and drives to take in the neighbourhood, and can give valuable advice as to your future route. I have found many civil and attentive *portiers* at other Norwegian hotels, but their stock of knowledge, as a rule, related chiefly to their own locality, and none showed themselves so generally well-informed as Louis Bruvold, of Hellesylt.

Having had a chat with him on the balcony of the hotel, which has a look-out on the fjord, and is reached by a flight of steps from the road, I thought I would stroll up the road and meet the plucky lady-walkers and their male friend. I had arrived about eight o'clock, and it was still broad daylight at ten when I saw the three girls come trotting along almost as fresh as though they had but lately begun their journey. And yet they must have walked nearly thirty miles that day. They declared that they were not much fatigued, and I rather think that the gentleman was the most tired member of the party. Certainly they seemed to prove the truth of Autolycus's song, 'A merry heart goes all the day,' for they were almost incessantly laughing. Whatever language they spoke in—and they were always chatting in one or other of three—the subject of their conversation seemed to be a humorous one. Well, it is a sad world; and it is pleasant to see people who are always gay. It was not till long after I had gone to bed that these young folks were at rest, as I heard them, through the thin partitions of the wooden house, still chattering and laughing till close upon midnight.

Hellesylt has a fine situation, not unlike that of Gudvangen, for the mountains that seem to enclose the waters below them are of much the same stupendous and precipitous character as those of the Nærö fjord. To the left of the village the torrent that traverses the ravine through which I had passed descends in a cascade of considerable height direct into the fjord, while to the right another river steals placidly out of another valley to the same bourne. The village lies partly along the shore, and partly on the side of the hill, where, on a prominent knoll, stands a plain wooden church with a spire, and the whole place looks well from the fjord.

Those who survey the scene may observe that on the right side of the great water-lane before them there seems to be a sort of cleft or indentation, and may be little aware at first of the fact that it marks the portal of what is beyond doubt the very grandest bit of scenery in Norway—the renowned Geiranger fjord. It was on the day after my arrival at Hellesylt that I explored this wonderful arm of the sea, as a small steamer belonging to the hotel was to make a trip to Merok in the afternoon. I was again rather unfortunate in the weather, for there was a drizzling rain at intervals nearly all day which

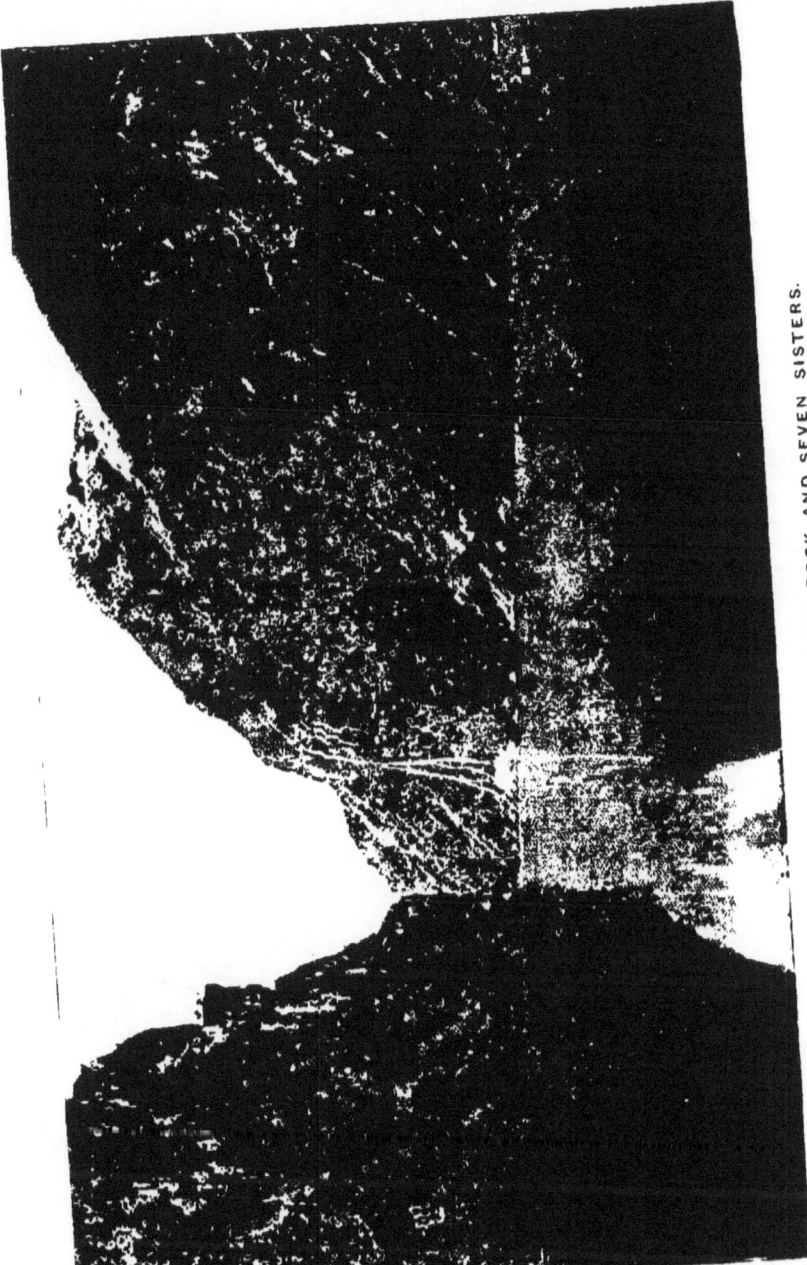

THE GEIRANGERFJORD. PULPIT ROCK AND SEVEN SISTERS.
(Pag. 187.)

greatly spoiled the pleasure of the voyage. Yet the charm of the Geiranger consists in near rather than distant views, and nothing but an impenetrable mist—and this happily was absent—could shut them out.

And what a scene it was! Others that I had beheld in Norway were fine, grand, even sublime, but no adjective has yet been coined that could adequately convey an idea of the stupendous magnificence of the Geiranger fjord. Perhaps, after all, simple facts will most clearly explain the character of this marvellous scene. Imagine then a dark waterway absolutely placid, and in no place more than a few hundred yards wide, bordered on either side by gigantic walls of grey and black granite from four to five thousand feet high. They shoot up in a line so straight that a stone dropped from the summit must fall direct into the water. And these mighty precipices extend all along the course of the fjord for many miles, until at last both shores circle round and join in a vast amphitheatre. Under their deep shadows the vessel creeps silently on, while the voices of the passengers are hushed by the solemnity of the spectacle. It must, indeed, surely be impossible to pass through this dark and awful avenue without being profoundly impressed by its weird and grandiose aspect. It is one of those rare scenes of Nature which overwhelm the mind that contemplates them.

Only when the eye has become to some extent

familiarised with this truly sublime spectacle can attention be given to the many curious details which the passage of the fjord reveals. Several lofty waterfalls descend from the summits of these giant rocks, but the most noted of them is somewhat disappointing. This is called the 'Seven Sisters,' but only four or five streaks of water, side by side, are visible. Possibly the others make their appearance when the snows are beginning to melt. Elsewhere the rocks are singularly stained with great patches of black, as though giant hands had poured vast quantities of ink down their sides. At another point a curious projection overhead takes the form of a pulpit, and is so called. But the most striking eccentricity of this mighty range is the position of a farm perched high up among the crags. It stands 1600 feet above the level of the fjord, and is reached by an almost perpendicular path with the aid of stanchions and chains. There is some pasture-land even at this immense altitude, but probably nowhere else in Europe has any human being ever chosen such a singular eyric.

The vast amphitheatre which forms the end and head of the Geiranger fitly closes this magnificent gorge. Its proportions are as symmetrical as they are massive, and it contrasts pleasingly with the bare rocks we have passed, as it is richly clothed with wood and verdure, and a splendid torrent, the Otta, rushes down its centre. Below we see the pretty village of Merok, with its curious octagon church on a knoll behind it, and here we land. The amphitheatre above Merok is scaled by means of the most wonderful road in Norway. It goes in windings up the mountain in countless bends, and extends for many miles. At almost every turn it crosses the torrent of which I have spoken, and every bridge that spans the stream gives a view of magnificent cascades. Following one of the by-paths you come to a waterfall of grand dimensions, the Storfos, but the waters are boiling and roaring around you on every side. At an elevated point, many hundred feet above the fjord, there is a terrace and look-out (*udsigten*), and here I was obliged to terminate my walk, as I had to catch the steamer on her return voyage. But it is by no means the end of the road, which goes much higher, and is intended at last to join the Gudbrandsdal highway to Trondhjem and Lillehammer. The descent is as interesting as the ascent, as it presents fine views of the fjord and the dark walls by which it is enclosed. Unfortunately the bad weather prevented me from seeing them to the best advantage, but still the clouds that hung about the heights gave them a peculiar, sombre grandeur. The return voyage on the Geiranger is quite as impressive as that made in the opposite direction, and as the rain had now ceased I had a more favourable view of the scene.

One trifling circumstance enabled me to realise the immense height of these gigantic cliffs. The steamers are always followed by a flock of gulls, on the look-out for food, and one of these birds, either satisfied or disappointed by its quest, left us to seek its nest high up among the rocks above. I watched the bird as it flew up the side of the mountain, its white form and flapping wings standing out clearly against the dark grey rock. Little by little it diminished in size, until, when only half-way up the height, it appeared no bigger than a butterfly, then a mere white speck, and ere it had reached its home it had wholly vanished from sight. I arrived at Hellesylt late in the evening, after a trip that convinced me that the very finest and most impressive scene in Norway was the mighty Geiranger.

[A new route is now open from the Nordfjord to the Geiranger which, I believe, is much more interesting than that *via* Horningdal. A fine carriage road has been completed from Hjelle, at the eastern end of lake Opstrynd to Grotlid and thence to Merok. It is 41 *kil.* from Hjelle to Grotlid, and as much more to Merok. There is good accommodation at several points of the route, and the scenery in many parts is of the most magnificent kind. It seems an important addition to 'The Best Tour.'— May 1896.]

CHAPTER XIX.

BY THE HJÖRUND FJORD TO AALESUND.

I HAVE already said how much indebted I was to the good-natured and intelligent 'interpreter' of the Hellesylt hotel for the useful information he gave me, and I have to thank him for inducing me to take a route which is not often pursued, but which is, beyond doubt, by far the best to follow after leaving Hellesylt. From that place the tourist bound northward invariably makes his way to the Romsdal, and it is customary to take the steamer from Hellesylt to Söholt, drive thence to Vestnæs, and take the steamer again to Veblungsnæs and Aandalsnæs. There is, however, a very much better way of making the journey, for it enables you to see one of the most remarkable scenes in Norway. This is the route via the Nebbedal and the Hjörund fjord, and it is that which I adopted.

I started from Hellesylt on the morning after my expedition to the Geiranger in a comfortable *carriole*, and re-ascended the road through the ravine which I had previously traversed as far as the Nebbedal, which now lay to the right. This part of the journey was not quite so satisfactory as that which was to come. For one thing, the Nebbedal road was quite the worst I had yet travelled upon. It was a mere country cart-track of the stoniest and ruttiest kind, all up and down, with scarcely a dozen yards of level ground for many miles. I wondered how a station *carriole* could be allowed to ply on such a rough road. So I alighted and walked in front of my conveyance, a more agreeable mode of locomotion than the process of being banged and jolted about over the loose stones. For the scenery of the Nebbedal a very few words will suffice, as the valley is utterly bare, is monotonously straight, and presents very few picturesque features. A stream of no great beauty passes through it, broadening in many places into lakes or tarns, and altogether it seemed to me about the dreariest bit of country I had yet seen. It is entirely uninhabited except by the occupants of one or two rude *sæters* here and there, and the fields, such as they are, appear to afford poor pasture for the few thin cattle we met on the way.

The only human beings we encountered in the valley were two children, who seemed wilder and more timid than the mountain-goats. I noticed them, a girl and a boy, squatting on the hillside and gazing down on me with wondering and half frightened looks. I beckoned them to come to me, and held out my bag of sweetmeats as a temptation. It was some time before they could comprehend my purpose, but presently the little lad crept shyly down the mountain, and then, I need hardly say, we soon came to an understanding. He accepted the handful of sweets which I gave him with a grave look and no excitement. He did not doff his hat or thank me, and it was I who had to take the initiative in giving the friendly hand-shake, which so invariably seals such transactions elsewhere in Norway. The poor lad doubtless was not ungrateful, but probably it was the unprecedented novelty of the experience that thus made him forget his 'manners.'

The Nebbedal ends in a very narrow pass, a mere cleft in the rocks, which is the one really fine point in the valley, and as soon as you have got through this, you enter upon a new and much more pleasing scene, and besides have the advantage of a civilised road over which you can drive in comfort.

I was now in the Norangdal, which is justly celebrated for its beauty, and presented a complete contrast to the barren valley behind me. It is richly fertile everywhere, abounding in fine trees and meadows brilliantly green, and now and again I passed what looked like a respectable and thriving farmstead. But the most remarkable feature of the Norangdal is its mountain scenery. Here I had come upon something quite new. The heights that skirt the Norwegian fjords and vales are, as a rule, the borders of vast table lands, and their ridges are more or less straight or take the form of huge shoulders. But here in the Norangdal the mountains terminate in peaks and pinnacles, or what are known in Switzerland as 'horns' and 'aiguilles.' Few of these are capped with snow, though snow lies in patches on their sides, but their sharp crags assume a hundred fantastic shapes. The drive ends at Öie, a village that lies a short distance from the Norang fjord, which comes in sight not long before its shores are reached. I had timed my journey so as to catch the steamer that was due to start from Öie at 5 P.M., and as I arrived at the hotel about 3 P.M. I was able to dine comfortably.

The inn is a very good one, and has the services of the best English-speaking waitress I had yet met. This young woman had, indeed, lived for some time in America, a country which every year absorbs a large proportion of the Norwegian population, and was remarkable for her good manners. I had always found the attendants at all hotels civil and obliging; but this particular damsel gilded the refined gold of her courtesy, so to speak, by calling me 'sir.' It is a curious fact that with all their natural politeness, with all their hat-lifting and hand-shaking, the Norwegians never address a stranger by any title of respect. They seem to have no equivalent for 'your honour,' or 'monsieur,' or 'mein Herr,' or any of those other verbal forms with which the inferior in rank salutes his superior elsewhere. Yet you are never struck with the idea that they wish to appear insolent or even familiar or independent. They accost you with a certain easy self-possession

ÖIE ON THE NORANGFJORD.
(Page 196.)

which is at once dignified and deferential, and is simply the expression of a native good-breeding inherent in the race. So I was a little amused with the Öie waitress's perpetual 'Yes, sir' and 'No, sir,' though it seemed to come as naturally from her as the less formal address of her fellow-countrywomen.

The steamer arrived about an hour late, but I was glad of the delay, as it gave me a little time to sit by the waterside and enjoy the beautiful prospect before me. The weather had been gradually improving, and it was now a lovely afternoon, so that the scenery showed to advantage in the sunlight and the clear atmosphere. The fjord on which Öie stands is a small offshoot of the Hjörund fjord, which crosses it at right angles, so that the water here looks exactly like a lake completely environed by mountains. These mountains are all of the same peculiar character as those I saw in the Norangdal, being topped with sharp peaks or jagged needles. One very conspicuous mountain, the Slogan, with a summit almost as acute and precipitous as that of the Matterhorn, stands immediately over Öie, and is said to be a particularly stiff climb.

The steamer that conveyed me from Öie was the *Söndmör*, a vessel quite equal in comfort to any of its sisters, and commanded by a captain of the most genial type. In a very short time we emerged from the Norang fjord, and found the Hjörund fjord extending both to our right and left in all its majestic splendour. The shorter section, which lay to the right, ends at Bjerke, which could be seen in the distance. The more extensive branch going northward was our route, and it formed a long vista of rugged peaks such as those surrounding Öie. Between these points glaciers appeared in several places, and altogether the range presented an outline more varied and picturesque than any to be seen on the Hardanger or the Sogne fjord.

As the northern extremity of the Hjörund is approached you seem to be going out to the open sea, for there is a wide stretch of water ahead with little land in sight. However, as the steamer advances to the mouth of the fjord it is found to be still upon the inland sea, for there is rock and crag on every side, though much of this is inferior in height to the mountainland we have left behind. We cross this plain of water, the Hjörund fjord closing upon us like a gate, and make in the direction of a rocky shore, which I am told is the island of Sulö. The larger vessels that come this way take their course through the wide Stor fjord to the west, but the *Söndmör* makes the more interesting passage of the extremely narrow channel which separates Sulö from the mainland. There seems to be hardly room for two vessels to pass each other in this strait, but the water is so deep that it is safe for the steamer to come close to the shore.

The voyage continues to lie among a perfect labyrinth of rocky islands, many of which are utterly barren and inhabited only by sea fowl, while on others there are small groups of cottages or one lonely hut. I am now in the midst of that coast scenery which fringes the shores of Norway for a thousand miles and more from south to north, within that rocky barrier which acts as a breakwater to the ocean, and fulfils the tempting promise of the steamship companies, who assure the public that a voyage along the Norwegian coast is made in perfectly smooth water. There is a certain sameness in such voyages, but they have a peculiar charm of their own in fine weather. However, I had considerable experience of them on my return journey, so I will reserve what else I may have to say on this subject for a future occasion.

Meanwhile our destination was Aalesund, and at about eight o'clock in the evening it came in view. It appeared to be a town of considerable size, and stretched in a long line of houses piled up in picturesque irregularity along the shore before us. We seemed to be making immediately for its centre, and I calculated that in a few minutes we should reach it. The captain, however, told me that we should not enter Aalesund that way but on the 'other side.' I did not understand his meaning at first but soon discovered it. Aalesund is situated on a long narrow strip of land encompassed by the sea on three sides. We were approaching it from the south and the port lies in the north. So presently our course was altered; we turned the western point of the peninsula and so worked round to the north side of the town.

There the entrance of the harbour, with its white lighthouse capped with a red roof, appeared in sight, and above the walls of the breakwater rose a small forest of masts and funnels, which, with the masses of wooden houses painted in various light tints, the whole being backed by a range of distant grey mountains, formed a very pretty scene. In fact the view of Aalesund from the water at this point was quite the most picturesque bit of 'composition,' as an artist would call it, that I had seen in Norway. It was just 'posed' for a picture, and our marine landscape painters would do well to put it on canvas. I am enabled, by the courtesy of Messrs. Valentine, to give a 'bird's-eye' view of the situation of this singularly-placed town, but its aspect in 'profile' is much more picturesque, and I recommend it to the attention of both the painter and the photographer.

On landing I made a hasty supper at Schjeldrop's hotel as I wished to see something of the town. It was now about nine o'clock; but that long daylight which is so precious a possession of Norway at this time of the year, and the duration of which was protracted in the much higher latitude I had now reached, was favourable to a ramble. The sun was only just declining towards the horizon as I set out on my stroll through the streets of Aalesund, and it was as beautiful an evening as could

AALESUND.
(Page 199.)

well be desired. The main thoroughfares run the length of the peninsula and by-streets branch off to the shore on either side. The place wears the same air of prim neatness and modest beauty that I noted in Stavanger. There are no quaint old houses with carved fronts, bay-windows, and gabled roofs, such as you see in the old towns of France, Belgium, and Germany, yet the house architecture is pleasing to the eye: there is nothing ugly, dull, and commonplace about it. Wandering up one of the by-lanes, I presently found myself in an avenue bordered by trees, and this led to a public promenade neatly laid out and winding round the foot of a massive hill, called the Axle, which rises at the point where the Aalesund peninsula joins the mainland. Following the walk along the shore I passed a small church and cemetery, and thence the road becomes a rough path extending far along the coast. From this promenade, and especially from the higher ground, the views are enchanting. The eye wanders over a vast space of water out of which rise rocky islands, and far away are discerned the bold outlines of the peaked and jagged mountains of the country I had left.

The sun was now setting behind a huge mass of rock out at sea; and the heights to the east glowed with that rich purple tint which when reproduced by the painter seems almost an exaggeration of Nature. Experience has told me what these too beautiful effects of colour imply.

In mountainous countries I have always known them to presage heavy rain on the morrow; but it is worth while even to endure the bad weather that too often follows this lovely phenomenon for the sake of the enjoyment which it gives to the eye while it lasts. So I sat watching the glow of the sunset on the hills till it gradually faded away, leaving the rocks it had illumined once more cold and grey. Then in the soft twilight I sauntered back to the town and my quarters, and at eleven o'clock, while the sky was still clear and blue, retired to rest.

CHAPTER XX.

THE ROMSDAL.

The *Söndmör* lay in the harbour all night, and was to resume her voyage at seven o'clock in the morning. She could therefore convey me to Aandalsnæs for the Romsdal, the next point I wished to reach, and whither she was bound, but I had intended to travel by land, if the weather should prove favourable, of which I had grave doubts. And my apprehensions were only too well justified, for, on awakening at an early hour, I found the rain descending heavily. There seemed every prospect of a wet day; so, packing my baggage, I made at once for the port, and went on board the steamer. I would advise future travellers, however, to carry out the intention I had formed, and drive to the Romsdal along the coast, *via* Söholt and Vestnæs, as thereby they will vary their route, and avoid doing the same steamboat journey twice over.

As it was, I took the latter course, and it was the best I could adopt under the circumstances. However, I saw little or nothing of the scenery during a great part of this voyage, as everything was obscured by mist and rain. Yet the wet morning had its consolations. In the first place I enjoyed a capital breakfast in the cabin with the cheery captain and his first officer, for I was the only saloon passenger up to that time, and after the meal, I made myself snug in the comfortable little *rogelugar*, or smoking-cabin, on deck, and through the open door surveyed as much as I could of the passing scene. It was not much for a time, but it was interesting to see how near we passed to the rocky islands, with their population of gulls and other sea-birds, and there was a certain charm, too, in the sight of the distant mountains whose forms loomed ghostlike through the mists.

The weather improved when we touched at Vestnæs on the Molde fjord, and was better still when we arrived at Molde itself. I greatly admired the appearance and position of this place, with its fine background of forest-clad hill. It was to be the most northerly point of Western Norway that I proposed to touch before bending my course southward and homeward; and as, in fact, I did visit it again, I will say what I have to say about it hereafter. It was almost the first occasion on which I had to go over the same ground twice, but this duplication had its advantages, as will be seen when I come to speak of my second visit to Molde.

We stopped at the two piers connected with the town, one opposite the Alexandra Hotel and the other about half-a-mile off in front of the Grand,

and took on board from both a large number of passengers. Molde, in fact, is a place much frequented by both natives and foreigners, and I could see at a glance that it must be a delightful spot for a long stay.

Among the passengers who embarked on the *Sündmör* was one whom I shall take the liberty of calling the Genial Grumbler. A highly respectable old gentleman he evidently was, a man of means and leisure, who entered readily into conversation, and gossiped affably and cheerfully about the weather and things in general. It was not until we touched on the subject of travel in Norway that his character as a Genial Grumbler came out. Norway! He knew the country by heart, and from end to end. He had visited it every year for the last thirty years, and the place was ruined, sir, positively ruined. I was sorry to hear this, and the G. G. was sorry to say it. Yes; the country had been utterly spoilt by tourists. It was overrun now, modernised, vulgarised, in short, ruined. Asked to state his reasons for this pessimistic view of things, he replied that when he first came to Norway, there was not such a thing as a railroad or steamer to be seen; half the new roads now existing were not made; there were hardly any hotels, and the people were as honest and simple as they were now extortionate and cunning.

I granted that no doubt great improvements ('improvements!' sniffed the G. G. scornfully) had been introduced into the country, but certainly the character he had given to the people was quite contrary to my experience. Ah! I should live among them as he had done; then I would see what they had become. However, it did not appear that he had any definite charges to bring against the good Norsk folk, so I presumed that his sweeping assertion as to their deterioration in character was a slight exaggeration. It was plain that he felt a warm and sincere affection for the people, and the source of his discontent soon became apparent. He rented a fishery somewhere in the interior, and this season he had had very poor sport. So he had come away in disgust, and had sought to get rid of his disappointment by change of scene. But the tourists were worse than the trout. While the latter were scarce, the former were only too abundant, and the G. G. was now fleeing from them as fast as ever he could, being on his way back to his fishery.

In spite of his dislike of modern improvements, as applied to Norway, my new friend, having had his grumble out, proved a most agreeable and intelligent companion, and gave me a great deal of interesting information respecting the country and people. So the time passed very pleasantly in profitable chat during the voyage.

The steamer crossed the wide waters of the Molde fjord to Vestnæs, at which we had touched *en route* from Aalesund, and thence our course lay eastward, and brought us to the entrance of the Romsdal fjord. This is a very fine narrow waterway, bordered by towering mountains, like so many of the same kind that I had viewed elsewhere, but not presenting any feature of special novelty until we near the head of the fjord. There the twin villages of Veblungsnæs and Aandalsnæs, one on either side of the river Rauma, come in sight; and presently we obtain a glimpse of the famous Romsdalshorn, with its bold peak peering over the summits of other mountains. Veblungsnæs runs along the shore at the foot of a grand mass of mountain with snow-capped peaks—the Vengetinderne,—and the view of it with its surroundings is more like a bit of Switzerland than anything I had yet seen in Norway. In fact, the scenery of the Romsdal is very Swiss in character, which is not to be said of any other part of the country. I know it is not unfrequently the injudicious habit of travellers to compare Norway with Switzerland to the depreciation of the former. But this is hardly fair. Norway is no more like Switzerland than the Upper Thames is like the Rhine, but has a beauty and a character all its own. It is Norway in fact and nothing else. As I have said before, however, the scenery of the Romsdal has certain features in common with that of the Alps, and this will be made more clear when I come to describe it.

We passed Veblungsnæs, and stopped at its sister village Aandalsnæs, where there is a good and convenient quay, which was crowded with *carrioles* and other vehicles ready to take passengers up the Romsdal. A good deal of touting is carried on here, a thing rarely practised elsewhere, and a young man followed me about like a shadow, persistently pressing me to engage his vehicle, though I told him repeatedly that I was not 'going on' just then. He tried hard to tempt me to take a drive up the Romsdal and back, and I had some difficulty in shaking him off.

The fact is I had decided to dine and spend a few hours at Aandalsnæs, for it was now about 1 P.M., and I did not propose to start again on my travels till the evening. So I accompanied my friend the Genial Grumbler with a companion of his, a Norwegian gentleman, to one of the two Bellevue hotels which contend for the patronage of visitors to the Romsdal.

There is a story connected with these hotels, and it is curiously illustrative of Norwegian customs. Once there was only one Bellevue, and it was owned by a proprietor named Aandahl, who died while his eldest son was absent in America. The hotel was then purchased by a Mr. Caspar Lossius, together with a piece of land close to it. In the meanwhile the son returned from the States with his family, and under the Norwegian law of succession claimed the right of purchasing his late father's property. This, it appears, he was entitled to do if the claim were made within a certain space of time, I believe three years, and that term had not yet expired. So Mr. Lossius had to give up the hotel, and it is now 'run' by Mr. Aandahl under its old title of the Bellevue. Yet Mr. Lossius was not to be beaten. He had still the piece of ground, so he built a hotel of his own upon it, and called it also the Bellevue, there being apparently no copyright in the name.

It was to Aandahl's Bellevue that I resorted with my friend the G. G., partly because I preferred to support the 'old house,' and partly because I was a little disgusted with the proprietor of the other for having utterly spoilt, I hope only for a time, the appearance of the place, by running up a long, ugly barrier of wood across the boundary of his property where it stood in all its unsightly bareness. The new Bellevue is a large and showy hotel, not built in the pretty tasteful style of most Norwegian houses of the same class, with pendent eaves carved in Arabesque designs, but in a clumsy barn-like shape, and with a polygon turret or out-look at the top, the whole being painted a hideous yellow ochre. Above all, I could not forgive that abominable hoarding which seemed made all ready for the exhibition of flaming illustrated placards, vaunting the virtues of somebody's pills and somebody else's soap, though happily not yet used for such a purpose. So I would not go to the new Bellevue, though I believe that, as a matter of fact, it is a very well-conducted establishment.

As it was, we fared well enough at the old Bellevue, and I was much amused with Mr. Aandahl's large family of Yankeefied children. They spoke English with a curiously mixed Norwegian and American accent, but quite fluently. I found them playing at croquet outside the hotel door, or rather they were about to indulge in that mild pastime, as one of the little damsels told me, 'Yes, sir, I guess we are just going to start.'

I left Aandalsnæs at about seven o'clock in the evening. The G. G. and his friend went on in a carriage and pair, and I was captured at last by the persevering *skydsgut* who had been touting for custom earlier in the day. Nor had I any reason to regret having yielded to his importunities. His *carriole* was all that could be desired, with a comfortable seat, good springs, and a capital horse, and the price I agreed to pay for the short journey I was about to take was the regular post fare. He did not go with me himself, but placed me in the hands of his father, who proved a perfectly efficient driver. It seemed that the reason of his eagerness to get a job for his *carriole* was that his father was bound for the Romsdal on some business connected with a *sæter*, and this worthy person afterwards tried hard to persuade me to go further than I wanted to go, with an eye to 'killing two birds with one stone,' that is, making his own journey as well as a little profit out of it. Who shall blame these good people for their desire to do the best they could for themselves? Certainly I did not, for I lost nothing by it.

The Romsdal has a world-wide fame, and all those who know anything whatever about Norway are familiar with the features of this enchanting valley. Nor do I think that it has been at all overpraised, though the G. G. seemed to be of that opinion. Probably he did not like the Romsdal because it is so much liked by his enemies, the tourists. However, I have to thank him for the special zest he imparted to my enjoyment of its beauties. I had heard the Romsdal so enthusiastically extolled that I ran some risk of being disappointed by it. So when the G. G. denounced it as a 'humbug,' and said that it 'could not hold a candle' to many other places in Norway that he knew of, I expected that it would hardly prove to be up to the mark of its general reputation. Thus I was agreeably surprised to find that the valley was really the gem of beauty it had been represented to be. That is to say, from the entrance at Aandalsnæs to the foot of the Romsdalshorn, a distance of some eight miles, it presents a scene more strikingly picturesque in some respects than any other to be found in Norway.

The view of the Romsdalshorn itself all the way up this part of the valley is most remarkable. The mountain stands boldly out before you, topped with a round shoulder like a camel's hump, from which rises a lofty peak or sugar-loaf, which shoots straight up in sheer precipice on every side. It would seem from a distance as difficult to climb as the Matterhorn itself, and there was a time when it was thought to be quite inaccessible. Indeed it is only of late years that the first recorded ascent has taken place, and since then artificial aids have been provided to facilitate the labour of scaling the summit. From its peculiarly isolated position there must be a superb and extensive view from the top. The height of the Horn is only about 5000 feet, but it looks much higher than many mountains of inferior altitude.

On the other side of the valley the Romsdalshorn has a rival in peculiarity of form and dignity of aspect. This is the Troltinderne, a mountain of greater magnitude, whose summit consists of not one peak only, but many, or rather a series of 'aiguilles,' which give the ridge the appearance of a gigantic saw lifting its huge teeth to the sky. The Troltinderne is higher than the Romsdalshorn by some 700 or 800 feet, but it only appears so from distant points. The imposing forms of the two combine to give a remarkable stateliness to the valley, which in other respects pleases by its exquisite verdure, the richness and abundance of its foliage, and the beauty of the brawling river Rauma which rushes through it. Soon after you enter the Romsdal another lovely valley, the Isterdal, opens to the right. This is overshadowed by the Troltinderne on the one hand and the Vengetinderne on the

THE ROMSDALSHORN.
Page 211.

other, a mountain also with jagged peaks, which forms such a fine background to Veblungsnæs, as seen from the fjord.

In the midst of the Romsdal, within some two or three miles of Aandalsnæs, and in view of every one of the grand and beautiful objects I have mentioned, the two valleys and all the mountains, stands Aak (pronounced Oak), one of the very choicest spots in all Norway. It was formerly a hotel, but the property was bought up some years ago by Mr. Wills, of Bristol 'bird's-eye' fame, and the hotel buildings are now his private residence. The situation of this enviable estate is unsurpassable, but I rather wonder that the owner has not made more of it. The house, which stands on a prominent hill in the midst of the valley, is not at all attractive in appearance, but this, one might think, would be the very spot for the erection of some edifice of really stately and sightly form and proportions, a *château* or *châlet*, designed by a skilful architect, which would look well in the landscape. Nothing short of a building of the most imposing or picturesque kind, and in the best possible taste, would justify such an alteration; but here, if anywhere, is the place for it.

It is when the foot of the Romsdalshorn is passed that the depreciating remarks of the Genial Grumbler are to some extent justified. Here the Romsdal ceases to keep up its high character, and degenerates into a mere rugged ravine of the ordinary sort, of which the traveller has seen miles upon miles in the course of his tour. I do not say that these narrow winding valleys are without interest or charm, but naturally they are dwarfed by the grander scenes presented elsewhere. The Romsdal, however, is not to be judged by these tamer sections of it; it bases its reputation on the superb tract between Aandalsnæs and the Horn, and the magnificent scenery further up between Ormeim and Stueflaaten. Yet even in the interval there is much to admire. Some very pretty waterfalls are seen by the roadside, and the valley is strewn in several places by tremendous boulders and masses of rock, many of which must weigh tens of thousands of tons, that have become detached from the mountains and are now adorned with mosses and wild-flowers, and miniature woods of fir which have managed to take root in their crevices.

I arrived at Fladmark, a small station about twenty miles from Aandalsnæs late in the evening and decided to make it my resting-place for the night, chiefly for the sake of the company of the worthy G. G., who had arranged to stay here. We took a walk together for some miles up the valley, the character of which continued the same as I have described, and on our way we passed several more pretty fosses. One of these had a singular appearance, as a side view made it look as though it were gushing out of some hole in the rock and vanishing into the mountain, which of course could not be. As a matter of fact, we found, as I expected, that it flowed through a very narrow cleft, which could not be seen in profile, and that its actual source was far up at the top of the mountain. These rambles in the Norwegian valleys indeed always disclose some curious freak of nature, the study of which forms a welcome relief to the excitement of watching and admiring the bolder scenes.

It was in this pleasant stroll by the side of the brawling river, with the soothing murmur of the waterfalls in our ears, and the gentle twilight of the Norwegian summer-night dimly illumining the landscape, that the kindly G. G. gave expression to his true feeling of affection for the beautiful land to which his heart had been ever constant. He loved Norway at once like a father and a child, and it was only because he could not shake off the influence of his earliest associations with the country when it was but little known save to wanderers like himself, that he so resented the changes and improvements which had been demanded and enforced by its growing popularity. He was too sensible, however, not to acknowledge that these alterations were inevitable, and too candid to deny, after all, that they were for the advantage of the country and its people.

On the following day my good friend and his companion left by the *diligence* for the remote region where he resided. This *diligence* was the only one I had yet come across in Norway, and it plies on the high-road from the Romsdal to Lillehammer, the direct route to Christiania. I myself felt strongly tempted to go part of the way with the G. G., not only for the pleasure of his company, but in order to explore the beauties of the upper Romsdal, which are said to be as fine as those I had seen at the other end of the valley. But time did not admit of this excursion, and I was reluctantly compelled to leave Stueflaaten unvisited. I would advise future travellers, however, to proceed further up the valley before retracing their steps. According to information that I could trust, it is well worth while to go as far as Ormeim. At that point the road attains a great elevation, and commands, I was told, superb views, while there are two waterfalls to be seen near the roadside—the Vermefos and the Slettefos—which are very easily accessible, and are among the most beautiful of the second rank in Norway.

As it was, I purposed to drive back as far as Horghjem, and walk the rest of the way to Aandalsnæs. This plan I carried out. My driver of the day before wanted to take me on in the direction of his *sæter*, and did not see his way to drive me back so short a distance as Horghjem, so we had a friendly parting, and I engaged another *carriole*. It was to be my last, and it was quite the worst I had yet hired. Never shall I forget that *carriole*, and the torture it inflicted on me! It was lamentably shaky in the springs, and although the road was good enough it jolted and bumped so violently whenever my *skydsgut* urged his horse into a trot that I was compelled at last to make him go at a walking pace. Never was I more glad to get to the end of a journey than I was when I reached Horghjem. This is a very small station, a mere place for changing horses and obtaining light refreshments, and it was here that the only instance of an overcharge which I experienced during the whole of my tour occurred. But it was not a very great matter. On my way 'out' I had stepped into this station for a drink of milk and was charged fifteen *öre*, or twopence, for it. Now I asked for another drink, and twenty *öre* was demanded. I laughingly pointed out the discrepancy, but it was taken gravely enough, and the trifling overplus was duly offered. Perhaps it was only an accidental mistake after all.

While planning to walk from Horghjem to Aandalsnæs, a distance of about ten miles, I did not see exactly how I was to get my baggage transported. You cannot 'post' your portmanteau or knapsack in Norway as in Switzerland, but now and then a good-natured traveller will take it on for you, and I had done this little service more than once myself for pedestrians. As it happened I had no need to solicit this favour, for the *diligence* from the south had just arrived at Horghjem, and the conductor readily consented to convey my traps to Aandalsnæs. It is a characteristic fact that no charge was made for the carriage.

Thus relieved I started on my walk, and took my time over it. The Romsdal—that is the true Romsdal—is not to be hurried over, and seeing it now as I did on foot and at leisure I had a much better opportunity of enjoying its beauties than before. I frequently sat down by the roadside, not to rest, but to survey the scene—the wonderful peaks and pinnacles of the Troltinderne, the strange, bold form of the Romsdalshorn, and the exquisite landscape that encircles Aak. The great charm of the Romsdal consists in its 'foreground.' Painters complain that this is too often wanting in Norway. The mountains, as a rule, rise sheer out of the plain or the fjord, and there is no fringe below to 'set them off.' No such fault is to be found with the Romsdal scenery. The lower ground is so richly wooded, and not alone by firs and pines, that the mountain views always rise out of a lovely bower of foliage. Thus with a broad, foaming river at his feet, a forest on the hillside beyond it, and the grey rocks shooting up thousands of feet in the background, the artist has as beautifully composed a scene as he could wish to depict.

It was not until late in the afternoon that I arrived at Aandalsnæs, thoroughly pleased with my walk. Once more I dined at the 'old' Bellevue, and then I went up to the balcony on the topmost floor, which commands a noble view of the Romsdal fjord, to smoke my pipe and watch for the arrival of the steamer. It appeared in sight long before it could reach the quay, and I strolled leisurely down to meet it.

CHAPTER XXI.

MOLDE.

The steamer which was to take me from the Romsdal was named the *Rauma*, after the river which traverses the valley, and it was distinguished from other vessels of its class by being painted white, whereas the colour most in fashion among the fjord boats appeared to be black. In all other respects the *Rauma* was like its sister vessels, that is, thoroughly comfortable and well built. I had heard it said that the Norwegian steamers were dirty and ill-kept. This may have been the case in former times, but it is not the fact now. No British man-of-war ever looks more trim and neat than these smart fjord boats, which are always well provided with convenient seats and lounges, deck awnings, saloons, bars, smoking-rooms, ladies' cabins, and occasionally sleeping-berths. Nor in any hotel do you get better living than on board the steamers when long trips necessitate your taking meals *en route*; and for one thing they are especially remarkable, that is the excellence and cheapness of their wines. The charges, indeed, for all meals are very moderate—a good breakfast generally costing one *krone* fifty *öre*,

MOLDE.
(Page 220.)

and dinner two *kroner*, which is about the average hotel price.

And here let me put on record a very small matter, yet one characteristic of the care and courtesy shown towards their passengers by the captains of the fjord steamers. I had accidentally left my felt hat behind on board the *Söndmör*, coming from the Romsdal, having substituted for it a travelling cap. I gave it up for lost, but yet thought I might as well try to recover it, if possible. So when, two days afterwards, the *Söndmör* touched at Molde again, I asked the captain if he had seen anything of my missing hat. To my great surprise he said, 'Yes,' he had it, and there and then went down to his cabin and fetched it. Indeed I was told that whatever you might leave on one of these steamers, whether valuable or not, you might consider it as safe as if it were still in your own possession.

The *Rauma* is a fast boat, and did the voyage to Molde in good time. I need not say much about the trip, as I had gone over the same waters before. After passing through the fine Romsdal fjord we entered the broader Molde fjord, touched once more at Vestnæs, and again arrived at Molde.

And now the advantage of my first sight of that place, to which I referred at the time, became manifest. I may say here that although Norway is much more frequented than it used to be, and attracts larger numbers of foreigners every year, it is not overcrowded by tourists at the early period of the summer at which it was my good fortune to travel. Thus I never found any place—even those most resorted to—'full'; there was no sleeping in cottages or farm-houses; not often even in *dépendances*, much-less on billiard-tables and in passages as one sometimes has to do in Switzerland and other tourist countries at the height of the season. This sort of thing happens occasionally in Norway too, but not in June, or even early in July. I was, however, now coming to a place which is greatly frequented by both natives and foreigners, and besides it was the middle of July, when the tourists begin to arrive in large numbers. So I was not surprised to hear that Molde was 'full,' and for the first time in my tour felt a little anxious on the subject of quarters.

The Grand Hotel has a particularly fine situation overlooking the fjord, and enjoys a high reputation; but I heard that the Grand had been 'choke full' all the week, and had turned away many visitors only the day before. This news I got from the captain, and he further told me that he intended to touch first at the Grand Hotel landing-stage, and then go on to that opposite the Alexandra. This was a useful 'tip,' as will presently be seen. Sure enough, when we arrived at the 'Grand' quay the landlord of the hotel, who was waiting for us on the pier, at once called out that his house was almost full; in fact he had only one double-bedded room left.

'I will take it!' promptly cried one of a couple of young gentlemen who were travelling together.

'All right, sir,' replied the landlord. 'It's No. 31.'

'Have you nothing else?' meekly inquired a 'pale young curate' on board, who appeared to be travelling alone.

'No,' said the landlord; 'but I could get you a double-bedded room in another house.'

'But I only want one bed,' pleaded the youthful cleric.

'You can have this room,' responded the Grand host, 'if you pay for both beds.'

The reverend young gentleman did not seem prepared to indulge in such extravagance, and was silent. Nevertheless he and nearly all the other passengers landed at the Grand pier, thinking, in their innocence, that this was the only place of disembarkation at Molde. But, thanks to my previous visit, I knew better, and so remained on board to be conveyed to the other landing-place opposite the Alexandra. Indeed I was the only one who got off there, and when I inquired of the hotel porter if I could have a bed, he replied with great alacrity, 'Oh yes, sir.' The fact is, by keeping to the steamer I had outstripped the other passengers, for the Grand is situated nearly a mile from the centre of Molde where the Alexandra stands. Now it appeared that the people of the last-named hotel were bitterly jealous of the rival establishment, and highly resented the proceedings of the *Rauma's* captain in touching first at the opposition place. Consequently I was received by them, so to speak, with open arms, as the one faithful traveller who had stuck to the 'old house,' was assigned the best bedroom vacant, and generally well-treated.

Soon after I arrived the unfortunates who had been crowded out of the Grand began to drop in. There was something humorous in the situation, though I could not help pitying these hapless wanderers, who had had to trudge all the way through the town, getting their baggage conveyed as best they could, in search of a shelter for the night. The landlord stood on his dignity. 'Beds, oh no! he was quite full. If they went to the *Grand*' (with a sarcastic emphasis on the name) 'they might stop there. He had no room.' The man's pride was hurt. He did not like to be turned into a makeshift and convenience. Besides was not his hotel the oldest in Molde?—and as for the *Grand*—paff!

Then there was a pretty scene. Among the applicants for admission was an English clergyman, one of the best sort; elderly, grey haired, mild of speech, yet dignified in demeanour, dressed in a sober suit of black with the familiar clerical wide-awake, he appeared what he was—a perfect specimen of the good old-fashioned country parson. In soft persuasive tones he addressed the angry landlord. He had ladies with him, delicate and tired, surely the landlord would not turn them away. Could he not find room for them somewhere? He would be so much obliged. He was a perfect stranger to that part of the country and knew nothing about the hotels. If he had known that there was so good a hotel as the Alexandra he would have been only too happy to seek its hospitality, and so on. Thus the gentle-speaking clergyman softened the landlord's heart at last. The native Norwegian good-nature asserted itself, and in the end vacant rooms were found, and no one was turned away.

I have dwelt on this little incident chiefly as a characteristic illustration of Norwegian manners. Of course the moral of it is the old saying about the 'soft answer' which is universally applicable; but nowhere does a little civility go further than in Norway as a means of getting over all difficulties. Almost every previous traveller has noted this. Your hardy Norseman will not be driven or ordered about. He does not openly resent bullying, but he simply opposes to it a quiet, passive resistance. I can confirm the assertion of others that the traveller is much more likely to get what he wants in Norway, whether it be his dinner or his *carriole*, when he is in a hurry, by lifting his hat and saying '*Vær saa snild*' (Be so good) than by giving orders in a peremptory tone or indulging in irritation. As a retort to such an attitude the Norwegian says nothing, but he also does nothing. He is essentially

P

a good natured fellow, and an appeal to his courtesy or his sympathy is irresistible.

It is not surprising that there is such a run upon Molde. In my humble opinion it is one of the most delightful places in Norway. There is nothing grand or savage or overwhelming about it. It is soft, gentle, reposeful, a soothing resting-place to fly to after all the excitement and fatigue of travel, when the limbs are weary of wandering and the mind of wondering. There is, however, nothing at all remarkable about the town itself; it has little even of the modest picturesqueness of Stavanger or Aalesund. It consists of one long main street and a few by-lanes, and the houses and public buildings are of the most ordinary character. The two hotels already mentioned are perhaps the most imposing structures in the place—the Alexandra being rather ornate in its external decoration, and the Grand stately and well proportioned. There is also a neat wooden church with a handsome steeple in the upper part of the town, the interior of which is chiefly remarkable for a fine altar-piece by a modern painter. Plenty of shops are to be found in the main street, but there is no great display in them of attractive objects, except in the case of a few that lay themselves out to tempt the tourist with jewellery, toys, and specimens of Norwegian produce and industry, or articles of *bric-à-brac* and curiosity. There is one shop, next door to the Alexandra, which makes a show of furs that is really irresistible. Nowhere else had I seen such a sumptuous display of bear, fox, lynx, cat, and other skins, such exquisite rugs and quilts and cloaks of eider-down and wild-bird plumage. Inspection of this lovely collection is freely invited, but though no one ever presses you to buy anything, it is almost impossible to leave the shop without having been tempted to secure some of its treasures. The prices, though large in some cases, seem fair, and are all marked on little tickets fastened to the goods. There is also a very tempting bazaar a little further down the road where you can get thousands of varieties of Norwegian carved and modelled work, and where ladies can procure complete dresses made up in the style of the native costumes, charming things for a fancy ball.

There are several piers and quays and warehouses along the shore, for Molde does a very fair amount of small shipping business; and some capital floating baths, close by the Alexandra, will be found a great luxury by the British visitor—such things being not so common in this much-watered land as they ought to be.

But it is in its surroundings that the chief charm of Molde lies. Take its front to begin with. Every part of the town looks out upon a vast expanse of water, which presents the appearance of an immense lake, perhaps five miles across, and twenty or thirty from end to end; and on the opposite shore of this great lake, if it may be so called, is ranged a panorama of mountains that skirt its entire length. An outline plan of this tremendous array of peaks and horns and fjelds is to be obtained, but it would be useless to mention the unfamiliar names, many of them difficult to pronounce, of the more conspicuous summits thus defined. But one readily recognises as old friends the sugar-loaf crown of the Romsdalshorn and the sharp needles of the Troltinderne in the middle of the range.

The hills behind Molde abound in the most delicious walks. They form a broad and lofty slope, and are clothed to within a short distance of the topmost ridge with a wealth of wood and undergrowth. You have the choice of rambling in neglected wildernesses, or following the well-made roads and paths which wind up to the heights. There are several well-placed 'bellevues' on different levels. The most easily accessible of these is Reknæshaugen, a canopied terrace standing in the midst of a little public park, intersected with winding walks; or you can go further up to the Varde, a wooden pleasure-house about half-way to the top of the hill, and thence it is an easy walk to the summit of the ridge Tor Stuen, whence a magnificent and widened prospect of the mountain-ranges is obtained on the one hand, and a grand view of the ocean and the rocky islands that fringe the coast on the other.

Then, again, for walking and driving there are

excellent roads skirting the margin of the shore for scores upon scores of miles, and by one route, a whole day's journey, it is possible to make the entire circuit of the peninsula on which Molde stands. Trips by steamer may also be frequently made across the water to Vestnæs—a very pleasant run in a launch—or to the Romsdal, or along the coast southward to Aalesund, or northward to Christiansund. Most of the vessels which have been, or are going, to Trondhjem and the North Cape, put into the Molde fjord on their way, and lie off the town for an hour or two, while every private or tourist steam-yacht on a voyage in Norwegian waters touches here as a matter of course. The number of the latter has greatly increased of late years, and a very good investment indeed is a passage taken in one of these handsomely appointed vessels. I preferred to make my own way across the country, but I readily admit that a fjord voyage in a first-class steam-yacht has much to recommend it. It is impossible, however, to do justice to the beauties of Norway without making journeys through the country by land, and for these the yacht-cruises afford too little time.

While I was at Molde the *Ceylon*, a handsome and well-known vessel, came in after a voyage to the North Cape. Her passengers landed, but did not stay long, though she was delayed for a time by the accident of losing her anchor, which somehow slipped off its cable in the process of being cast.

From the shore we heard the rattle of the chain and then a sudden silence, which told what had happened, and during the remainder of my stay several boats were engaged in the attempt to recover the lost anchor.

There is, indeed, always something going on in front of the hotel, and this makes it so pleasant and cheerful to lounge in one of the cosy basket armchairs in the verandah, and smoke your pipe after breakfast, or take your coffee after dinner, or idle about there at any time. The people passing to and from the steamers, or engaging *carrioles* and *stolkjærres*, or settling up with the *skydsgut*—the luggage being taken down to or brought up from the landing-stage, and the vessels and boats, large and small, arriving and departing, with that grand, wide expanse of water ever before you, now rippling under the breeze, now lying blue and glassy when the winds are at rest, and the long range of snow-topped mountains stretching for miles upon miles along the distant shore—here is a scene full of animation, of which you can never weary.

I had come to Molde to rest or lounge, not to travel or toil, and I would strongly advise all who follow me to do the same, giving themselves at least a couple of days for absolute idleness in this delightful place. It is generally a good class of people that you meet at Molde. The 'rushing' tourist, eager to get as much as he can for his money, is not to be found here. He just takes a peep at the place, and goes away, as a rule sniffing at it, because there is nothing 'big' and 'grand' about it. The Norwegian visitors are always pleasant companions when, as is usually the case, they speak English; and the English themselves are, for the most part, persons of taste, who have been travelling with intelligent eyes. In fact, it is only the traveller possessed of some artistic feeling who cares to stay long at Molde; it is too 'tame' for the conventional tourist.

It was a beautiful evening when I arrived, and I had a fine view of the panorama of mountains across the fjord. Again there was a glorious sunset, and once more it was followed by a wet day. Yes; the wettest of all the days I had spent in Norway. It was no mere drizzle at intervals as when I crossed the Moldestad hill, or when I steamed up the Geiranger, or rambled in the Romsdal, but a long and persistent heavy down-pour. The view was utterly obliterated, and the plain of water before us might have been the open sea, so entirely bereft was it of any opposite coast, while a thin veil of mist diminished the horizon of the water itself. A humorous fellow-visitor compared it to a view of the Isle of Dogs from Greenwich on a foggy day, and indeed it was not much better.

Hoping that the weather would improve, I put on my waterproof, and ventured upon a stroll up the hill road of which I have already spoken. It is reached from an open space in the centre of the town to the left of the church, and through an avenue of trees which leads to the woods. You can see that it is a favourite promenade, for at intervals of every few hundred yards you come upon one of a series of benches, each of which is marked by a number—'Benk No. 1, Benk No. 2,' and so on— like mile-stones.

I was making for the Varde, and after walking for about half-an-hour I came upon some grounds and a villa-like house which I took to be a public garden and restaurant. But I soon found that I was trespassing, for a gardener lifted his hat and said, 'privat,' and I afterwards discovered that I had wandered into the demesne of the British Vice-Consul. Of course I promptly beat a retreat, but I saw enough of the place to be able to testify that it is a very charming one indeed. It was, in fact, a real garden, the only one I had seen in Norway. It abounded in handsome trees and shrubs and flower-beds, with neatly gravelled walks, and on a fine day must have appeared a perfect little paradise. Indeed I saw it afterwards from the road to better advantage, and I must say I envied its possessor. Standing on the slope of the hill, and commanding the beautiful view of sea and land which I have described, and backed by the dark pine-woods above, it enjoyed an unsurpassable situation.

The road up the hill rose in easy windings, but though well made it was now very sloppy and slippery with the rain, so that the walk became somewhat toilsome. However, I had the convenient 'benks' to rest at, and I still hoped that the weather might pick up. But it did not; it went from bad to worse, and by the time I had arrived at 'benk No. 10,' I saw that I was getting into the clouds, for a thick mist spread along the upper part of the hill completely effacing the summit. I mounted as far as the Varde, however, and took refuge in the little refreshment house, which was occupied only by a solitary man, its keeper, who seemed surprised, but glad, to see me on such a shocking day.

And here again there was some evidence of Norwegian lack of enterprise, such as I have noted more than once before. The Varde is a very nice place, with a well-built house, and a charming look-out when there is something to look at. One would think that hundreds of people must come up here on a fine day, and need refreshments after their long pull up the hill. Many if not most, of these people, too, would no doubt be English, unable to express themselves in the Norsk tongue. Yet there was nothing to be got at the Varde but tea and coffee, aerated waters and biscuits, and bread and butter, while the keeper of the house did not speak a word of our language. So I contented myself with a cup of coffee—and very good coffee it was—and conversed as well as I could with the hermit of the Varde by dumb signs. After I had rested and refreshed myself I descended, as it was hopeless to attempt to go further up, and made straight for my comfortable quarters at the Alexandra.

The next day the weather was all that could be desired. The sun was shining brightly when I rose early to try those most welcome floating baths near the pier. A long wooden footway conducts you to the double row of little bathing-rooms, where rough but sufficient accommodation for your toilet is provided, and there is a square of clear cold water for your dip. I had often—unfortunately not being a swimmer—taken my morning bath in the fjords wherever I could get a bit of shallow water, but I had generally to improvise the bathing-place for myself, as at Gudvangen, where near the pier I 'spotted' overnight a barge with a long rope attached to it, which afterwards came in very handy to keep me out of the deep water. Those enviable beings who can take headers from the shore or from boats have plenty of opportunities for a morning plunge in Norway, but the water of the fjords is often rendered icy cold by the melted snows that come down to it from the mountains, and it is not safe for persons with weak hearts or those liable to cramp. A young gentleman lost his life from one or other of these causes some months ago at Utne in the Hardanger.

My pleasant holiday was now fast drawing to an end. At two o'clock that afternoon the *Nordstjern* was due from Trondhjem, and by this steamer I was to proceed to Bergen on my way home.

Fortunately she was very late, having been detained for a heavy loading at Christiansund, and did not put in an appearance till about four in the afternoon. So I had the greater part of the day to spend at delightful Molde, and I made the best use of my time. Re-ascending the hill, now in glorious weather, I once more visited the Varde and then pursued the path to Tor Stuen, the summit of the ridge, whence I was able to survey that magnificent double view of sea and land of which I have before spoken. There was no need to hurry my return, as I could not possibly miss the steamer, for the course the vessel must take was visible for many miles, and I should be able to make her out a good hour before she could come in sight of Molde. So I loitered at my leisure on the hills, and arrived at the hotel in ample time to dine, as there was yet no sign of the *Nordstjern*. I was even able to take another walk after dinner along the shore, and turned back only when I saw the smoke of the steamer in the distance.

CHAPTER XXII.

BY THE COAST TO BERGEN.

The *Nordstjern* was a big, bulky screw steamer, of an old-fashioned pattern, with a somewhat blunt cutwater, like that of a barge; but these old slow-going boats are very comfortable. Her cabin accommodation and 'table' were excellent, and she had the additional advantage of a good clear deck, where you could take quite a long walk from one end to the other. She had, too, plenty of nice cosy nooks, where you could lie, sheltered from sun and wind, and was altogether as nice a vessel for making the interesting coast trip I was about to undertake as could be wished.

There was a good deal to do before we could get under weigh; many barrels and sacks and loads of timber to be taken on board, not to speak of passengers' luggage, which included such a quantity owned by one party, that it might have been thought that they were 'moving house' rather than travelling. Long boxes, evidently containing salmon-rods, however, suggested that they had been on a fishing expedition up the country, and salmon-fishing in Norway is not to be done with any success in a day or two. Indeed, I afterwards made acquaintance with one of the fishers, an English gentleman, who told me that he leased a salmon-river, and had had very poor sport that season, as in two or three months he and his friends had killed only thirty or forty fish, as against three or four hundred in the previous summer. Herein he was more successful than another Englishman, who rented part of the river in the Suldal, and had had only one salmon in a fortnight, as I was told when I was at Sand.

At last we were off, and fair Molde gradually faded from our view. We weighed anchor at 5 P.M., on a beautiful afternoon, the 'sun shining with all his might' upon the sea, and made for the broad fjord which opens out to the west of Molde, in the direction of the German Ocean. The detention of the vessel was a piece of good luck, and for the reason I am about to state.

We had hardly been half an hour on our voyage when we descried a strange sort of haze on the water in the distance. On so bright a day it could not be fog or mist, but what else it was no one could say. It was not long, however, before we discovered its nature. It was smoke—the vapour of not one funnel, but many—and presently this dense cloud was tipped by a forest of masts. 'Why,' exclaimed one of my fellow-passengers in a tone of great excitement, 'it is the German fleet!' And the German fleet it was, or rather the squadron which was escorting the Emperor William, who, in his yacht, the *Hohenzollern*, was then making a cruise in Norwegian waters. Here was a treat that we had little anticipated. It was expected that in the course of a few days the German Emperor would arrive at Molde, but he had not been looked for so soon. Rows of Venetian masts had been erected at one of the landing-places, but these were not yet decorated, and no other preparations had been made so far for his Majesty's reception. So he would take the good folk of Molde by surprise.

It was a fine sight, this stately flotilla of ironclads, with the Imperial yacht in the centre, and a long line of dark, vicious-looking torpedo-boats bringing up the rear, as it slowly steamed in procession along the fjord between the grey mountains, and came nearer and nearer to us every minute. With an alacrity of which I should hardly have thought Norwegian seamen capable, our rigging was decked with all the flags that could be mustered on board, and the proper salutes were made and responded to, as one after another the monster ships passed us. Grand and graceful these vessels looked, for they were of the older and more sightly type of ironclad rather than the newer and uglier sort. I could not see a turret-ship among them, but they all carried tremendous guns slung broadside, and seemed formidable foes for any hostile fleet afloat. We did not catch sight of the Emperor himself, though of course we scanned the *Hohenzollern* eagerly with our glasses, but all the decks were crowded with officers and men, evidently enjoying the beautiful scenes through which they were passing. One by one these stately warships glided by, steaming so near to us that we could command a perfect view of all their external arrangements, and then, when the last torpedo-boat had passed our stern, we hauled down our bunting, and watched the fleet gradually receding into the distance till it vanished behind its own cloud.

After this interesting experience our voyage was uneventful, but it was none the less pleasant for all that. This cruise along the rugged coast of Norway, in and out among its grey rocky islands and over a sea as placid as a lake, is full of charm if not of variety. Yet to my taste there is no more monotony in it than the constant sight of the broad and boundless ocean. It is a different but equally pleasing sensation to watch these giant rocks gather and separate and assume new groupings and forms as we approach and slip past them, and note the strange lonely situation of cottage and lighthouse and church upon the barren granite islands. Here and there you see a scattered cluster of houses that might be called a village, and a strip of green that might be termed a meadow, and now there is a little offing with a barque or two at anchor in it, but there is otherwise hardly any sign of human existence. The sea-birds skim and drop and rise again in our wake, or fly away to unknown haunts, with shrill cries and flapping wings, but for the rest all is silence in the calm, rock-begirt waters.

Most of these craggy rocks and barren islands have names of their own, familiar enough, no doubt, to those who navigate the waters from which they lift their gaunt, grey forms, but strange and meaningless to the foreigner. Now and again one is tempted to ask what such or such a huge pile of granite is called, more perhaps for the purpose of identifying it on the map, so as to see what progress we are making, than for any particular interest which the object itself excites. But there is one great rock, encountered near the entrance to the Nord fjord, which cannot be passed by without attracting special notice and inquiry. We are threading an extremely narrow passage, and to our right rises, sheer out of the dark water, a huge wall of granite, tremendous in its proportions as the giant cliffs of the Geiranger itself. Its summit stands nearly three thousand feet above our heads, and it presents this remarkable peculiarity that the top considerably overhangs the base. Well may we ask the name of this wonderful giant, and we learn that it is no other than the famous Hornelen.

No one can fail to feel profoundly impressed by these wild solitudes, or to wonder what sort of lives their inhabitants can lead, so far away from any 'camp of men,' cut off from all news of the world, and obtaining the very necessaries of life who knows how ? As a matter of fact, they are fisher-

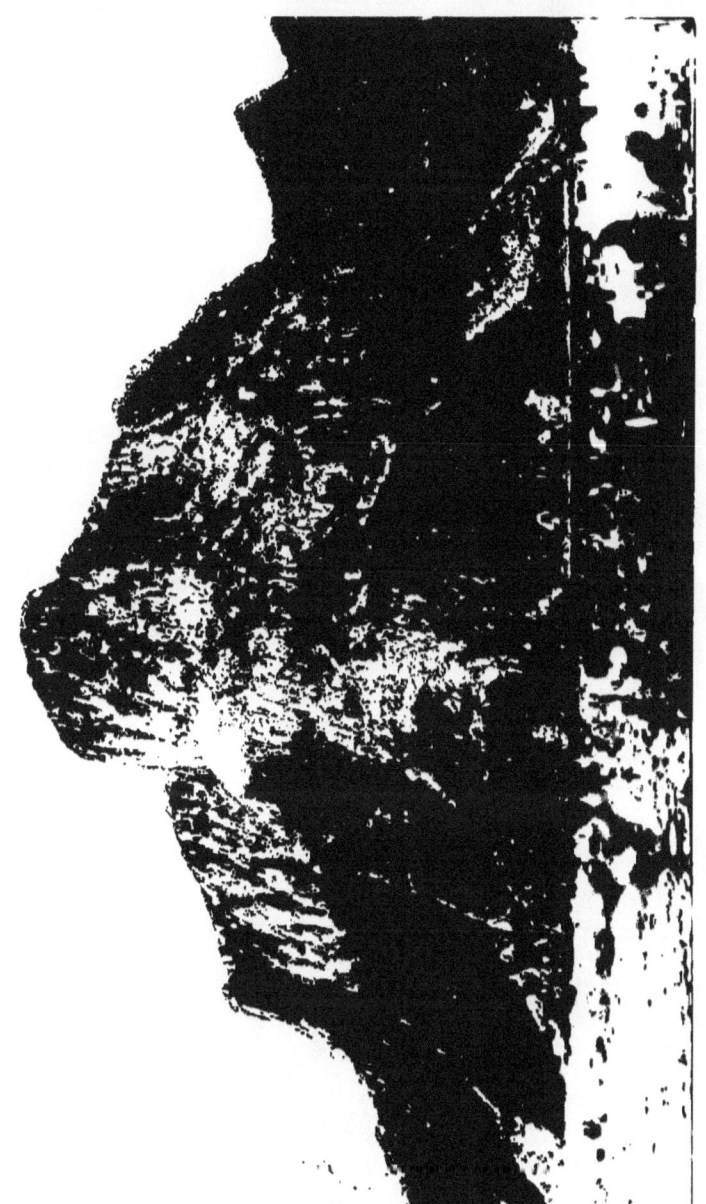

HORNELEN
(Page 240.)

folk or farmers, and many of them are sufficiently comfortable and well-to-do. They go to and fro in their barques and boats; they make nothing of a voyage to Molde or Bergen for marketing purposes; and, pious, devout people as they are, they will sail or row many miles, starting even at the early northern dawn, in order to attend divine service at the little wooden church on that grey rock far away down the fjord. Here is piety indeed—the sort of religion that makes men and women devote to it labour and fatigue, and even risk danger for the sake of it. That is the sort of faith we must all respect, and nowhere can we find a nobler or more impressive example of it than in these wild Norwegian waters.

A beautiful evening and another splendid sunset ended this day, and we turned in to our comfortable berths to awaken in the early morning still among the rocky islands, but well on our way to Bergen. It was hard to say exactly where we were, but at intervals I could see the openings that led to the fjords which I had traversed many days before, and the ranges of distant mountains overshadowing the Sogne and other districts. It was not without a certain feeling of sadness that I saw these landmarks of my pleasant tour disappear one after the other; but it is ever thus when a holiday is coming to an end, and it is well when one can console one's-self with the reflection which it was my privilege to enjoy, that the journey had been

Q

prosperous and profitable down to the last. For the weather was still brilliantly fine, the deck and the sea were bathed in genial sunshine, and the voyage we were making was as delightful as any voyage could well be. And now the habitations on these lonely rocks became more and more numerous. Here and there the eye rested on stretches of comparatively fertile and cultivated land; barques and fishing-smacks sailed by us in increasing numbers; in fact many signs betokened that we were nearing our destination.

At one o'clock the bell rang for dinner and we went below, so that I did not see the first view of the great port for which we were bound, as the vessel turned into the fjord that gives access to it. But when I reached the deck once more the scene lay disclosed in all its beauty before me.

CHAPTER XXIII.

BERGEN.

I have visited Bergen three times—first after the voyage just described, secondly in the summer of 1891, on my way from Stavanger, and lastly on the return at the end of my second tour. The most interesting of these trips was the voyage from Stavanger on board the *Lindholm*, a particularly comfortable steamer, apparently much used by German merchants and others frequently making the journey between the two ports, and therefore more than usually well provided with luxuries, such as matting and arm-chairs on deck, and a *table d'hôte* of a specially liberal character. The route, too, is much more attractive than that by the outer channel traversed by the larger steamers, for this local vessel threads the maze of islands that stud the coast, and touches at many spots of great beauty little known to ordinary tourists. The waters here and there are exceedingly narrow, and their scenery is of the most imposing character. Several busy and picturesque little fishing villages are passed by the way, and one gets a good view of the important port of Haugesund, which lies along the shore of a narrow river-like channel, in which the steamer passes down an avenue of ships more than a mile in length.

Bergen is situated at the foot of an amphitheatre of hills, not so high as those I had seen elsewhere, but still bold and abrupt, and its outline is not less picturesque than that of Aalesund, and much more so than that of Stavanger. Foreshortened as it was to our view we could not see at first that it is built on a long peninsula, extending far out into the fjord, and bordered on either side by a fine harbour. The water to our left is the Vaage, and it is crowded with steamers and ships, whose masts make a thick forest, while the larger Pudde fjord to the right is comparatively clear, being studded here and there only with a few boats and yachts.

Now we enter the Vaage, and see what Bergen is really like. The sight is not disappointing. Wharves and quays and warehouses are not very presentable objects as a rule, but those of Bergen would delight the eye of any artist. The buildings on both shores are old and quaint; on one side there are ancient towers and turrets and long rows of tall storehouses, while on the other long narrow lanes, in which the buildings are supported by colonnades of wooden pillars, lead down to the water-side. Overhead on every hand tower steep hills clothed with foliage and sprinkled with villas and cottages on the terraces cut across them, and up among the

BERGEN, FROM FLÖIFJELDET
(Page 242.)

heights appear pleasant outlooks giving promise of many a noble prospect.

The *Nordstjern* is moored along-side the quay, and at two o'clock we bid her farewell and land. I had selected the Hotel Bergen as my resting-place for the night, and did not know that I could have reached it in two or three minutes by crossing the harbour in a boat. As it was, I walked thither, sending my luggage on, but I was glad to do so, as I was thereby enabled to see something of the town.

I first skirted the Tydskebrygge with its warehouses, its army of barrels, and its long strings of dried cod-fish hanging on fences, and then turned into a wide open space at the head of the harbour where the fruit and fish markets are held. This leads to a wide street or 'place,' Torvet, surrounded by handsome shops, the first turning out of which is the long narrow Strandgade, at whose remoter end my hotel is situated. It is a strange sensation after creeping along the quiet coast for so many hours thus to enter a busy noisy town; for Bergen here is very noisy indeed from the clattering of cart-wheels on its stony roads, and the footways are crowded with people passing to and fro. There are first-rate shops in the Strandgade, which is indeed the 'shoppiest' thoroughfare in Bergen, and at every few yards I get a peep down the vistas of those quaint lanes, with their timber colonnades, that lead so picturesquely to the harbour. Now I come to a massive and ancient building, Muren, with an archway over the road, and traversing this I soon find myself at the door of the Hotel Bergen. There I have very comfortable quarters, and I find attached to it a *café* of the regular continental sort, with a bar and a smoking-room.

Opposite the Bergen is Smeby's, a house much frequented by English tourists and largely patronised by Cook's excursionists. These are situated in a quarter handy for reaching the fjord steamers, but very noisy from the traffic passing over the stony road. Elsewhere, in a quieter part of the town, and not far from the railway station, are two hotels of the first class, Holdt's and the Norge; and here, too, is a capital middle-class house, the Nordstjern, where I took up my quarters on the occasion of my last visit.

I had but a short time for seeing the notable sights of Bergen when I first touched at that place; but the town and its neighbourhood are extremely interesting, and in 1891 I arranged to spend two days there in order to examine them more completely. I was indebted to one of the Bennett family for much kind attention and useful information, and it was due to his courtesy that I was enabled to make a very pleasant excursion on the evening of my arrival.

There is, in fact, no more agreeable jaunt from Bergen than that which takes the visitor to the beautiful estate of Fantoft, some three or four miles distant. This place may be reached by the Bergen-Vossevangen Railway from Fjösanger station, but it is preferable to go by road, as it is a charming ride through the fine broad valley, at the head of which Bergen lies, and which contains several pretty sheets of water. Fantoft itself is the property of Mr. Gade, the American consul, and consists of a richly-wooded piece of country spread over a group of hills and dales, the higher ground commanding delightful prospects of lake and river scenery. It is upon the loftiest of these summits that you find the building for which Fantoft is most famous, the curious old *Stavekirke*, which stood for many centuries at Fortun near the Sogne fjord, and which, being threatened with destruction, was purchased by Mr. Gade and transported to its present position; for these old wooden churches can easily be taken to pieces and put together again, and in several parts of the country there are examples of such transfers as that which brought the old Fortun church to Fantoft.

This is, perhaps, the very finest specimen extant of the quaint ecclesiastical architecture of Norway, and, probably restored here and there, is in a perfect state of preservation. There is a touch of paganism in its pagoda-like roofs, and the strange dragon-shaped wings with which their ridges are finished off, and its whole appearance is bizarre and grotesque, but not without a certain harmony and grace. The dark interior, with its massive wooden pillars and open ambulatory surrounding the building is also full of character, resembling no other kind of ecclesiastical edifice in Europe. Visitors are admitted at all times to see the church and wander about the well-kept grounds in which it stands, and from the top of the hill they survey a wide landscape in which Mr. Gade's large white mansion is a conspicuous object. If you drive to Fantoft along one side of the valley, you can vary the journey by returning along the opposite road, and this leads either direct into Bergen or takes you up to the lofty heights of Floifjeldet, from which a fine bird's-eye view of Bergen and its fjords is obtained.

In was on a brilliant summer evening, ending with a splendid sunset, that I made this excursion to Fantoft, and it was well that I did not delay it, for by the following day the weather had broken up, and it rained from morning till night. I do not regret this wet day, and for more than one reason. In the first place, Bergen is famous for its rain. It is said to be the wettest place in Europe, having a heavier annual rainfall than any other town on the continent. When I first visited it the sky was blue and the sun was shining, and I had no chance of seeing what Bergen rain was like. Now I had ample opportunity of witnessing this phenomenon, and certainly it was remarkable. Never had I seen such rain anywhere. Not only did it fall from clouds to earth, but the mid-air seemed to hold it in volumes. You could see it hanging suspended in great masses of mist, which every now and then burst and discharged their contents in heavy showers. The vast basin of mountains in which Bergen lies seemed filled with moisture, as though the atmosphere was one great sponge which yielded torrents at the least squeeze from the hand of the wind.

There was another reason why I was indifferent to the wetness of this day. I had seen all that was best worth seeing out of doors in Bergen, but had not yet visited any of its interesting public buildings. Of these there are several, ancient and modern: more than one excellent museum and picture gallery, and some edifices of great historic interest. It was the latter that I wished most to inspect, and I took advantage of this wet day to visit the famous Hanseatic house in the Tydskebrygge and the adjacent Valkendorf Tower and Kongshall.

The Hanseatic house, or museum, is the property of Mr. W. J. Olsen, a Bergen merchant, and stands in the Finnegaard on the Tydskebrygge. It is the last remaining habitation occupied by that notorious ring of German traders who settled down in Bergen in the fourteenth century, and monopolised its commerce for some two or three hundred years, until their power was finally broken in the eighteenth century. All the rest were burnt or otherwise destroyed; and it is said that even in the German

Hanse Towns themselves there is not one of the ancient leaguers' houses left standing. Not that the Hanseatic house on the Tydskebrygge is very old. It dates only from the early part of the eighteenth century, and was built after the last great fire which devastated that quarter. But it is a perfect example of the Hanseatic merchant's place of business and residence, and it is to be seen exactly in the condition in which it was left by its last occupant. The exterior is embellished with carvings, and its surface is painted in green and red, colours freely used also in the various rooms through which the visitor is conducted. Here we find the merchant's business office and his manager's bureau, the apartments used by the clerks, and the bedrooms of all. These last are, perhaps, the most curious of the whole suite, for the beds are constructed like the berths of a ship, and are closed on one side with hinged or sliding doors, while, on the other, shutters open to a passage beyond, to enable the female domestics to make the beds without entering the men's rooms. For the Hanseatic community was, or was supposed to be, strictly celibate, in order to prevent its members from intermarrying with Norwegians, and thus allowing the natives to obtain a share of the monopolised trade.

The house is called—and is—a museum, for it contains a vast quantity of curious articles formerly used by the old merchants, such as their scales and weights, the latter being of two sorts, for buying and selling; their clocks, lanterns, candlesticks, fire-engines, snuff-boxes, washing bowls, drinking-cups and tankards, machines for chopping cabbage, and staves with bags for making collections in church. Here, too, we saw the lamps which were fed with cod liver oil, not yet used for medicinal purposes; decorations made of strips of dried codfish, the arms of the leaguers—half an eagle and half a cod—and a cornucopiæ in which again the cod took the place of fruit and flowers. One old ledger lay open on a desk, containing, no doubt, the record of many a fraudulent transaction; and elsewhere we saw the merchants' strong-box made of oak and bound with brass, in which their valuables would be transported from time to time to their native towns in Germany. It had three separate locks, so that it could be opened only by the application of three separate keys in the possession of as many persons, for these astute folk were too suspicious of each other to entrust any one of their number with the sole custody of the common safe.

We had the privilege of being conducted over the museum by Mr. Olsen himself, a highly intelligent gentleman, who speaks English well, and who seems to take a great pride in his collection. He told us that the German Emperor, when he recently visited the place, offered to purchase it, but was respectfully informed that it was not for sale at any price. 'No,' exclaimed Mr. Olsen, with warmth, 'the house belongs to Bergen. It is a portion of our history, and we will not part with it.'

It is but a step from the Hanseatic Museum to Valkendorf's Tower, the grim old fortress which stood just outside the German merchants' gates, for the Hansers' quarter was jealously walled and guarded, and from which this robbers' den, as it was considered, was at last bombarded. The tower is now used as an arsenal, and is stocked with old-fashioned arms and accoutrements which would raise a smile on the lips of any officer from Woolwich. A subterranean passage leads from it to the Kongshall, the palace erected by King Haakon Haakonsön in the thirteenth century; but this is, I believe, blocked up. We crossed a courtyard to get to the palace, and were guided over the building by a courteous young soldier, the son of a respectable solicitor of Bergen, but here, as he laughingly told us, 'only a number.' The Kongshall had been left for centuries in a state of ruin and neglect, but for some years past it had been undergoing a process of restoration. It consists mainly of a fine spacious hall, very early Gothic in style, together with a handsome crypt. There is a confusion of scaffolding and loose planks in it at present, but it will soon be put into repair for use as a public place of assembly.

These three buildings are the most interesting edifices in Bergen, and are well worth seeing. No charge is made for inspecting them, though the visitor is expected to put something into a box at the Hanseatic house, and that something a *krone*. As you are shown over the others by soldiers, a very small 'tip' will suffice, and none is necessary if, as in my case, you happen to fall into the hands of a gentleman private.

In fine weather the day may be agreeably wound up with a visit to the Nygaardspark, a well-kept pleasure-ground overlooking the town, where a very fair entertainment is usually given on the boards of an open-air theatre, while the visitors promenade under the trees on the terraces, or sit consuming light refreshments. When I first went to the park there was an excellent orchestral performance by a band of young lady instrumentalists from Christiania, and on the second occasion a concert by Bergen musicians, enlivened now and then by solo scenes, in which a native comedian gave us a very favourable example of Norwegian humour, especially in the character of an old fishwife narrating her grievances. Music, I believe, is also to be heard sometimes at Nordnæs, the extreme point of the Bergen peninsula, which is neatly laid out as a public ground, and commands a fine view of the fjord.

As I was twice in Bergen on Saturday mornings, I was enabled to see the fishmarket in full swing. It is a very animated scene, often described. The harbour was crowded with smacks and boats from those lonely isles I had passed on the coast, and these were loaded with fish of every sort and description, from the tiny sprat to the gigantic hake, as big as a man. Cod, herring, and mullet there were also in abundance, and the prices charged for these dainties were something almost inconceivable, a few *öre* being sufficient to purchase enough fish to last a family for a week. Bargaining for fish is always amusing, and it is conducted here by the buyers hanging over the railings that guard the margin of the harbour, and haggling with the fishermen below. The women, of course, had a good deal to say for themselves, but the men were grave and sententious, and I could not see that there was any wrangling, or even much excitement, over the various transactions. The Norwegians take things very quietly, whether in business or pleasure.

There was little display of native costume at the market, but some of the fisherwomen, or *fiskerpiger*, were picturesquely attired in a blue woollen gown, with an opening in front, showing a peep of gaudy handkerchief, and wore a thick muffler round the throat, with a peculiar round cap, broad at the crown, and having a white band across the brow. They looked well in groups of two or three, all carrying the gaily painted *tine* or box, without which no Norwegian woman can travel or market. They seemed rather warmly clad for summer weather, but as they pass so much of their lives at sea in open boats, doubtless their costume was suited to the climate.

I am still of opinion that it is quite the best

course to leave Bergen as a *bonne-bouche* for the wind-up of a tour in Western Norway, but I would advise my readers to allow at least two or three days for the visit. Not only is the town itself full of picturesque bits and objects of antiquarian and historical interest, but there are many lovely walks to be taken on its heights, and pleasant trips to be made across its waters, while the neighbourhood abounds in attractive drives, and a run along the wonderful railway, with its fifty-four tunnels, which connects it with Vossevangen, ought on no account to be omitted.

There is another good reason why Bergen is the best place to finish up with. It is impossible to leave Norway without carrying away many souvenirs of this beautiful country in the shape of its products. The shops are full of things both ornamental and useful, which are well worth having, and many of which cost twice as much elsewhere, and it is not convenient to carry these articles, sometimes bulky, about the country. So at Bergen you may best do your shopping and buy your presents, and then all you need do is to have them packed and put on board. And here let me say, while I am on this subject, that while the traveller may in some cases be able to buy certain articles cheaper elsewhere there need be no fear of any imposition or extortion being practised on him at Bergen itself, where prices are no higher as a rule than in other parts of the country.

One incident which I have to relate speaks volumes for the integrity of the people, and it is among the most remarkable facts of my tour. I had purchased some furs and other articles at the well-known house of Brandt in the Strandgade, paid for them, and ordered them to be packed and sent to my hotel. In due course they arrived, and I had them sent to the steamer. But during my voyage home I unpacked them, as I thought I could enclose them more conveniently in another receptacle. What was my surprise to find at the bottom of the box in which the shopkeeper had deposited my purchases, a small paper packet evidently containing money! I opened the paper and found that it enclosed two silver coins, accompanied with a memorandum in the following terms:—'It was 2 Kr. too much, Sir.'

Thus it appeared that by some miscalculation I had overpaid, or had been overcharged, the small sum in question, and the shopkeeper or his assistant had had the honesty, of his own accord, to return it! And this too in the case of a tourist who, it was known, was just about to leave the country, perhaps never to be seen there again, and who could not by any possibility have otherwise discovered the mistake. The matter, no doubt, is a small one in itself, but it is very significant. Where else would such scrupulous honesty have been displayed?

There are many other shops besides Brandt's worth patronising, where the customer is sure to be fairly dealt with. But Bergen ought not to be left without a visit to Bennett's, where almost everything that Norway produces is to be procured, not to speak of circular tickets and coupons and thousands upon thousands of photographs. Nor should I omit to add that excellent service of the same kind is done by Mr. T. Beyer, whose establishment has existed since 1771, and whose shop in the Strandgade is abundantly supplied with everything that the tourist can require. He, as well as Mr. Bennett, publishes a time-table of railways and steamers, in English, which will be found by the traveller much more useful and intelligible than the rather confusing *Norges Communicationer*. Mr. Beyer has also a branch establishment in the Carl Jonans Gade at Christiania, where he is represented by a courteous and efficient manager. Tourists save themselves an immense amount of time and trouble by taking counsel of these well-informed and obliging agents.

It is needless to say much about my voyage along the coast from Bergen, as it was of precisely the same character as that which I had made from Molde. The same bright sunshine followed me all the way, as we continued to thread the same archipelago of rocky islands that skirts the whole coast for a thousand miles, from Stavanger to the North Cape. It was once more for Stavanger that I was bound, thus completing the circuit of Western Norway, and there I arrived at seven o'clock in the evening, having started from Bergen at noon.

A large crowd was assembled on the quay to witness the arrival of the *Eldorado*, and in the midst of it I recognised the sturdy figure and genial face of my good friend Captain Pedersen, who had come down to meet me on my return. I need hardly say how glad I was to see the brave old mariner again, and to thank him for his advice, which had enabled me to make the most satisfactory route, as I am convinced, that can be chosen for a tour in Western Norway.

The *Eldorado* was to stay a couple of hours at Stavanger to discharge and take in cargo, so I had time for a little jaunt with my worthy friend. We made the most of the opportunity, and, taking a boat, rowed across the fjord to Bjergsted, a public garden, prettily laid out on the slope of a hill, with a refreshment house and a band-stand. Thus my last two hours in Norway were pleasantly spent, and my last act was to grasp the hand of the best and most interesting companion I had found in the whole course of my travels in his beautiful country.

And so I bade farewell to Norway. The sun was setting as the steamer put out from Stavanger, and as we glided down the Bukke fjord the shores became more and more shadowy in the twilight till they vanished like ghosts in the gloom, and under a dark blue sky we entered the open sea.

CHAPTER XXIV.

A SECOND TOUR—CHRISTIANIA.

In the summer of 1891 I revisited Norway, mainly for the purpose of satisfying myself that I was fully justified in setting forth the tour described in the foregoing pages as the 'best.' I also desired to ascertain whether my favourable impressions of the first and least-known part of my route, namely that between Stavanger and Odde, stood the test of comparison with my later experiences. In both respects my original ideas were confirmed. Not only was I assured by persons who knew the country well that it would be impossible to make within a short space of time any other tour equalling in beauty and interest that which I have indicated, but I was more than ever charmed with the scenery of the Suldal and the Bratlandsdal. Hence I now put forward this story of my travels with greater confidence than I should have felt if I had not visited Norway a second time.

On this occasion I began at Christiania and traversed Telemarken. Then I revisited some of the scenes of my first tour for the purposes I have mentioned. That portion of the round which was new to me is exceedingly beautiful and interesting, but it does not include any fjords, properly so-called. It derives its charm chiefly from the picturesqueness of the lake scenery and the luxuriance of the vegetation which is the glory of Southern Norway. A tour of this sort is necessary for those who wish thoroughly to understand the character of the country as a whole, and it therefore forms an admirable 'supplement' to the journeys and voyages among the fjords.

On their way to Christiania, the Wilson steamers touch first at Christiansand. This is a port almost at the extreme point of the south coast, originally built some two-and-a-half centuries ago, but retaining few traces even of such limited antiquity, as, of course, it has met with the usual fate of Norwegian towns—destruction by fire. It is now laid out in squares and blocks like certain American cities, and cannot be said to present many attractions. But its environs are very pretty, and it is worth while to take a stroll among them, for which there is sufficient opportunity, as the steamer arrives at 10 o'clock in the morning and stays to discharge and take in cargo till about 4 o'clock in the afternoon.

It was a brilliant sunny morning when the *Tasso* arrived at Christiansand, and, accompanied by a fellow-traveller, I went ashore and proceeded to take a walk up the country. A fine river, the Otteraa, flows through the town, and the pleasantest ramble is up the course of this stream as far as you can go in the time at your disposal. The river makes its way through a wide and verdant valley, the Ravnedal, which becomes more and more narrow as you ascend it, until it forms a ravine between abrupt cliffs, from the summit of which one looks back upon a charming scene, embracing the course of the Otteraa to the sea, and a distant view of Christiansand. Retracing our steps we came to a ferry, crossed the river, and varied our walk by returning by the main road to the town. It is a pleasant little excursion on a fine day, and no doubt might be continued with advantage by those who intend to enter Norway by the Sætersdal route, which is sure to become popular one of these days when the carriage road to Telemarken is completed.

At 4 o'clock we set out again and shortly afterwards entered the Skaggerak. We stood well out from the land, so could only see the coast in dim outline, and long before we had neared the fjords which lead to the Norwegian capital the sun had set. The Skaggerak, as a rule, is a very nasty bit of water, but it was kind enough to us on this occasion, and a tranquil voyage on its bosom enabled us to enjoy a good night's rest until about 5 o'clock in the morning, when we awoke to find ourselves alongside the quay at Christiania.

If Christiania is not a very interesting city that is its misfortune rather than its fault. It has been burnt down over and over again, nearly all its relics of the past have been destroyed, and the only wonder is that it is so bright and cheerful as we find it. The 'devouring element' has been merciless to the Norwegian capital. It has spared much of ancient Bergen, and has not deterred the good people of Stavanger from building up their town again on something like the old lines. But fire has made a clean sweep of the old wooden houses of Christiania, and has terrified the inhabitants or their Government into erecting a city of brick and stone, which is handsome enough, no doubt, but has nothing of the true Norwegian colour and tone about it. The principal portion of the town is mostly laid out with straight regular streets, of which the Carl Johans Gade is the principal and finest, containing the best hotels and shops, and many large private residences. This great thoroughfare runs the whole length of the city, from the eastern railway station to the royal palace, which is not a striking example of architecture, but stands in a splendid position at the summit of a slope. The Carl Johans Gade is intersected at right angles by the streets before mentioned, and here and there are fine open spaces, some pleasantly planted with trees. The gardens in the upper part of the Carl Johan are particularly beautiful in their luxuriant foliage, and at the back of the palace there is a well-kept park.

But, as I have said, there is nothing very remarkable or characteristic in the aspect of the capital.

It is very much like an average continental town, such as we see by the score in France and Germany, but without those fine old cathedrals, churches, hôtels-de-villes, and antique mansions which give so many touches of picturesque contrast to their more modern surroundings. The ecclesiastical edifices of Christiania are in fact simply hideous, and the only public buildings of an imposing character are the Basilica-like Storthing, or Parliament House, the University, and some of the departmental offices.

But one relic of antiquity Christiania possesses, and this alone deserves to attract visitors from almost any distance. I refer, of course, to the unique and deeply interesting Viking ship which is on view in a shed at the rear of the university building. This wonderful *trouvaille*—dug up some years ago from a mound near Sandefjord, at the entrance of the Christiania fjord, in which it had been marvellously preserved in the blue clay for over a thousand years, has been described again and again, and a full account of it and the circumstances under which it was brought to light may be found in a little pamphlet in English by Professor O. Rygh, antiquary at the university of Christiania, which may be obtained gratuitously at Bennett's and elsewhere. It is not necessary, therefore, that I should enter into minute details with regard to it. Everybody knows that it is a huge boat some 80 feet long and 16 feet wide at the broadest, that it contains in its centre the death chamber, resembling a hut, in which its captain was laid to rest, that you see in it or about it every sort of appliance and implement used by its crews : the oars they rowed with, the apertures and rowlocks from which these were worked, the mast, the rudder, planted not in the centre of the stern, but on the starboard side, and even the very beds in which the men used to sleep, the same in shape exactly as those now in use in the hotels and private houses, just as the form of the ship itself is precisely that of the boats in which we are rowed on the fjords to this day.

The sight of this ancient vessel is one of the most suggestive in the world, and it is impossible not to feel deeply impressed by it. It is difficult to realise to the mind the stories of the old sea-kings, their strange adventures by sea and land, their naval battles and their piratical visits to our own shores. They seem to savour of the legendary and the mythical, and one is almost inclined to doubt whether these hardy Norsemen ever crossed the German Ocean at all. But here we are brought face to face with an unquestionable evidence of their reality. Here is one of the ships in which these old rovers certainly did traverse the North Sea to harry our shores. How they managed to do it, however, is a question that seems more puzzling after we have set eyes on this ancient boat than it was before. It appears almost incredible that such a frail craft, stoutly built though it is, could have lived in such stormy waters as those which divide

Britain from Scandinavia, rigged with one square sail, scantily provisioned as she must have been, and delayed on her voyage by contrary winds for weeks and perhaps even months.

She could have done but little in the way of tacking, and my friend the old Stavanger captain told me that in a dead calm her rowers would not make more than six knots an hour at the outside. Yet make these voyages she did, and sailors and warriors contrived to live in her somehow, probably existing on *fladbrod* and *öl*, and dried fish, which pack close. So there she stands, a substantial witness to the truth of history.

Christiania is amply provided with hotels, the Victoria and the Grand being of noble dimensions, a little dear perhaps for Norway, but giving the visitor the best accommodation. Midway between these first-class hotels and those of the cheap sort stands the Scandinavie, in the Carl Johans Gade, and at this most comfortable and moderate hostelry I put up in company with two gentlemen I had met on board the *Tasso*. Here you can take your meals at fixed prices or *à la carte*, and when I state that the charges for a good dinner are from 1 *kr.* 50 *ö.* to 2 *kr.* it will be seen that the guest at the Scandinavie is not likely to incur a heavy bill. I should add that the cookery is excellent, especially in the matter of fish, of which there is always a large variety, consisting chiefly of salmon, trout, mackerel, flounders, and herring.

After a good breakfast I repaired to the headquarters of Mr. Bennett, the tourist agent in the Store Strand-gade, as I desired to obtain certain information for my new tour. The house is a very old one, and must have been among the few that escaped the great fires of the past. A double flight of steps leads up to the main door-way, giving entrance to a series of long rooms, where the tourist may find everything he can possibly require for his coming journey. For those, indeed, who desire to travel comfortably in Norway, a preliminary visit to Bennett's is indispensable. Mr. Bennett, the founder of the house, which has existed for the best part of half a century, is now somewhat advanced in years, and the business is mainly conducted by two of his sons, the third and eldest having charge of the branch at Bergen. These gentlemen have every conceivable sort of information about Norway at their fingers' ends, and nothing can exceed the courtesy and patience with which they are always ready to impart it. They have also at their command every possible contrivance and facility for travelling purposes, being able to provide not only coupons for locomotion and hotel accommodation, but cars and carriages of all kinds, guides and other books innumerable, an inexhaustible collection of photographs and specimens of Norwegian art and industry without number. Many thousands of tourists pass through their bureaux during the season, and I have never heard yet of any one who sought the advantage of their services without being thoroughly satisfied.

I think it only fair to pay this tribute to Mr. Bennett's agency, as I myself derived great benefit from it, and have to thank his sons for the good-nature with which they placed at my disposal facilities for seeing the objects of interest in and about Christiania in a short space of time. These gentlemen kindly lent me a comfortable carriage and pair for a tour in the environs of the city, and in this on the first day of my visit I set out with one of my companions on a round which the Bennetts had made out for me.

It was indeed a most interesting little journey of some seven or eight hours, and I strongly advise those who may hereafter begin their tour in Norway at Christiania to follow in my footsteps. We started from the Carl Johans Gade at 10 A.M., and rattled through the stony streets to the northern suburbs. It was only on reaching the latter that anything remarkable was to be seen. The environs of Christiania are more than pretty. One is struck by nothing so much as by the abundant foliage one sees everywhere. Norway is by no means a land of gardens, as I have pointed out elsewhere, but here the eye encounters in all directions little bits of park-like scenery which remind one not unfrequently of the country scenes of old England. And in the midst of these green wooded spots stand stately mansions of no mean architectural pretensions, villas which are not monstrosities, and other residences pleasing to the eye. Certainly the Norwegians build with taste, and acquit themselves creditably in stone and brick, as well as in their more favoured wood.

The first stage of our tour was St. Hanshaugen, a neat building standing in some prettily laid out grounds, on a slight eminence, about 280 feet above the sea. Here is a reservoir for the water supply of the city, and above it rises a tower from which a fine view of Christiania and its fjords and hills is obtained. Next we drove on through many a pleasant country lane to Oscarshall, a small palace belonging to the king, in the midst of a very English park, and by the fjord side. It is a neat modern castellated Gothic building, painted white, and contains a series of 'show' rooms, stored with a vast number of interesting relics of Scandinavian history, and some excellent pictures and portraits.

Within a few minutes' drive of Oscarshall we came to an enclosure in which the king has collected several curious examples of Norwegian architecture. The most notable of these is Golskirke, one of the finest specimens of the old wooden churches of the country, dating from the twelfth or thirteenth century, and brought hither from Hallingdal. It is remarkable to see how perfectly the wood is preserved both within and without, and one cannot but be struck by the harmony and grace of the

GOLSKIRKE AND OLD HOUSES.
(Page 264.)

construction of the edifice, with its sloping roofs resembling the tiers of a pagoda and its tapering spire. The walls are covered with pieces of wood cut into the shape of the scales of a fish, and set close together, a contrivance which has at once a pleasing appearance and must be effectual for carrying off the rain. Hard by the church stand two old farm houses and a *stabur* or storehouse, also brought bodily from Telemarken and the Gudbrandsdal, which are most perfect specimens of their kind, and are filled with curious appliances of Norwegian domestic life.

On resuming our journey we passed through some extremely pretty country of the same soft, park-like character as that which we had previously seen, and as the road gradually ascended the views of Christiania and its neighbouring waters, studded with islands and lively with shipping, became more and more extensive and picturesque. We are now bound for the high hill, about 1400 feet above the sea, on which the Frognersæter stands. The road winds in zig-zags through dense woods, cut away here and there to give a view, and terminates at last at the summit, where we find a lofty scaffolding which serves as an outlook. Hence naturally the prospect is the widest and finest we have yet seen. The panorama is magnificent, embracing the Christiania fjord for many miles, and extending far into the heart of Telemarken. The atmosphere was not very clear on this occasion, but at times it is said that from this point of view it is possible to see mountains seventy miles distant. Just below Frognersæter is Holmenkollen, where there is a capital restaurant, a place of great resort. An excellent *table d'hôte* dinner here agreeably wound up the tour, and all that remained was to rattle back down hill by a shorter road to Christiania.

Nor were the pleasures of this well-spent day exhausted by our tour in the environs. In the evening we visited the Tivoli gardens which lie off the main road leading to the king's palace. And very pretty convenient gardens they are, where the townsfolk are wont to gather on fine summer evenings and enjoy themselves. The pretensions of the grounds are not great, but they are sufficient. Everything about them is neat and in good taste. They contain a theatre and an open-air platform for musical and acrobatic performances, shooting galleries, and sheds for various harmless games, restaurants and cafés and bodegas, while tables and chairs are set about the grounds for the consumption of light refreshments. A *Börnefest*, or children's festival, was on foot on this particular evening, so that the proceedings were if possible even more decorous than usual. But the Norwegians are always well-behaved, and drunkenness and rowdyism at these popular resorts are wholly unknown. The good people take their pleasure cheerfully but stolidly in their national fashion, though it cannot be said that there is anything specially characteristic of the country in the entertainments they enjoy. Yet one thing struck me as being peculiar. In one of the bodegas, where wine and other liquors are consumed, the waitresses are young girls of from 16 to 18 years of age, dressed in picturesque national costume, and in several cases of very pleasing appearance. 'Mrs. Grundy' might be expected to look askance at these comely damsels, suspecting them to be there for no good; but the uncharitable lady, if she thought evil of these fair Norwegian handmaids, never was more mistaken. Not only are they quiet and modest in their demeanour, but they bear, I was told, the highest character for propriety of conduct. They are the daughters of respectable people, and are well looked after, and from the point of view of the 'fast' young man, are simply unapproachable. Norway, indeed, is a very moral country, and probably there is no capital in Europe where there is so little evidence of open vice to be seen as in Christiania.

I have further tribute to pay to the national character in connection with this visit to the chief city. Having need of certain official information, I had been furnished by a friend in London with an introduction to Herr Qvam, the minister of Justice. He was unable to tell me what I wanted to know, but he placed me in the hands of his son, who took me the round of the principal Government departments until I found the official who had the means of satisfying my inquiries. It was an interesting little tour, affording one an opportunity of obtaining a glimpse of Norwegian bureaucratic life, and making the acquaintance of the ministers then in power. The party in office were the Radical section, who had not long before defeated their opponents the Conservatives. But there was no trace of the characteristics generally attributed to democratic leaders in the manners of the bland courteous gentlemen with whom I came in contact, except perhaps that perfect simplicity and absence of affectation which should, but does not always, mark the 'men of the people.' It is indeed difficult to say which seemed the most polished gentleman of the three ministers to whom I was presented: Herr Qvam of the Justice department, Herr Konow of the Interior, or Herr Barth of the Post Office.

Their offices are plain buildings, situated in different parts of the town, and appeared to be fitted up with a strict regard to economy, as the furniture they contained seemed to be no more than was absolutely necessary for purposes of business. There was indeed rather a bare and cold look about them, and the work of the state appeared to be done in a calm leisurely manner. No one seemed to be particularly busy, and the staff of departmental clerks everywhere was to all appearance anything but excessive in numbers.

While on our way from one office to another, young Mr. Qvam took me into the Storthing or

Parliament house. It stands in the Carl Johans Gade, and is built in the Romanesque or Byzantine style. There is only one chamber, and the members hold their debates in a spacious and handsome hall exactly semicircular in shape, and with a large and very showy chandelier suspended from the ceiling. The seats are arranged in a horse-shoe, with the President's chair at the straight end. The house was in session when we entered, nearly all the 140 members being present, while the galleries were full of strangers, among whom were several ladies. Yet the debate in progress did not seem to be of a very exciting character. The subject under discussion was the proposal to construct a railway between Christiania and Bergen, a scheme which, I was told, had long been before the legislature, and was not likely soon to be adopted. An elderly gentleman was on his legs making what was probably a very business-like speech, on one side or the other, for he appeared to be listened to with profound and respectful attention. We did not stay long in the Storthing, as of course I could not understand a word of what was being said, but this short experience of Norwegian Parliamentary life made a favourable impression on me, as the proceedings at any rate were orderly and dignified.

During my stay in the capital I also called at the British Consulate, and had the pleasure of making the acquaintance of that accomplished gentleman, Mr. Crichton Somerville, the vice-consul, who gave me some useful information and introductions. Mr. Somerville is a high authority on all matters relating to Norway, and it was a satisfaction to hear his opinion that the route I proposed to indicate in these pages was indeed 'the best tour.'

I was further indebted for much courtesy to the sub-editor of the *Verdans Gang*, the most largely circulated paper in Norway, who received me in the absence of his chief. He was good enough afterwards, quite unsolicited, to insert in the paper a paragraph about my projected book, and this I found very useful when I was endeavouring to explain to natives of the country for what purpose I was travelling. As a sort of curiosity in its way I reproduce it here in the original:—

ENGELSK BOG OM NORGE.

En bekjendt engelsk Forfatter og Journalist E. J. Goodman, der i bisse Dage har opholdt sig her og fra tidligere Besög har godt Kjendskab til vort Land, vil i en nær Fremtid hos det bekjendte Londonnerforlagsfirma Sampson Low, Marston & Co. udgive et elegant udstyret Værk 'Den beste Rute gjennem Norge.'

CHAPTER XXV.

SKIEN TO THE VRANGFOS.

HAVING done all I wanted to do in Christiania I set out for my tour through Telemarken. There is a line of railway from the capital to Skien, the starting-place for the Telemarken route, and two trains a day, at 8 A.M. and 3.20 P.M., depart for the latter. The distance is 126 miles, and the journey occupies about seven hours, but I preferred to travel by the afternoon train, as it would still be daylight when I should arrive at Skien about 10.30 P.M. As on most Norwegian railways, there is no first-class, but only second and third, a sort of anomaly to which we are well accustomed in our own country, for it seems as difficult in Norway as it is here to persuade the common people that a second-class fare is not necessarily dearer than one called third. The first—I should say the second—class carriages are fairly comfortable, but the third are provided only with bare wooden seats.

I did not look forward with extreme pleasure to this long railway journey, for I had an idea that Southern Norway was at least comparatively flat and tame, but I was agreeably surprised to find that it was far otherwise. Rarely have I travelled by rail through such beautiful country as that which is to be viewed from the carriage windows all the way from Christiania to Skien. The landscape everywhere is strikingly picturesque, but that which lends the chief charm to the journey lies in the fact that from first to last, without any considerable break, the line skirts some fine piece of water, now a river, now a lake, and now an arm of the sea. For many miles the railway follows the course of the Christiania fjord and its tributaries, sometimes hugging the shore and nearly always within sight of it. But the most interesting section of the journey is found towards the end. Near Laurvik the line, which has been running south, takes a sudden turn to the west, and on reaching that town creeps along the border of the Farisvand, a long winding lake embedded in mountains clothed with luxuriant foliage. The scene, or rather succession of scenes, here presented is truly enchanting. The line passes through a series of rocky cuttings which hide the view for a few yards every few minutes, and then open, to reveal a landscape of exquisite beauty. A sheet of water backed by wooded hills is the general characteristic of these charming tableaux, but no two of them are precisely alike, and I was enabled to see them under the light of a glowing sunset, in which the western sky was a surface of gold barred by crimson and purple clouds, which threw the mountains into shadow and cast a variegated gleam across the waters. To realise these scenes to the mind of some readers, I would describe them as twenty Killarneys revealed, hidden, and revealed again as we sped along.

Once more my good fortune befriended me in giving me interesting travelling companions. For some miles I was greatly amused with the conversation of a female missionary, a Norwegian by birth, who had lived most of her life in America, and was now returning to her native land, where she intended to carry on her work of evangelisation. She was a pleasant, cheery person, and had many curious stories to tell of wonderful conversions; but her talk was not excessively theological, and she left me, at Drammen junction, convinced that she was a thoroughly good and earnest woman.

As soon as I had bidden adieu to the lady preacher, I struck up an acquaintance, which circumstances rendered far too short, with a German gentleman, a native of Hanover, who had resided for many years in the interesting country of Lithuania. Dr. Sauerwin—for I have no hesitation in mentioning his name—I found to be a man of great intelligence and wide information. An accomplished linguist, he spoke English quite perfectly; he was also an author and poet, and conversed with excellent judgment on all sorts of European literature. He has since done me the honour of sending me a copy of his verses in Norwegian dialect, besides writing me several interesting letters. I have always regretted that, as he had to alight at a place far short of my destination, I was obliged so soon to part with worthy Dr. Sauerwein.

But I was compensated for the loss of this pleasant companion by immediately picking up another in a young divinity student from Christiania, who was going to visit some friends at Skien. He, too, spoke English remarkably well, and he surprised me by stating that I was the first Englishman with whom he had ever conversed. He left me at Skien, but I had the pleasure of meeting him again with his friends later on.

Quitting the Faris lake the railway takes a bend to the south and then turns northward till it brings us to our destination. Skien (pronounced Stchien) is a large and busy town actively occupied in the making of paper from wood pulp, the material for which is supplied by the abundant forests of Telemarken. Its situation is picturesque, but it is not beautiful. It has suffered from fire perhaps more severely than any other Norwegian town, and very recently, too, for it was totally destroyed in 1886, and has since been rebuilt of brick and stone. It is excellently placed for business purposes, for it stands on a good navigable river, which connects the great chain of Telemarken lakes with a fjord opening to the sea. This river is, so to speak, half paved for several miles with timber rafts brought down from the forests, and, indeed, on all the lakes we shall see everywhere thousands upon thousands of these great collections of bare white trunks, stripped of their bark, massed together like a vast platform at the foot of some village, or being towed along by boats and steamers.

Skien, at the time when I visited it, could boast of a very creditable industrial exhibition, which had recently been opened. It was held in a large wooden building covering some 7000 square mètres of ground, which had been erected, as I was told, at the very moderate cost of £2500. Much of the contents was of the usual 'shoppy' character, consisting of pickles and potted meats, bottled beer and chandlery, but it also included a vast quantity of specimens of native industry and ingenuity well worth inspection. The carved wood and needlework were excellent, and the straw-plaiting of the peasant girls and children was marked by great taste in design. It was interesting also to see the high finish brought to bear on the construction of *carrioles* and sledges, the national means of locomotion in summer and winter. But the most attractive part of the Skien exposition undoubtedly was the display of local antiquities. Of these there was a very rich collection, chiefly from neighbouring Telemarken. The peasants sent old relics that had been in their families for centuries: furniture of all kinds, pottery and tankards, tapestry and embroidered linen, antique clothes and bridal costumes, and, most interesting of all, attended in person, attired in their quaint native dresses, to watch over their treasures. The Telemarken costumes are certainly among the most curious to be seen in Europe. They are very strong in contrasts of colour, and in make and shape the picturesque and the useful agreeably combine. I was fortunate to see so many of these quaintly attired natives thus gathered together, as I was afterwards rather disappointed in failing to come across much characteristic costume in the country itself. The ordinary work-day clothes of the Telemarken peasants seem to come from the universal cheap slop-shop; their 'full fig' is put away for high-days and holidays.

Some of the exhibits were of a very extraordinary character, and perhaps the most notable of all was a wonderful piece of tapestry, the property of the family of Opdal in Bö. It was six hundred years old, and had been in the possession of the Opdals for five hundred years, yet it seemed as fresh and strong as though but recently made. On a ground of dark green cloth were worked in silk and human hair a number of fantastic pictures of a religious character, such as the Crucifixion, the Adoration, the Resurrection, and so forth, while the whole was surrounded with representations of fruits and flowers in brilliant colour. It certainly was the best preserved piece of tapestry I had ever seen. Some of the needlework, a hundred and two hundred years old, was remarkably fine, and the colour as bright and delicate as anything produced by the Japanese. The collection was also very rich in old tankards, and included such quaint curiosities as ancient *primstavs* or sticks used as calendars and marked with the signs of the Zodiac, and flat boards for rolling linen with carved animals for handles.

Most of these relics were priceless—that is to say, their owners would not part with them for any money. But here and there a few of the natives showed themselves willing to dispose of their treasures for a consideration, and curiosity collectors had a fine chance of picking up a rare bargain. Disappointments, however, sometimes arose. For instance, one elaborately carved antique cabinet had been marked as for sale at the temptingly low price of 40 *kroner*, a little more than £2. Instantly, of course, it was snapped up, when to the buyer's chagrin it was found that the small price ticketed was a mistake, the amount actually demanded being not 40 *kroner* but 400! These and other curious facts were imparted to me by Mr. Didrik Cappelen, the President of the Exhibition, a gentleman of high position in Skien, who courteously took me round the show and explained everything in perfect English.

I am indeed indebted to more than one inhabitant of Skien for much kind attention, which I found of considerable service. It is in fact characteristic of the national good-nature that a Norwegian is always ready to do his best to serve you, and if he finds that he cannot do what you want of him, he passes you on to some one else who can.

Thus I brought an introduction to Mr. Torkildsen, Manager of the Credit Bank at Skien, who presides over the Telemarken Tourist Club, and in his absence, Mr. Hielm, the Chief Cashier, was indefatigable in his efforts to meet my wishes for information. It was he who introduced me to the President of the Skien Exhibition, and he further gave me a card commending me to the Chief Engineer of the Telemarken Canal Works. In fact, it was my experience in Norway that, paradoxical as it may appear, you sometimes fare all the better when the particular person to whom you are accredited happens to be out of the way, for he is pretty sure to have left behind a representative, who makes it a point of honour to do all in his power to compensate you for the absence of his principal.

In no case had I a more agreeable example of this delegated hospitality than when I visited Ulefos, my next destination after leaving Skien. It is desirable to explain here that my projected tour through Telemarken promised to prove the more interesting from the fact that I should have an opportunity of following an entirely new route by water and land, which at that moment was not yet completed, being still in the hands of the engineers. This new route consists partly of a great waterway through a chain of lakes connected by canalised rivers, and extending from Skien to Dalen, in the heart of Telemarken, a distance of nearly 100 miles. When opened, as it was expected to be in this present year, 1892, it would be practicable to proceed all the way by steamer in twelve hours. It is a most interesting and beautiful voyage, which is to commence at 6 A.M. and end at 6 P.M., and dating from this instant summer, it is destined, no doubt, to be among the most popular routes in Norway. In 1891 the works were in their last stage of completion, and I was told that they were well worth inspection. The total cost of them would be about £2,200,000.

From Skien to Ulefos the steamboat route was already open. The vessel left Skien at 3 o'clock in the afternoon, and her voyage began on the beautiful winding river which flows out of the Nordsjö lake between precipitous banks, clothed with luxuriant foliage. In a short time the steamer enters a very narrow passage, Löveid, and here it is stopped for a while by a series of locks which it will have to climb.

These form the first of the remarkable works by which the so-called 'canal' is rendered navigable. There are four locks in tiers rising one above the other, like those still more wonderful water-gates at Trollhatten on the Göta canal in Sweden. It takes about half-an-hour to pass through the locks, and the traveller has the choice of landing and stretching his legs on shore, or of standing to watch the water coming boiling and foaming in through the flood-gates in cascades of the purest white and emerald. Having emerged from the topmost lock, the steamer at once enters the great Nordsjö lake, from the broad bosom of which is viewed a succession of scenes that recall in some measure memories of our own Windermere and Ullswater. When about two-thirds of this lake have been traversed, a point is reached which may be regarded as the commencement of the new route proper. The old route passes northward to the further end of the lake, where the traveller lands at Næs, and thence proceeds to Hitterdal and Tinoset, and to the mighty Rjukanfos, a journey often taken, and one, no doubt, of great interest. The new and more direct route through Telemarken starts from Ulefos, which is now reached, and where last year we found it necessary to land, as the waterway was not yet navigable for large vessels. Here, on the river Sogna, there is another lock and a fine fall by its side, but small by comparison with those to be seen further up the channel.

Ulefos is the headquarters of the engineering staff, and it was here that I had one of my most agreeable experiences of Norwegian courtesy. The Chief Engineer, Mr. Fenger-Krog, was absent, and so, too, was his second in command, Mr. Ström, but they had left behind an excellent substitute in Mr. Ingvar Kristensen, who responded to my desire for information with an alacrity that might almost be termed enthusiastic. It was somewhat late in the evening when I arrived, an hour at which the

LÖVEID: TELEMARKEN CANAL.
(Page 28)

officials knock off work and go home, but it was enough for Mr. Kristensen that I wished to see the works that night and he was ready to take me to the most interesting spot at once. This was at a point about two miles distant, and in a very short time my kind host, as I may call him, had had a trap brought to the door and we were starting for the next locks. The road runs parallel to the river Sogna, which has been deepened for the steamer traffic, and the scenery of which is pretty but not otherwise remarkable. It is only when the Eidsfos is reached that there is something really striking to be seen. There is a lock here, and the river beside it takes a leap of some 30 or 40 feet, the large volume of water giving it an imposing appearance. But my companion assures me that this is a very small affair compared with what is to come. We alight from the car, and I am conducted by a footpath along the river side for about half a mile, when my ear detects a distant rumble of falling water, indicating that we are approaching a foss of more than ordinary dimensions.

We are in fact getting near the Vrangfos, a fall of which the world as yet has heard little, but which is beyond doubt destined to be one of the most noted in Norway. Indeed, Norwegians themselves have hardly yet become familiarised with its name, for in subsequent stages of my journey I met many travelled and educated natives who had never even heard of the Vrangfos. The fact is, it is a new waterfall, being artificially caused for the purposes of the canal works. At this point the river formerly descended in a series of rapids, but the construction of the locks, four in number, like those at Löveid, necessitated the damming up of the flood to such an extent that the river, here about 120 feet broad, takes one leap to a depth nearly as great as its breadth. It is, indeed, a grand sight, this magnificent cataract tossing and foaming over the rocks, and rebounding in clouds of spray, which the breeze carries far along the river bank, and roaring with a thunderous voice that drowns all other speech.

The Vrangfos deserves to be called the Schaffhausen of Norway, and probably will be known as such hereafter. In some respects, indeed, it surpasses the famous falls of the Rhine, for, while not so broad, its height is, I believe, nearly twice as great. Its surroundings are most pleasing, as from almost every point of view it is set in a rich frame-work of foliage. At the time when I visited it, it was approachable only by land, but from the present summer it will be one of the most interesting points of the steamboat voyage. The vessel will have to wait here for about half-an-hour in order to get through the series of six locks, and during this pause the passengers may land and survey at their leisure the Vrangfos, which lies side by side with the locks. A long wooden bridge traverses the stream at the head of the fall, and this is a fine point of view, as the torrent rushes under your feet and precipitates itself in stupendous volume into the lower bed. Then you may cross the river and view the mighty foss in profile from the opposite bank, and probably sooner or later a path will be cut to the level of the stream, so that the fall may be seen at its best from the base.

Climbing a steep hill by a path through the woods my companion and I presently reached the main road where we found the *stolkjærre* which had brought us from Ulefos, and in which we now returned. At the door of Aaheim's hotel, which has a pleasant look-out on the river, I parted with my excellent friend, Mr. Kristensen, the most courteous and attentive host I had met even in hospitable Norway.

CHAPTER XXVI.

TELEMARKEN BY WATER.

PENDING the opening of the new waterway, which at this stage still required deepening in parts, it was necessary to proceed for some distance by road. I had, therefore, to take a drive of about twelve miles from Ulefos to Strengen, where the voyage by steamer would be resumed. Starting at about 9 A.M. from Aaheim's hotel in company with two Norwegian ladies, I drove by the river side for some miles, noting the strong wooden booms that mark the course of the new channel, and passing several more locks. The scenery all the way is very lovely and of varied character. Now the road traverses thick pine woods, now it emerges into an open plain bounded by forest-clad hills, now it winds through a dark narrow ravine or creeps round the margin of a lake. The open country about Lundefaret gives a fine view of the distant snow-sprinkled Lifjeld. Then the valley contracts, and, at the end of it, Strengen comes very suddenly in sight.

Strengen is a small scattered village with a *skydstation* which serves the purpose of an inn.

But it is a busy place, or rather was so, for but few travellers will pause there when the steamer route is complete. At present a large number of visitors arrive to catch the boats, and as one *carriole* or *stolkjærre* after another drove in, depositing its passengers and their luggage, the little station became quite a lively scene. The travellers resorted to the house for light refreshments, and sat about the porch and in the balconies above, while the horses were being taken out of the cars, and the latter were being collected in a crowd upon the open space along the quay. The luggage was stacked under a shed ready for shipment, and barrels and sacks and loads of timber were being brought down for transference to the steamer. The vessel was an hour late, being due at noon, but not arriving till 1 P.M., and it was nearly two o'clock before we started on our voyage.

The steamer was the *Bratsberg* and belonged to an English company who own certain copper mines of the same name near the Bandak Lake. It is rather a rough little boat, but sufficiently commodious on deck, though the saloon below was not large enough to dine more than some eight or ten passengers at a time. As we started at the hour for *middagsmad*, we missed some of the scenery of the Flaavand, the first of the series of lakes upon which we entered; but fortunately this was by no means the finest portion of the voyage. Soon after coming on deck we found that we were near-

T

ing the head of the lake, and then we entered another narrow channel, upon which the steep mountains closed in with very grand effect. These transitions from the broad waters of a lake to the confined gorges through which the connecting rivers flow give interesting variety to the voyage, and they are several times repeated. The next lake entered is the Hviteseidvand, and here the scenery becomes more and more imposing. The mountains rise higher, sometimes to 3000 and 4000 feet; their outlines are less monotonous, and there are great masses of them standing boldly out from the water in ever-changing form. At one point the lake closes in, having a very narrow channel, and here it is crossed by a curious drawbridge, giving passage from either side of a road. The steamer is skilfully navigated to thread the central arch of the bridge, the arms of which are raised to let us through, and remain stretched up high in the air after we have passed, as we shall have to retrace our steps.

We have now reached one of the prettiest stages of the voyage. We are steaming up an arm of the lake out of the direct course which we have to follow in order to touch at an important village called Kirkebo, which lies at the head of the Hviteseidvand. Kirkebo is certainly one of the loveliest spots in this part of Norway. Its situation by the lake-side commands a magnificent view of a grand amphitheatre of mountains, beautiful in form, stately in dimensions, and clothed with wood and verdure from base almost to summit. Between these mountains there are glimpses of valleys and glens suggestive of other picturesque scenes, while in Kirkebo itself, with its pretty-looking hotel in the foreground, there is an appearance of comfort which indicates that it must be a pleasant place for a short sojourn. To those who like nice out-of-the-way spots for sketching, or fishing, or honeymooning, or general loafing about, I confidently recommend a visit to Kirkebo.

After the steamer has done its business at this little lake-side paradise, it returns through the drawbridge, which then folds its arms again. Now we take a sharp turn to the right and once more enter another and perhaps the finest of all the narrow channels between the lakes. Here the rocks rise on either hand very precipitously, and we seem at times completely land-locked. But there is nothing naked and savage in the mountain sides. Everywhere the clefts and ledges bear clumps of green foliage, constantly presenting to the eye the sight of hanging woods and gardens, which stand reflected in the placid waters, sheltered from every wind that blows.

Here, as elsewhere, we see vast stretches of those timber rafts of which I spoke at Skien. There were acres upon acres of them spread along the margin of the lake at Kirkebo, and here in this channel, the Skarpström, we see a long strip of timber poles in mid-stream. And now, in connection with these, a curious little incident occurs. There are two men in a boat busily doing something at the extremity of one of these rafts. They have got a rope which they are attaching to one of the trunks, and as we steam towards them they row alongside and fling the other end of the rope on board, then putting off. It seems a mysterious proceeding, but the purpose of it soon becomes apparent. In a moment the rope's end is secured to our stern, and, as we proceed, we detach one of the strips of timber; this in turn drags another into its wake, and that a third, and so on until we find at last that we have got behind us a long tail of white pine trunks, about twenty in number, which spin along in the wash of our screw, the head of each trunk raising a little fountain of its own as it cleaves the waters. This addition to the impedimenta of the steamer does not appear at all to retard its progress, and so the vessel pants along with this singular tail till it reaches a point some miles distant, where two more men put out in a boat and relieve it of its charge. The *Bratsberg*, indeed, seems to be a good-natured sort of steamer, ready to take anything in tow, and it has rendered the same service to a rowing boat which has brought two peasants from a lake-side hamlet. But this time the *Bratsberg's* kindness has a melancholy result. Whether the boat's rope was rotten or ill-secured, certain it is that, after racing along for some miles in the rear of its patron, the little craft suddenly is seen to be adrift and tossing helplessly in the wash of the steamer many yards behind. The captain could not stop to recover the lost boat, but we were told that he certainly would have done so had he not been encumbered by his pine-tree tail. The poor men who owned the boat looked rather blank when they saw it bobbing about in the water far behind; but there was no fear of their losing it. It would go ashore somewhere, no doubt, safely enough, and the men would get some one at another village to come back with them and help them to recover it.

On emerging from the Skarpström we enter the Bandaksvand, the last and longest of the series of lakes. The first reach of this water is as picturesque as anything we have seen hitherto, for the surrounding mountains are bold and fantastic in shape, and their sharp peaks and ridges present forms to which various fanciful names are given. You are led by some Norwegians to expect that the Bandak will prove to be the finest of all the lakes, but it is really not so. A considerable stretch of it is rather monotonous in outline, though the mountains are finely grouped at the head, where stands Dalen, the terminus of the steamboat voyage.

Dalen is a favourite resort of the Norwegian tourist, and, lying as it does in the very heart of Telemarken, it is well situated for those who wish for a convenient centre from which to make excursions. The village is scattered about a plain at some little distance from the lake, and contains two or three decent hotels, of which the Bandak is the most generally recommended; but there is another—Lastein's—of very attractive external appearance, which stands immediately on the lakeside by the steamboat pier, and at this I decided to put up, nor had cause to regret having done so. The accommodation is excellent, and the people attentive; in fact, my worthy host, evidently desiring to make me 'feel at home,' immediately after my arrival put before me a file of the *Sheffield Daily Telegraph*, for a recent fortnight or so, which had been left behind by an English visitor. It was very kind of him, and, of course, he could not be aware that I was a slave of the press only too glad to get rid of the sight of a British newspaper for a time.

It had been my good fortune to meet on board the *Bratsberg* a party of young Norwegians, two gentlemen and two ladies, who were making a tour from Christiania *en route* for their home in Christiansand, and one of whom was that divinity student whom I had met in the train on my way to Skien. They amused me at intervals during the voyage by singing some of their national melodies as part songs, and the pretty plaintive airs, so characteristic of the country and its people, lent an added touch of charm to our romantic surroundings. Then they playfully struck up 'God Save the Queen' with Norsk words, as a

BANDAK LAKE.
(Page 293.)

special compliment to their British companion. Our national anthem, I may remark by the way, is much more cosmopolitan than is generally supposed. It is not only claimed by England, but by Germany and Switzerland. I was travelling in the latter country once on board a steamer when a party of Swiss began to chaunt the familiar air, and all loyal Englishmen present immediately raised their hats in token of respect for their sovereign, to whom they thought a tribute was being paid. But there was an Irishman on board, a regular 'wearing-of-the-green' nationalist, and he refused to uncover. He looked a little foolish when he discovered that the patriotic Switzers were singing not 'God Save the Queen' but 'God Save our Fatherland.'

On the day after our arrival at Dalen, I agreed to accompany the merry Norwegian party above-mentioned on an excursion to the Ravnejuv, which is the chief 'lion' of the district. I had heard much of its wonders and was assured that it was a sight not to be missed. My Norwegian friends, who had come provided for a walking tour, decided to perform the little expedition on foot, the distance being seven English miles each way, so they started first, and I followed in a *stolkjærre*, as it is practicable to drive part of the way. A good easy zig-zag road ascends the steep mountain side immediately above the hotel, and it is a pleasant ride to the top. Having reached the summit of the ridge, you cross a plain, and in a short time find yourself at the village of Eidsborg, where there is an excellent specimen of a *stavekirke*, similar to those to be seen at Borgund, Hitterdal, and in the king's grounds near Oscarshall. The exterior, with its coat of fish-scales and its tiers of pagoda-like roofs, is well preserved, though many centuries old, but it is said that the interior has been restored and is not worth seeing. I therefore merely took a walk round the quaint edifice and then pushed on, leaving my car behind, for there is only a footpath hence to the Ravnejuv.

On the way I picked up the Norwegians, and we walked on together. It is a charming ramble through woods and among fine rocks, and after a short climb the road descends some hundreds of feet below the level of the highest ground at Eidsborg, which stands 3400 feet above the sea. In fact, we are approaching the edge of one of the most terrific precipices in Europe, and that precipice is the Ravnejuv. It is indeed a singular freak of nature. A wall of rock perfectly perpendicular stands above the valley to the height of more than 1000 feet, and spreads over a space of about 100 feet, the mountain side on either hand being of the ordinary steep character. It is a very 'giddy height' for those whose heads are not steady enough to allow them to look over the edge with comfort, but even for rather nervous persons the position should have no terrors, as the brink of the great precipice is protected by a natural parapet of rock, over which any one can gaze downward in perfect safety. And the scene from this margin of the plateau is very beautiful. Far below, the roaring, foaming river Tokke winds in a perfect horse-shoe round the foot of a mountain which rises beyond it to a great height and is densely covered with forests of pine and fir. It is altogether a very remarkable and striking 'belle vue,' and, no doubt, will be one of those days as well known to English travellers as it is to Norwegian tourists.

A summer-house or outlook was being built near the top of the precipice, and this will be a welcome refuge in bad weather. It was on a delightfully fine afternoon that we visited the place, and there was just breeze enough stirring to facilitate the favourite amusement of the more frolicsome frequenters of the Ravnejuv. The wind when in the right quarter rushes up the cliff with more or less force, so that light objects thrown over the brink, instead of descending to the depths below, are blown back again and far above the heads of the throwers. To fling various articles into the gulf and watch what the wind will do with them is a pastime that, no doubt, delights childish visitors of all ages—from seven to seventy. I am not ashamed to confess that the party of whom I was one were for a short time fascinated by this frivolous amusement and eagerly watched the paper discs and spirals spinning and twisting in mid-air, and the lumps of turf or fragments of wood shooting up like rockets above our heads. A pastime of this sort is harmless enough so long as it is not overdone and does not tempt those who take part in it to do mischief or 'make a mess about the place.'

We had a pleasant walk back to Eidsborg, where at a farm-house we all partook of milk, *flöde-melk*, drinking it from wooden ladles out of a common bowl, Norwegian fashion. I gave up my *stolkjærre* to the two ladies of the party, whereat one of them —who rejoiced in the pretty name of Borghild— exclaimed, clapping her hands, 'Oh, this makes me so happy!' and walked down to Dalen with their friends. I was sorry to hear during the evening that they did not intend to stay there that night, but had resolved to push on *en route* to Christiansand through Sœtersdal. Notwithstanding their long walk, these hardy young Norsewomen were full of pluck and activity, and, like their male companions, they shouldered their knapsacks and marched off on their journey as fresh as though it was the first of their day's work. But though bereft of their company, I was not destined to pass the evening in solitude, for I met another Norwegian student at the hotel, and we sat till a late hour on the balcony overlooking the lake, smoking our pipes and conversing in German.

CHAPTER XXVII.

TELEMARKEN BY LAND.

AFTER crossing the plain over which, as I have said, the village of Dalen lies scattered, and which forms the bottom of a vast basin encircled by lofty mountains, the rough road becomes smooth, for here commences the new land route through Telemarken. It forms a short-cut as compared with the more circuitous way *viâ* Mogen and Aamot, but passes through scenery quite as fine as that to be viewed from the old road. At the end of the Dalen valley it strikes off sharply to the right, and seems to be taking you to the foot of the Ravnejuv. Indeed, I was hoping that it would do so, as I wished to see that wonderful precipice from its base. But you only get a distant glimpse of it, which your driver points out as you take another sharp turn to the left, and begin to ascend the mountain side above the roaring, foaming Tokke. Up and up the road winds in long zig-zags through the forest until you come to a point far above the bend which brought you out of the Dalen valley.

And the scene all this way is truly magnificent. Comparisons sometimes better realise the character of a country than descriptions, and to those who have travelled in Scotland I would say that the scenery of this part of Telemarken resembles nothing so much as the finest Highland landscape, such as that about Blairgowrie and the pass of Killiecrankie. In fact, one traverses many a lovely glen as beautiful as the Trossachs for mile upon mile, until coming to scenes of an entirely different character. There is a wealth of wood in this romantic region, and not alone of fir and pine, though these predominate. Larch, ash, oak, birch, alder, and beech appear here and there among the evergreen, and the under-growth of fern and bracken is as luxuriant as any to be found in our British woods.

After attaining a considerable height the road descends, and presently there suddenly appears in sight the long Börtesvand, a fine lake, which commences in the district of Mö. Hereafter the journey will be continued by car along the margin of this water, but in the summer of 1891 the road was not yet finished, and it was necessary to alight and take boat at Mö. There is a modest little station here, and on its walls is displayed a notice that a new hotel had just been opened at the other end of the lake, a welcome announcement to those who might be arriving as I was within an hour or so of dinner-time. A boat was all ready to convey me along the lake, and it was a very pleasant little voyage of some five or six miles on a fine, warm morning. It terminated near the head of the lake at Börte, and within a few yards from the shore could be seen the new hotel aforesaid, which, like the road leading to it, was not yet finished. It was a neat but unpretending little inn, and I had some doubt whether it would in its undeveloped condition be able to give adequate satisfaction to a keen and healthy appetite. The hotel had only been opened three days, and I found that I was the first Englishman to visit it. The walls were bare, there was an air of newness about everything in the place, and the builders were still at work on the rear of the premises.

Nevertheless, Börte was ready for me, a genial landlord welcomed me, and a strapping serving wench, in picturesque native costume, with much blue and red and white about it, replied with suggestive confidence to my demand for *middagsmad*. There are episodes in my travelling experience which I have been accustomed to call 'memorable meals'— that is to say, exceptionally good repasts which one happens to get just at the right moment and in the most unlikely places. I turned up once at a little way-side inn, at a very out-of-the-way spot in Belgium, and found that the landlord and cook was an *ex-chef* at Claridge's, who served me with a dinner worthy of a first-class Paris restaurant. This was certainly the most 'memorable meal' within my recollection; but the little dinner at Börte deserves to take high rank among such pleasant reminiscences. For it proved to be the very perfection of the best Norwegian cookery. It began with an extremely nice light soup. Then came a dish of *fiske-böller i hummeroos*—that is, fish-balls in lobster sauce. Oh, those fish-balls, I shall never forget them! Imagine a number of small puddings, each about as large as a bantam's egg, composed of some fresh fish, with the bones extracted, and rolled into a paste, and these floating in a creamy sauce, in which a fresh lobster had been cut up into little pieces. They were simply delicious, and I am afraid to say how many of them I ate. Then came a plate of *carbonada med sylte töi*—or mincemeat fritters with jam. These are dainties which they give you pretty nearly everywhere, but nowhere else had I tasted anything like the *carbonadas* of Börte. They were prepared and cooked absolutely to perfection, and I thought of them long afterwards with many a sigh of regret at past joys, never perhaps to be renewed. A splendid *omelette aux confitures* wound up this admirable little repast, and a bottle of excellent *öl* washed it down. Blessings on thee, Oh, worthy host of Börte: may thy skill never grow less and thy custom wax greater day by day!

It will readily be supposed that I was in a humour to enjoy my resumed journey, which was rendered not the less agreeable by the fact that I was provided with a new and particularly comfortable *carriole*. I was being driven also over another section of the new road, which was as level as a billiard table, and the scenery for several miles was charming. At Heggestol you come upon the old road, which is not so good, being ill kept in places, and of that 'switchback' character of which I have spoken elsewhere. A little beyond this point too the views around are less interesting than before, and at last you enter a very barren valley, almost destitute of attractions. Nor was I greatly 'taken' with Nylænd or Grungedal, my destination for the day. It was situated on the border of a lake flanked by somewhat monotonous mountain ranges—not by any means a place to stay at for any length of time, though it is said that the fishing is good there. The hotel is a very decent one, but not up to the mark of that at Börte in the victualling department. The waitress here was a very handsome Telemarken girl, who looked well in her pretty native dress. She spoke English and chatted affably. And I had also the pleasure of the company of another German-speaking Christiania student with whom I agreed to drive the next day as he was going my way.

We soon got out of the comparatively uninteresting part of the Grungedal, and the scenery became once more as fine as ever. The road now began gradually to rise, and little by little we attained a considerable height, for we were approaching one of the most elevated stations in Norway, the well-known Haukeli-Sæter. This, however, was some distance off, and meanwhile we decided to rest and dine at Botnen. Our surroundings continue to improve as this place is neared. We pass through fine narrow valleys, and by the side of streams that go dashing grandly over boulders of rock, and here and there fall in magnificent cascades, and we catch sight of more than one fine foss, the most beautiful of all being the Vafos, which descends from a great height on the opposite side of the valley in a series of leaps.

We are charmed with Botnen. It stands on an elevated position above a lake bordered by high wooded mountains, and has a plain-looking but apparently substantial and comfortable hotel, near which is erected an extremely pretty and highly ornate imitation of a *stabur*, fitted up with refreshment- and bed-rooms, and with a covered balcony all round it. In the open yard in front of the hotel stands a strange withered beech tree, with many branches, which, blanched and stripped of its bark, has a quaintly ornamental appearance. We bait fairly well at the hotel, and then prepare to resume our journey. Our intention is to walk the rest of the way to Haukeli-Sæter, a distance of twelve miles, but I am encumbered by a heavy bag, and it is necessary first to arrange for its transmission. I would have hired a *carriole* for the purpose, but there is no vehicle to be had, the only car being engaged by a Danish gentleman and his wife, who are making a honeymoon journey. But the diffi-

HAUKELISÆTER.
(Page 305.)

culty is soon surmounted. The Danes are good-natured and promise to take my bag for me, and so we start unencumbered.

The road still mounts, but as we get to higher ground the whole aspect of the scenery changes. Gradually the woods become thinner; soon hardly a tree is in sight, and at last none at all. But we are compensated for this loss of vegetation by the striking appearance of the barren mountains. These are of great height, and their summits are thickly besprinkled with snow in patches, giving to the dark rock, on which they lie, all the semblance of marble. At their feet are dark placid lakes or tarns which reflect the mottled crests as in a looking-glass. It is a grand wild scene, which follows us all the way to Haukeli-Sæter, and is seen there at its best. The Sæter is not at the highest point of the road, for the latter begins to descend within a mile or two of the station, and the incline is continuous all the way to Röldal.

Haukeli-Sæter is a place of great resort. It is not much visited by English tourists from the Telemarken side, but many of those who have been to Odde come up to it and return viâ Seljestad and the Horrabrækker, described in an earlier part of this volume. It has very fine bracing air, and is therefore famous as a sanatorium. Indeed, it is said that a week or two passed at Haukeli-Sæter is as beneficial as even a longer residence at any marine watering-place. The accommodation here is excellent in every way. There is a good substantial hotel, supplied with every comfort, and it has a commodious *dépendance* across the road. It was into the latter that we were first introduced, and being taken to the upper floor I was for the moment a little alarmed at the sight I saw there. For, opening on to the corridor, was a range of quite the smallest bedrooms I ever beheld in my life, and I confess I viewed the prospect of having to be boxed up in one of these rabbit hutches—for they were little more—with something like dismay. I did not measure any of these closets, but I should say that none of them were of greater dimensions than eight feet by four. They were, in fact, something like the sleeping cabins in a ship; in fact there were, if I recollect rightly, two tiers of berths in some of them.

However, my mind was soon relieved. These 'little-cases' were never used, except under great pressure of business, and fortunately just then Haukeli-Sæter was not yet over-crowded. So both my companion and I were accommodated with good large bedrooms on the ground floor, and were made as comfortable as weary travellers could desire. We had had a little rain on our march from Botnen, but the evening was fine, and a beautiful sunset lighted up the snow-patched mountains across the dark lake which lies at the Sæter's feet. It was something of a novel sensation to find oneself once more seated at a large *table d'hôte*, and hearing one's native tongue talked on every side, by ladies and gentlemen from Bayswater and Kensington, from Manchester and Liverpool. I had long been out of the track of the British tourist, for very few English people make their way through Telemarken, not one in fifty names in the visitors' books being that of a subject of Her Gracious Majesty, Queen Victoria.

The Norwegian student had arranged to spend a few days at Haukeli-Sæter, so on the following morning I started alone for that which must be the end of my second tour for present purposes. I was bound for Röldal, and thence would make my way through the Bratlandsdal, and the Suldal to Stavanger, and go over other portions of my old route with the objects that I have previously explained. It was again a delightful drive down hill to Röldal, over an excellent road, which has not been completed many years. The picturesque barren scenery was gradually changed to landscape more verdant, and, as Röldal is neared, the road winds down the mountain sides, through wooded valleys and ravines as fine as any that I had seen near Dalen. Here I was among familiar scenes, as the great Röldal lake lay stretched at my feet, and in the distance I descried the gap that marked the portal of the Horrabrækker pass with Breifond hotel perched upon the hill side at its entrance.

But I must say no more about these later stages of my second journey, as I have embodied my experiences in that which has gone before, correcting what I had already written, and adding such new facts as came subsequently under my notice. Suffice it to say, that the first portion of this second tour was to me not less interesting than the journey I took in 1890, and that Telemarken, though not possessing natural features so distinctly characteristic of Norway as the regions of the great fjords, is still extremely beautiful, and well deserving of a visit by those who have 'done' the Hardanger and the Sogne and desire something new.

[Under the title of 'New Ground in Norway' a book has been published for me, giving a full account of my travels in the Ringerike, Telemarken and Sætersdalen, during the summer of 1895. I was accompanied by Mr. Paul Lange, one of the most accomplished amateur photographers in Europe, and my volume is illustrated by beautiful reproductions of his views. That which I have lightly touched upon in these last few pages is much more amply described in my new book, which is the first that has ever been written in English about South Norway under its present conditions of travel. Many parts of Telemarken not mentioned here are included, and the portion relating to Sætersdalen is entirely new.—May 1896.]

SUMMARY OF THE TOUR.

I NOW propose to give a summary of my first tour with a view of indicating the best route for future travellers who have only about a month at their disposal, and desire to confine their wanderings to Western Norway. I do not say that I could not have improved upon my plan of travel; that I might not have saved time here and spent it more profitably there; but I am satisfied that the *general outline* of the tour was the right one, and I shall not hesitate to point out where those who pursue it in future may do better than I did.

June 26.—Arrived at Stavanger at 6 A.M. Saw the town and environs, and started by steamer at 1 P.M., arriving at Sand at 5.30 P.M. Put up at Rasmussen's Hotel.

June 27.—Went by rowing-boat to Saude and back, and again slept at Sand.

> *Note.*—Those who wish to make the most of their time would do well not to stay at Sand, but, after spending an hour or two there, to take a conveyance and go on to Oset the same evening, so as to be ready for the steamer the next morning.

June 28.—Left Sand at 6 A.M. Drove through the Suldal; arrived at Oset at 8.30. Started at 9, and arrived at Næs at 11. Left Næs at noon, drove through the Bratlandsdal, and arrived at Haare about 4.30 P.M. Put up at the Breifond Hotel.

June 29.—Left Haare at 10 A.M. Drove to Seljestad, arriving at 1 P.M., and dined there. Started again, and arrived at Odde at 5 P.M. Put up at Præstegaarde's Hotel.

> *Note.*—The Hardanger Hotel is that chiefly patronised by English tourists.

June 30.—Spent the day in an excursion to the Buarbræ.

> *Note.*—On arriving at Odde you will have time to make a trip to the Buarbræ and back the same evening, and the next day might be devoted to the Skjæggedalsfos. If time permit, the sledge journey across the Folgefond, described in Chapter X., may also be made.

July 1.—Left Odde by the steamer *Hordaland* at 7 A.M., touching at Vik and Ulvik. Arrived at Eide at 4.30, and drove to Vossevangen, arriving about 8 P.M. Put up at Dyksten's hotel.

> *Note.*—It might be worth while to stay the night at Eide in order to visit the Vöringfos the next day, and go on to Vossevangen the following morning. Fleischer's is considered the best hotel at Vossevangen.

July 2.—Spent the morning and afternoon at Vossevangen. At 4 P.M. drove to Stalheim, arriving about 8.30 P.M.

> *Note.*—It might be well, while at Vossevangen, to take a run on the railway to Bergen and back, or to stop at one of the many pretty places on the line, returning to Vossevangen by the evening train.

July 3.—Took a walk from Stalheim on the ridge above the Nærödal, and slept at a *sæter* in the mountains.

> *Note.*—This, I need hardly say, is an excursion which few tourists are likely to make. They will probably prefer to limit their walk to the end of the branch valley at the Jordalsnut and return thence to Stalheim.

July 4.—At 6 P.M. drove through the Nærödal to Gudvangen, arriving at 7.30. Put up at Hansen's Hotel.

> *Note.*—The tourist would do better to *walk* early in the day to Gudvangen, having his baggage sent on, and either spend the rest of the day there, walking or driving to Bakke and back, or go on by the steamer in the afternoon at once.

July 5.—Spent the day at Gudvangen and took a walk to Bakke and returned.

July 6.—Left Gudvangen by the steamer *Alden* at 5 P.M. and arrived at Lærdalsören at about 8.30; had supper at Lindström's Hotel, and went on board the steamer again at 11 P.M.

> *Note.*—Those who have time would do well to spend a day or two at Lædalsören and make excursions by road to Borgund church, and by steamer to Marifjæren and the Sogndal. If they go to the latter they need not return to Lærdalsören, but may take the Sogne steamer thence to Vadheim.

July 7.—Left Lærdalsören by steamer at 3 A.M., sleeping on board, and arrived at Vadheim at 1 P.M. Dined there and drove to Sande, arriving at 6.30 P.M., and putting up at Sivertsen's Hotel.

> *Note.*—A short stay at Balholm, and a trip up the Fjærland fjord to the Suphellebræ and back are strongly recommended.

July 8.—Left Sande at 10.30 A.M. and drove to Förde, arriving about 2 P.M. Dined at the other Sivertsen's Hotel, and drove to Nedre Vasenden, arriving at 6 P.M. Went by steamer to Skei, arriving about 8.30 P.M. Put up at the hotel there.

> *Note.*—If the traveller goes by the steamer belonging to the Stanley Hotel at Fuglehaug he would put up at that house; it will make little difference.

July 9.—Left Skei about 11 A.M. and drove to Egge. Dined there at 1 P.M. and drove over the Moldestad hill to Utvik, arriving about 6 P.M. Then crossed by the *Gordon* steam-launch to Faleide.

> *Note.*—If the steam-launch be not available the passage across the fjord must be made by rowing-boat, and probably there would be other tourists with whom the traveller could join. It might be better to go (by boat) to Olden or Loen instead of Faleide.

July 10.—Went by steam-launch from Faleide at 10 A.M. to Loen, and thence drove to Loen lake, and made an excursion on it by boat, spending the day there, and reaching Faleide about 8 P.M.

> *Note.*—A somewhat longer time than I spent there should be devoted to this district. It would be well worth while to go to Visnæs from Faleide, Olden, or Loen, and drive to the Opstrynd Lake and take a boat on it.

July 11.—Left Falcide at 10 A.M. and drove to Kjos, arriving about noon. Went by boat to Grodaas, and dined at Raftevold's hotel. Left at 4 and drove to Hellesylt, arriving about 8 P.M., and put up at the hotel.

> *Note.*—You can drive from Kjos to Grodaas, but the excursion by boat on the Horningdal Lake pleasantly varies the journey. (See also p. 192.)

July 12.—Went by steamer at 3 P.M. up the Geiranger fjord to Merok, and walked up the zig-zag road and back, returning from Merok by steamer at 6 P.M.

> *Note.*—It would be much better to go early in the morning by rowing-boat to Merok and spend the rest of the day there, proceeding much further up the zig-zag road than I did, either walking or driving. If necessary, sleep at Merok, and return to Hellesylt the next day.

July 13.—Left Hellesylt about 11 and drove through the Nebbedal and Norangdal to Öie, arriving about 3.30 P.M. Dined at the hotel there, and went at 5 P.M. by the steamer *Söndmör* through the Hjörund fjord to Aalesund, arriving about 8.30 P.M. Put up at Schjeldrop's Hotel.

July 14.—Left Aalesund at 7 A.M., and went by the *Söndmör* viâ Vestnæs and Molde to Aandalsnæs, arriving about noon. Dined at Aandahl's Bellevue Hotel, and at 6 P.M. drove through the Romsdal to Fladmark, arriving about 8 P.M., and stayed at the hotel there.

> *Note.*—It would be better to drive from Aalesund viâ Söholt to Vestnæs, and take the steamer thence to Aandalsnæs. In the journey up the Romsdal, too, drive as

far as Stueflaaten or Mölmen, remaining at one or other for the night, and returning to Aandalsnæs the next day. To enjoy the scenery of the Romsdal, *walk* from Aandalsnæs as far as the foot of the Romsdalshorn, and from Stueflaaten or Mölmen to Ormeim.

July 15.—Left Fladmark at 10 A.M. and drove to Horghjem and walked to Aandalsnæs, arriving at 5 P.M. Left by steamer *Rauma* at 6.30 P.M. and arrived at Molde at 10.30 P.M. Put up at the Alexandra hotel.

> *Note.*—Some persons prefer the Grand hotel, but both are recommended. The Grand has the more quiet, the Alexandra the more lively, situation. Visitors would do well to give themselves two days at least at Molde.

July 16.—Spent the day at Molde in very bad weather.

> *Note.*—Others may be more fortunate. If so they might start early and go up to the Varde and Stor Tuen, and afterwards drive round the peninsula.

July 17.—Made excursions about Molde, and left at 5 P.M. by steamer *Nordstjern* for Bergen.

July 18.—Arrived at Bergen about 2 P.M. and spent the rest of the day there, shopping, walking about, etc.

> *Note.*—Bergen, with its neighbourhood, is much too interesting to be hurried over, and the traveller should time his visit so as to enable him to spend two or three days there.

July 19.—Left at noon by steamer for Stavanger. Arrived there at 7 P.M. and started again at 9 P.M.

July 20.—All day at sea.

July 21.—Arrived at Hull at 4 A.M.

The carrying out of the above scheme of travel will, I need scarcely say, be dependent on the success of the traveller in catching the local steamers. As I have stated elsewhere, I happened to be particularly fortunate in this respect, being on no occasion delayed long at any station. But others may not be equally lucky, and I would recommend the traveller to make the most careful inquiries in advance to ascertain on what days, and at what hours the steamers are to start from points for which he is bound. The *Norges Communicationer* will give him a certain amount of information on this head, but it is not very easy to make out, and not always to be depended upon. I have generally found it the safest plan to consult the landlord or *portier* at the hotel at which I have been staying as to the best means of getting on from the next place, and even the next but one. In travelling in Norway, however, you must often leave your future movements to chance, and if you are detained a day or a couple of days anywhere, you must make yourself as comfortable as you can where you are, and get away when you have the opportunity.

I will now append in tabular form an itinerary of my route, stating the mode of conveyance, the time and length of each journey, and the fare by car or steamer. The figures quoted are only approximately correct, but they will give the reader some idea of the cost of travelling in Norway, and the distances to be travelled. I may note further that the car prices are the *carriole* fares. The *stolkjærre* rates are about fifty per cent. higher, but two passengers are taken for a fare and a half. The steamboat prices are also for one person, but two people, if related to one another, are carried for a fare and a half. It will be noted that the cost of some car journeys is higher in proportion than others. This is due to the fact that you pay more on bad and hilly roads than you do on good and level ones. I have not included in this statement any reference to a few by-excursions that I made, thinking it sufficient to give particulars respecting the main route only.

Journey.	Conveyance.	Time.	English Miles.	Fares.
		Hours.		*s. d.*
Stavanger to Sand,	Steamer	5½	40	4 6
Sand to Oset,	Car	2¼	13	2 4
Oset to Næs,	Steamer	2	14	1 10
Næs to Haare,	Car	3	16	3 1
Haare to Odde,	do.	7	34	5 10
Odde to Eide (*viâ* Vik and Ulvik),	Steamer	9	80	3 3
Eide to Vossevangen,	Car	5	24	4 10
Vossevangen to Stalheim,	do.	5	24	4 8
Stalheim to Gudvangen,	do.	1½	8	2 2
Gudvangen to Lærdal,	Steamer	3	28	3 4
Lærdal to Vadheim,	do.	10	52	5 10
Vadheim to Sande,	Car	1½	10	2 0
Sande to Nedre Vasenden,	do.	5	27	6 10
Nedre Vasenden to Skei,	Steamer	2	14	2 2
Skei to Utvik,	Car	5	34	8 0
Utvik to Falcide,	Steamer	1	7	1 2
Falcide to Hellesylt,	Car	6	32	9 4
Hellesylt to Merok and back,	Steamer	3	28	2 6
Hellesylt to Öie,	Car	3½	16	2 9
Öie to Aalesund,	Steamer	4	32	3 7
Aalesund to Aandalsnæs (*viâ* Molde)	do.	7¼	50	6 2
Aandalsnæs to Fladmark and back,	Car	5	34	5 10
Aandalsnæs to Molde,	Steamer	4	30	2 4
Molde to Bergen,	do.	20	200	22 6
Bergen to Stavanger,	do.	7	100	11 0

I also append a summary of my second or supplementary tour in 1891. This, as I have shown elsewhere, may be combined with the first and 'best' tour, but there are few who are likely to have time for such a journey. The Telemarken tour had better be reserved for a second visit, and I shall indicate how it may be rendered, by extensions, even more interesting than the route I adopted.

July 6.—Arrived at Christiania at 5 a.m. Visited places and objects of interest in the town, including the Viking Ship. Went to the Tivoli Gardens in the evening. Put up at the Scandinavie hotel.

July 7.—Drove to Hanshaugen, Oscarshall, Golskirke, and Frognersæter, and dined at Holmenkollen.

July 8.—Went by 3.20 p.m. train to Skien, arriving at 10.30 p.m. Put up at the Grand hotel.

> *Note.*—The visit to Christiania may be shortened. I was detained there by special business. If the traveller intends to confine himself to Telemarken it will be a good plan to go by train to Kongsberg and drive to Hitterdal and Tinoset, take the steamer there on the Tinsjö lake to Strand, drive to Krokan, and walk or ride to the Rjukanfos, which many regard as the finest waterfall in Norway. But in taking this journey it is necessary to go back to Strand, Tinoset, and Hitterdal, and reach the new waterway *via* the Hitterdal and Nordsjö lakes, as there are no other means of getting across Telemarken except by rough mountain paths. [This route is fully described in my book 'New Ground in Norway.' (See p. 308.)—May 1896.]

July. 9.—Visited the Skien exhibition, and went

at 3 p.m. by steamer to Ulefos, arriving about 5 p.m. Went to see the Vrangfos. Put up at Aaheim's hotel.

July 10.—Drove at 9.30 a.m. to Strengen. Started by steamer at 2 p.m. for Dalen, arriving there at 9 p.m. Put up at Gastein's hotel.

> *Note.*—As I have explained elsewhere, the journey from Skien to Dalen will in future be made entirely by steamer through the lakes, and the traveller can start at 6 a.m. from Skien, unless he prefers to stay a day there. The neighbourhood is pretty, and the pulp works interesting.

July 11.—Drove up to Eidsborg and walked to the Ravnejuv and back to Dalen.

> *Note.*—It is pleasant to devote an entire day to this excursion, but not necessary. By starting early the traveller may get back in time to proceed on his journey the same day.

July 12.—Drove to Mö, and went by boat to Börte. Thence drove to Nylænd and put up at the Grungedal hotel.

> *Note.*—In future it will be practicable to drive all the way to Nylænd from Dalen, but the traveller should by all means stay to dine at the hotel at Börte. In fact, it would be a good plan to stop for the night at Börte or at Heggestol rather than Nylænd, as the latter is not an interesting place.

July 13.—Drove from Nylænd to Botnen and walked to Haukeli-Sæter. Put up at the hotel there.

> *Note.*—If the traveller has stayed the night at Börte or Heggestol he will find it pleasant to spend the next at Botnen, and have a short journey of twelve miles the next day to Haukeli-Sæter.

July 14.—Drove to Röldal and thence through the Bratlandsdal to Næs (Suldal).

Here I came upon the route previously described, and continued it with variations to the Sogne fjord. I did this, as stated, for a special purpose, and do not recommend the tour to others, as it will take them too much over old ground, if they have already made the 'best' tour. From Suldal it will only be necessary to go to Stavanger, and so home. The time spent in Telemarken may, however, be very profitably extended by sojourns of two or three days at such charming places as Kirkebo, Dalen, and others, and by excursions from those centres. Sooner or later the carriage road through Sætersdal will be completed, and then a tour in Telemarken will be well wound up with a journey by land and lake to Christiansand. In that case the route to Haukeli-Sæter, etc., will be omitted.

I do not propose to give any table of distances, fares, etc., in Telemarken, as the journey through that district will be made under different conditions from those that prevailed when I visited it, by the completion of the new water and land routes. Besides, ample particulars on every head and in the minutest detail will be found in the capital guide-book, *The most picturesque Routes in Southern Norway,* published by the Skien Telemarken Tourist Club, and to be bought at Christiania or Skien, or of Messrs. Gall and Inglis, London and Edinburgh, price 50 *öre,* or sixpence. One specially valuable feature of this guide-book is the information it gives as to the prices charged at the various hotels in Telemarken.

These charges, as well as those of hotels in other parts of Norway, vary considerably, but nowhere are they extravagant, while everywhere they are below the average in other parts of the Continent frequented by tourists.

The price of a bed for the night ranges from 1 to 2 *kroner*, sometimes it is 1 *krone* 50 *öre*. For breakfast you pay from 1 *kr.* to 1 *kr.* 50 *ö.*, and the same for supper; dinner from 1 *kr.* 50 *ö.*, to 2 *kr.* 50 *ö.*, but the average is 2 *kr.* A cup of coffee or tea is generally charged from 30 to 40 *öre*; a bottle of ale from 20 to 30 *öre*, and a small seltzer 25 to 30 *öre*. Wines, both French and German, are good of their kind and cheap, owing, no doubt, to the lightness of the duties and the facilities for importation by sea. Spirits you cannot get at any price. Service or attendance is often not charged in the bill, or at the most only 50 or 60 *öre*, sometimes for two or three days' visit. But no one who has experienced the attention of the hotel *portiers* can go away without giving these good fellows a small 'tip,' and a present of from 25 to 50 *öre* is always gratefully accepted.

As might be expected the charges of those old-fashioned country inns, to which I have more than once referred, are, as a rule, the lowest; but it is remarkable that some of the cheapest of the hotels in Norway, considering the accommodation they give, are in several cases those of the greatest pretensions. The highest prices are only about half as much as those at houses of corresponding position in Switzerland.

In fact it may safely be said that Norway is still, even on the regular tourist track, decidedly a cheap country to travel in, perhaps the cheapest on the Continent. I believe that a fairly careful traveller could easily get through—with hotel bills, car, and steamer fares included—for 15s. per diem, or less if he shares traps with a companion. What a walking man or woman, with a knapsack, could do a tour in Norway for I am almost afraid to say. Ten shillings a day, however, would be a liberal allowance.

Up to the present time therefore Norway presents every possible attraction to the British visitor—magnificent scenery, many novel sensations in the modes of travel, comfortable and cheap accommodation, English spoken nearly everywhere, and the most honest and courteous people in Europe.

FISHING IN NORWAY.

By the personal courtesy of Mr. Bennett of Christiania, for whose valuable advice and assistance so many tourists have reason to be grateful, and from particulars supplied by his excellent guide-book and other sources, I am enabled to give the latest information of a general, and in some instances of a particular, character as to the fishing to be obtained on the line of route indicated in the foregoing pages.

Those enthusiastic anglers who go out to Norway with a resolute determination to concentrate their energies on the sport most dear to them, and who desire to obtain the best that the country can afford, must be prepared to 'rough it.' They must seek the most out-of-the-way places, far from the beaten track, where the roads are little if at all better than pony tracks, where there are no hotels and few farmhouses, where they must live in the tents they have brought with them, and upon the potted and other provisions with which they have supplied themselves. As an example of an enterprise of this sort there is none better than that which will be found so brightly described in that amusing volume called *Three in Norway: By Two of Them.* Here we have a party of young sportsmen who 'meant business' both with their rods and their guns, but it is not for such adventurous travellers that the present book is intended.

If, then, one does not wish to go out of the way to live on the mountains and put up at *sæters* or under canvas, but desires to combine the comforts of travelling with the pleasures of sport—to journey, so to speak, with the guide-book in one hand and the rod in the other—it is still possible to enjoy the delights of angling with fair prospects of success and at very little cost. In the 'out-of-the-way' places trout-fishing is to be obtained easily almost anywhere, and often even without going through the form of asking leave. Elsewhere the facilities for this sport are abundant, and are generally to be secured by readily granted permission. At most places the fishing may be had gratis by applying to the landlord of the inn at which one sojourns. All the innkeepers and station-holders in Norway are landowners, and they have a right to dispose of any part of a river which is bounded by their property. In fact trout-fishing is, as a rule, to be had free at so many stations in Norway that it is practically unnecessary ever to pay for the privilege.

It is otherwise with salmon. This is very difficult to get, as most of the really good streams are leased out for several years. The price which a good salmon-river generally fetches per season averages about 1500 *kroner*. The best sport no doubt is to be got in the far North. The Namsen and the Vefsen districts are famous, as is also the Tana river beyond the North Cape. But nearly all the waters are leased. Nevertheless some salmon-fishing is occasionally to be obtained here and there, either by favour or by moderate payment, and a few places will be indicated where this privilege may be secured. For the rest the angler must make inquiries for himself as he goes along, and he will everywhere obtain at least courteous information if nothing else.

Following the route described in this volume, the first place at which fishing is to be got is in the neighbourhood of Stavanger. There is a railway from this town to the port of Egersund, and trains run each way twice a day, occupying three hours and twenty minutes in the journey—fares, 4 *kr.*, and 2 *kr.* 48 *ö*. At Thime, one of the stations (Bellesen's Hotel), there is some fishing, but it is better to go on to Egersund, where the landlord of the Jæderen hotel, close to the station, provides free salmon- and trout-fishing for visitors in the adjacent River Tengse. At Aaensire, near Flekke fjord, there is excellent salmon-fishing, and fair trout are to be got in the neighbouring lakes. The place to stop at in this district is Söiland, and the hotels there are Wahl's and Moy's.

On the Suldal route there is not very much to be done by the wandering angler. A magnificent river rushes through the Suldal to the fjord at Sand, but this is chiefly good for salmon-fishing, and is leased for several years.

At Næs on the Suldal lake there is fair trout-fishing in the neighbouring streams.

Trout is also to be got in the Röldalsvand, near Haare, and in the adjacent mountain lakes. If the travelling angler has time for a somewhat long excursion from Röldal, he will find at Botnen, on the Haukelid road, a more than usually good fishing-station. It is said that trout of twelve pounds' weight have been caught here. There are very comfortable quarters for travellers at the hotel, which has thirty or forty beds.

At Odde there is a 'little salmon-fishing' in the river, and also 'a little sea-trout' in the fjord; but the angler will not do much in this district.

Near Vik, in the Hardanger, salmon-fishing may sometimes be had by payment, the price averaging about £10 a week.

The prospects improve further along the Hardanger. At Eide is Mæland's hotel, and the landlord there can give free fishing, both salmon and trout, in the river skirting his property. 'Close to Eide,' says Mr. Bennett, 'is a river, about an English mile and a half long, issuing from a lake about three miles long, which is formed by another river, affording excellent trout-fishing, so that the angler may make Eide his headquarters for a few days. Very fine trout may be caught in Espeland Lake, three and a half hours' trip from Eide—that is, two and a half English miles to Graven church, and nearly three hours' climb thence to the lake. There is a good and clean farm-house, with one room and two beds in it, close to the lake.'

There is not much to be done at Vossevangen itself, though the village is situated on the border of a fine lake, into which a broad rapid river runs. But on the line of railway between Vossevangen and Bergen there are several stations where good sport is to be obtained. The best of these is near Evanger, where in the river Teidal both salmon and trout are to be had. Small trout also abound in the rivers and waters near Nestun.

On the road from Vossevangen to Stalheim the trout-fishing is excellent, and the best places for it are Tvinde, Vinje, and Opheim, all offering comfortable quarters.

I believe there is not much sport to be obtained in the Nærödal or at Gudvangen. At the last-named place I met two or three fishing men, but did not see much fish.

Lærdalsören is a noted headquarters for anglers, but it is necessary to go some little distance from this place to obtain good sport. Trout of from two to three pounds are caught in the river between Nystuen and Maristuen, and the trout in the lake in front of the station at the former place are celebrated for their fine flavour. At Husum, near the famous Borgund church, both salmon- and trout-fishing are to be had, and there are large sea-trout in the Aardal lake, two hours' journey from Lærdalsören. Klingenberg's Inn at Aardal is a favourite haunt of anglers.

From Vadheim on the Sogne fjord to Utvik on the Nordfjord the opportunities for angling are abundant. A not very long excursion may be made by steamer from Vadheim to Lervig in the Böfjord, where, says Mr. Bennett, 'very good salmon- and trout-fishing with fly and minnow may be had in the small river and lake. Also good trout-fishing in the Aksel and Espelandvand. Comfortable but limited quarters at Joh. Wolff's, who speaks English well.'

By road the next best fishing-station is at Sande, where Mr. Sivertsen will permit his visitors to angle in the river that runs past his property, as well as in several lakes and streams close to his hotel. While I was there two English travellers took several dozen trout between them in one afternoon.

The next station, Förde (Hafstad), is also good for trout, especially at a point about two miles' distant, where there are quarters at the Skjortan hotel.

The district of the Jölstervand supplies very fine trout-fishing, and it is to be obtained through the landlords at Nedre Vasenden, Ordal, and Skei. But here the traveller has to be a little careful, as there are rival claims to the fishing-rights in some of the waters, and it may be well to ascertain, if possible, who is really the rightful owner of the fisheries. A gentleman, during my visit to the locality, having obtained permission to fish, was interfered with and told that he was trespassing. This sort of difficulty is not common in Norway, but in the present instance it should be guarded against, as there is nothing a true angler dislikes so much as to be accused of poaching.

Crossing the Nord fjord one comes to that great tourist centre, Falcide, and at Tenden's Hotel ample information may be obtained as to the facilities for fishing in that neighbourhood. On the road northward there are large angling possibilities at Kjos and Grodaas on the magnificent Horningdal lake, and probably also in the smaller lakes and streams passed in the wild country all the way to Hellesylt.

From that place, whether the traveller goes on *viâ* Söholt or the Norangdal, he will have fine opportunities for his rod. Mr. Rasmussen at Söholt gives trout-fishing free in several rivers and lakes, and salmon-fishing in the Stordal and Stranden, at the charge of two or three *kroner* a day.

Mr. Bennett tells me of some particularly good trout-fishing, not generally known, which is to be had in a river called the Sjaastadelv near Bjerke, and not far from Öie, on the Hjörundfjord, a district not always visited, but one which ought not to be missed.

Near Aalesund there are some small salmon-rivers, such as the Valdal, the Sunelv, and the Nordal, where fishing is open.

Of the more frequented parts of Norway the Romsdal used to be the best for fishing, but it is said to be not so good now as it was formerly. At Aandalsnæs, Mr. Aandahl provides free salmon- and trout-fishing in the Rauma, and a man named Petersen has a boat for those who wish to try for sea-trout in the fjord. Up the valley at Horghjem and Fladmark there are good fishing facilities, and near Stueflaaten the trout are said to be large and fat. The best trout-fishing in the Romsdal, according to Mr. Bennett, is to be obtained from Mölmen, for about an English mile down the river, and in the lake Lesjekogen, the source of the rivers Rauma and Laagen. Good trout are also to be had in the mountain lake Aursjö, six or seven hours' walk from Mölmen.

In nearly all parts of Telemarken good sport is still to be obtained in the rivers and lakes, and full particulars of the best fishing places are given in the little Tourist Club Guide-Book previously noticed in these pages.

More precise information on this point is hardly necessary. The angler has but to take his rod with him and a good collection of suitable flies, and he will be rarely at a loss for sport of some kind at any station he may visit. Those mentioned above, however, are the most likely spots on the ordinary route. July and August are considered the best months for fishing in Norway.

INDEX.

AAK, 213.
Aalesund, 199.
Aamot, 299.
Aandalsnæs, 207.
Aardal, 152.
Accidents, 154.
Adventure in mountains, 135.
Aftensmad (supper), 37.
Akvavit, 174.
Almannajuvet, 48.
Arne fjord, 160.
Aurlands fjord, 150.
Axlen (Aalesund), 201.

BAKKE, 147.
Balholm, 153-159.
Bandaksvand, 293.
Barth, Mr. T. W., 64, 272.
Baths in fjords, 234.
Beds and bedrooms, 40, 306.
Begging, 22.
Bennett's Tourist Agency, 121, 246, 257, 266, 323.
Bergen, 243-258.
'Best Tour,' how discovered, 11.
Beyer's Tourist Agency, 257.
Bjergsted, Stavanger, 258.
Bjerke, 198.
Boathouses, 34.
Boats and boating trips, 43, 161, 183, 300.
Bojum glacier, 153.
Bondhus glacier, 95.
Borgund church, 151.
Börnefest, 270.
Börte and lake, 300.
Botnen, 304.
Botten, 70.
Brandt, C., Bergen, 256.
Bratlandsdal, 62-70.

Bredevandet, 20.
Bredhjem lake, 174.
Breifond, 70.
Bride's dress, 184.
Buar and Buarbræ, 88, 90, 108.
Bukken fjord, 17.

CANAL WORKS, TELEMARKEN, 283.
Cappelen, Mr. D., 281.
Carl Johans Gade, Christiania, 262.
Carrioles, 51, 216.
Cathedral at Stavanger, 19.
Cattle moving, 113.
Cemetery at Stavanger, 18.
'Cherub' logs, 6.
Cheese, 38.
Children, native, 169, 194, 210.
Christiania, 259-274.
Christiansand, 260.
Clothing for Norway, 171.
Coast scenery, 239.
Colour of fjord water, 31.
Confirmation, 83, 169.
Costume. *See* Dress.

Dagbog (day-book), 54.
Dalen, 293.
Dances, native, 157.
Daylight in Norway, 39, 200.
Diligence in the Romsdal, 215.
Dress, native, 26, 83, 130, 168, 184, 254, 280.
Drikkepenge (pourboire), 50.
Drink in Norway, 173.
Driving, dangers and inconveniences of, 53, 67, 154, 186.

EGGE, 172.
Eide, 120.

Eidsborg, 296.
Eidsfos, 285.
' Eldorado' steamer, 5, 257.
Engineer captain, 27.
Espelandsfos, 75.
Eugenie, Empress, 144.
Exhibition at Skien, 279.
Expenses of travelling, 321.

FALEIDE, 176.
Fantoft, 246.
Fares, 1, 55, 108, 116, 183, 316.
Farisvand, 276.
Farms, 21, 190.
Fishing, 131, 163, 237, 322-329.
Fishmarket, Bergen, 253.
Fjærland fjord, 153.
Fjords—Arne, 160.
    Aurland, 150.
    Bukken, 17, 27.
    Christiania, 276.
    Fjærland, 153.
    Förde, 167.
    Geiranger, 188-192.
    Graven, 120.
    Hardanger, 77.
    Hjörund, 197.
    Hylen, 43, 59.
    Lyse, 25.
    Mauranger, 92.
    Molde, 204.
    Nærö, 142, 149.
    Norang, 197.
    Nord, 176.
    Romsdal, 207.
    Ryfylke, 17, 27.
    Sogno, 142, 149-159.
    Sör, 77.
    Stor, 198.
Flaavand, 289.
Fladbrod (oatcake), 136.
Fladmark, 214.
Folgefonden, 76, 92-110.
Food. *See* Meals.
Förde, 167.
Fosses. *See* Waterfalls.
Frithjof's grave, 157.
Frokost (breakfast), 13, 43.
Frognersæter, 269.

GADE, MR. (FANTOFT), 247.
Gardens, 46, 126, 232.

' Genial Grumbler,' 205.
Geiranger, 188-192.
German Fleet, 237.
German speaking, 75.
Gjerde, 94, 97.
Gjvindvik, 161.
Glaciers—Bojum, 153.
    Bondhus, 95.
    Buar, 88, 90, 108.
    Folgefonden, 76, 92-110.
    Jostedal, 168.
    Suphelle, 153.
Godtskalk, the guide, 94.
Golskirke, 268.
Graasiden, 124.
Graven fjord and lake, 120.
Grimo, 112.
Grodaas, 182.
Grungedal, 303.
Gudvangen, 141-148.
Gula river, 163.

HAARE, 70.
Haarteigen, 107.
Handshaking, 50.
Hanseatic Museum, 249.
Hansen, Mr. (Gudvangen), 142.
Hardanger country, 75.
Hardanger fjord, 77, 82, 93, 111-119.
Haugesund, 243.
Haukeli-Sæter, 303.
Hay drying, 124.
Heggestol, 303.
Hellesylt, 186.
Hjörund fjord, 197.
Holmenkollen, 270.
Honesty, examples of, 172, 221, 256.
Horghjem, 216.
Hornelen, 240.
Horningdal lake, 182.
Horningdalsrok, 185.
Horrabrækker, 73, 307.
Horses, 53, 104.
House architecture, 16, 34, 71, 160, 201, 269.
Hotel accommodation, 36.
Hotels—Aalesund, 200.
    Aandalsnæs, 208.
    Balholm, 156.
    Bergen, 246.

INDEX.

Hotels—*continued*.
  Botnen, 304.
  Börte, 301.
  Christiania, 265.
  Dalen, 294.
  Egge, 172.
  Eide, 120, 326.
  Faleide, 177.
  Fladmark, 214.
  Förde, 167.
  Fuglehaug, 167.
  Grodaas, 183.
  Grungedal, 303.
  Gudvangen, 142.
  Haare, 72.
  Haukeli-Sæter, 306.
  Hellesylt, 186.
  Lærdalsören, 152.
  Molde, 222.
  Mundal, 153.
  Odde, 82.
  Öie, 196.
  Sand, 35.
  Sande, 163.
  Saude, 46.
  Seljestad, 75.
  Skei, 167.
  Stalheim, 134.
  Stavanger, 13.
  Sundal, 93.
  Ulefos, 287.
  Utvik, 175.
  Vossevangen, 125.
Hviteseidvand, 290.
Hylen fjord, 43, 59.

INDRE HAUGEN, 181.
Industries, native, 84, 226, 279.
Interpreter at Hellesylt, 186.
Isterdal, 212.

JAPANESE CERTIFICATE, 15.
Jölstervand, 167.
Jordalsnuten, 134.
Jostedal, 168.

KILFOS, 146.
Kirkebo (Telemarken), 290.
Kjelstadli, 185.
Kjos, 182.
Kongshall (Bergen), 252.
Konow, Mr., 272.

Kristensen, Mr. I., 284.
Krone (money), 21.

LAATEFOS, 76.
Lady travellers, 108, 176, 187, 295.
Læra river, 152.
Lærdalsören, 151.
Lakes—Bandak, 293.
  Bredhjem, 174.
  Börte, 300.
  Faris, 276.
  Flaa, 289.
  Graven, 122.
  Horningdal, 182.
  Hviteseid, 290.
  Jölster, 167.
  Langeland, 165.
  Loen, 178.
  Lone, 70.
  Nordsjö, 284.
  Opstrynd, 178.
  Ringedal, 87, 107.
  Röldal, 70, 307.
  Sandven, 77.
  Suldal, 57.
  Vand, 124.
  Vetle, 87.
Landmarks, 124.
Langeland lake, 165.
Language (Norsk), 23, 127.
Laurvik, 276.
Licensing laws, 173.
Lifjeld, 288.
Loen and lake, 178.
Lönehorje, 124, 133.
Löveid, 283.
Lundefaret, 288.
Lyse fjord, 25.

'*Mange-tak*,' 26.
Manners of the people, 25, 84, 89, 98, 113, 146, 172, 196, 206, 217, 225, 270, 281.
Marifjæren, 152.
Mauranger fjord, 92.
Meals in Norway, 13, 28, 37, 47, 93, 265, 301.
Merok, 190.
Middagsmad (dinner), 28.
Milk-drinking, 298.
Ministers of State, 271.
Mö, 300.

Mogen, 299.
Molde, 204, 220-235.
Moldestad, 174.
Money, Norwegian, 21.
Morkdalsond, 132.
Mundal, 153.
Music, Norwegian, 294.

NAALENEDAL, 136.
Nærödal, 133, 141.
Nærö fjord, 142, 149.
Næs or Næsflaten, 60.
Names and words, 23, 127.
'Nansen,' 96.
Nebbedal, 185, 193.
Nedre Vasenden, 167.
Norangdal, 195.
Norang fjord, 197.
Nord fjord, 175.
Nordnæs (Bergen), 253.
Nordsjö lake, 284.
'*Norges Communicationer*,' 30.
North Sea passages, 4.
Nygaardsparken, 253.
Nylænd, 303.

ODDE, 81-91, 109.
Öie, 196.
Öl (ale), 29, 97, 110.
Olden, 178.
Olsen, Mr. W. J., 249.
Opdal's tapestry, 280.
Opheim, 131.
Opstrynd lake, 178.
Öre (money), 21.
Ormeim, 214.
Oscarshall, 268.
Osen or Oset, 57.
Otta river, 190.
Otteraa river, 260.

PEDERSEN, Capt. C. H., 11, 257.
Phrase book, 127.
Portal (Suldal), 58.
Postal service, 120.
Procession of cars, 67.
Pronunciation of names, 23.
Pulpit rock (Geiranger), 190.

QVAM, Mr. 271.

RAILWAYS, 126, 255, 275, 325.

Rauma river, 212.
Ravnedal, 261.
Ravnejuvet, 295.
Red or Reed, 174.
Reknæshaugen (Molde), 228.
Religion of Norwegians, 83, 241.
Ringedal lake, 87.
Rivers—Bratland, 63.
Buar, 89.
Gula, 163.
Læra, 152.
Otta, 190.
Otteraa, 260.
Rauma, 212.
Sogna, 285.
Suldal, 56.
Tokke, 297.
Rjukanfos, 86, 284.
Roads, 64, 166, 174, 185, 191
Röldal and lake, 70, 307.
Romsdal, 207-219.
Romsdalshorn, 211.
Routes to and in Norway, 1, 11, 81, 92, 111, 117, 161, 193, 203, 243, 259, 275, 282, 299, 309.
'Rushing' tourists, 2.
Ryfylke fjord, 17, 27.

SÆBO, 117.
Salmon, 37.
Sand, 34-42.
Sand-fjord, 43.
Sande, 162.
Sandven lake, 77, 88.
Saude and fjord, 43.
Sauerwein, Dr., 277.
Sawmills, 123, 131.
Second tour, 259.
Seljestad, 75.
'Seven Sisters' foss, 190.
Shops, 83, 126, 226, 255.
Simodal, 115.
Sivlefos, 141.
Skaggerak, 261.'
Skarpström, 291.
Skei, 167.
Skervefos, 122.
Skien, 278-283.
Skjeidesnipa, 154.
Skjæggedalsfos 86, 107.
Skydsguts, 52, 68, 116, 181, 208, 216.

INDEX.

Skydstations, 54.
Sledging on the Folgefond 92-110.
Slettefos, 216.
Slogan, 197.
Soap, 42.
Sogna river, 285.
Sogne fjord ,142, 149-159.
Söholt, 193, 203.
Somerville, Mr. C. 274.
Sondefos, 98.
Sör fjord, 77, 111-115.
Sövde, 45.
Spender, E., 79.
Spisesal (dining-room), 35.
Staburs, 34, 131, 269.
Stalheim, 131-140.
Stavanger, 10-21.
Stavekirker—Borgund, 151.
    Eidsborg, 296.
    Fantoft, 247.
    Golskirke, 268.
Steamers, eccentricities of, 30, 88, 158, 167, 177.
Stolkjærres, 51, 62, 181.
Stor fjord, 198.
Storfos, 191.
Storm on a fjord, 49.
Storthing, the, 272.
Strengen, 288.
Stueflaaten, 214.
Suldal, 51-60.
Sulö, 198.
Sundal, 92.
Sunday in Norway, 83.
Sunsets, 80, 201.
Suphelle glacier, 153.
Sweetmeats, 170, 194.
'Switchback' roads, 166.

'Tasso,' steamer, 6, 260.
Tea-drinking, 38.
Telegraphs, 120.
Telemarken, 275-308.
Telephone, 143.
Tilsigelse stations, 54.
Timber, floating, 278, 292.
Tine (box), 26, 254.
Tivoli Gardens (Christiania), 270.
Tokheim, 110.
Tokke river, 297.
Tor Stuen (Molde), 228.

Torvet (Bergen), 245.
Tourist Club, 92.
Tourist hut (Folgefonden), 102.
Trille (carriage), 51.
Troltinderne, 212.
Trout fishing, 131, 165, 322-329.
Tvinde, 131.
Tydskebryggen (Bergen), 245.
Tyssedal, 86.
Tyssestrœngenefos, 87, 107.

Ulefos, 282.
Ulvik, 115.
Utne, 114.
Utvik, 175.

Vaagen (Bergen), 244.
Vaalandspipen, 17.
Vadheim, 162.
Vafos, 304.
Valbergtaarnet, 16.
Valkendorf's Tower, 252.
Vand lake, 124.
Varden (Molde), 228.
Vasenden, Nedre, 167.
Veblungsnæs, 207.
Vegetables, 29.
Vengetinderne, 207.
Verdans Gang, 274.
Vermefos, 216.
Vestnæs, 204.
Vettisfos, 152.
Vik, 115.
Viks, and Vikings, 115.
Viking ship (Christiania), 263.
Vinje, 131.
Vöringfos, 117.
Vossevangen, 124.
Vrangfos, 285.

Waage, 59.
Waitresses, 70, 75, 156, 196.
Walking in Norway, 180.
Waterfalls—Eidsfos, 285.
    Espelandfos, 75.
    Kilfos, 146.
    Laatefos, 76.
    'Seven Sisters,' 190.
    Sivlefos, 141.
    Skervefos, 122.
    Skjæggedalsfos, 86.
    Slettefos, 216.

Waterfalls—*continued*.
   Sondefos, 98.
   Stalheimsfos, 141.
   Storfos, 191.
   Tokheimsfos, 110.
   Tvindefos, 131.
   Tyssestrœngenefos, 87.
   Ulefos, 282.
   Vafos, 304.
   Vermefos, 216.

Waterfalls—*continued*.
   Vettisfos, 152.
   Vöringfos, 117.
   Vrangfos, 285.
   Weather in Norway, 3, 150, 248.
   Wills, Mr. (Aak), 213.
   Wilson steamers, 1, 260.
   Wire lines, 123.

YACHTING IN NORWAY, 229.

BY THE AUTHOR OF 'THE BEST TOUR IN NORWAY'

'NEW GROUND IN NORWAY,'
The Ringerike, Telemarken, Sætersdalen.

BY E. J. GOODMAN.

With about 60 Illustrations from Original Photographs by PAUL LANGE

REPRODUCED IN THE FINEST STYLE BY

Messrs. HUDSON & KEARNS, Printers of 'Navy and Army Illustrated,' etc.

The above-named work, gives a full account of the Districts of Ringerike, Telemarken, and Sætersdalen, and places of interest on the Southern Coast.

PUBLISHED BY GEORGE NEWNES (LIMITED),
SOUTHAMPTON STREET, LONDON.

AND

SAMPSON LOW, MARSTON & COMPANY (LIMITED),
ST. DUNSTAN'S HOUSE, FETTER LANE.

To be obtained at all Libraries and Booksellers, and of Messrs. W. E. BOTT & Co., 1 East India Avenue, London, E.C.

! HARDY'S 'GOLD MEDAL' RODS !
AND TACKLE ARE BEYOND COMPETITION ! ! !

Highest Awards in the World. 33 Medals.

THE BEST SALMON AND TROUT RODS MADE FOR NORWEGIAN AND SIMILAR ANGLING ARE—

The 'KELSON,' £12, 5s. | The 'CHOLMONDELEY-PENNELL,' £9, 5s.
18ft. Cane-Built Steel Centre. | 14ft. Cane-Built Steel Centre.

The 'HI-REGAN,' £10. | The 'SPECIALS,' £5, 16s. 6d. each.
16ft. Cane-Built Steel Centre. | 11 and 12ft. Cane-Built Steel Centre.

THE 'ALNWICK' GREENHEART RODS ARE SUPERIOR TO ALL OTHER MAKERS' WOOD RODS.

IMPORTANT.—If you want the best of everything in Rods, Flies, Tackle, etc., write us. Remember the 'Best' is always the Cheapest. it will pay you.

CATALOGUE FREE

Mr. J. J. HARDY, the Champion of the World, making his Record Cast of 49yds. 1ft. 9in. with an 18ft. Steel Centre Rod.

CATALOGUE OVER THREE HUNDRED ILLUSTRATIONS, 260 PAGES, **FREE!**

The 'FIELD' says:—"It ought never to be forgotten that it is to Messrs. Hardy, of Alnwick, we owe the supremacy we have achieved as rod makers."

HARDY BROTHERS, ALNWICK, ENGLAND.

RETAIL BRANCHES: } 5 South St. David Street, EDINBURGH.
12 to 14 Moult Street, MANCHESTER.

OSBORNE, BAUER & CHEESEMAN'S
CELEBRATED SPECIALTIES.

It Softens and Improves the Hands, Face, and Skin generally.

Sold by all Chemists and Stores, in Metallic Tubes, 6d. and 1/-. By Post from the Sole Manufacturers.

PREVENT CHAPS AND ROUGHNESS OF THE SKIN BY USING.

'GLYMIEL SOAP' (*Registered Title*).

A refined and delicately perfumed Toilet Soap, possessing all the properties of the world-renowned and celebrated 'GLYCERINE AND HONEY JELLY.' Admitted to be the leading preparation for softening and improving the skin of old and young. Useful in all seasons.
Price 6d. per Tablet, or Three Tablets in Box, 1s. 6d.

'NAFATHA SOAP' (*Registered Title*).
Perfected Coal Tar.

A DISINFECTANT SOAP SPECIALLY PREPARED FOR TENDER FEET, Etc. *Most useful to Travellers for arresting Gnat, Mosquito, and Insect Bite Irritation.*
RECOMMENDED BY THE MEDICAL PROFESSION.   WRAPPED TABLETS, 6d.

Sold by all Chemists, Perfumers, and Stores. Prepared only by E. CHEESEMAN—J. HOLDSWORTH & SON, trading as

OSBORNE, BAUER, and CHEESEMAN
Perfumers to the Queen

Proprietors of the 'Incomparable Smelling Salts' (as supplied to the Queen), 'Baby's Soap,' 'Bauer's Head (and Bath) Soap,' 'Sambuline,' etc. etc.

19 GOLDEN SQUARE, REGENT STREET, LONDON, W.

For information regarding Norway Travel write to

BENNETT'S
TOURIST OFFICE

CHRISTIANIA, BERGEN, DRONTHEIM,
STAVANGER, or MOLDE

For Thirty-five years the only Tourist Office in Norway

NO FEES CHARGED

Bennett's Book of Preliminary Information for Tourists intending to visit Norway (Illustrated) *Gratis and Post Free.*

HOLBROW & CO.

Outfits for Norway and Sweden

A SPECIALTY.

HOLBROW & CO.,
40 DUKE STREET, ST. JAMES'S, LONDON, S.W.

M^CCALL'S PAYSANDU OX TONGUES

In Tins from $1\frac{1}{4}$ lb. to $3\frac{1}{4}$ lbs. each.

HOTEL RÖLDAL, RÖLDAL

On the Hardanger—Telemarken—Bratlandsdal Route

FIRST-CLASS HOTEL.   **CENTRAL SITUATION**
1400 FEET ABOVE THE SEA LEVEL.

2 Reception Rooms, Large Dining Saloon, 36 Bedrooms, 50 Beds.
Good opportunity for Shooting and Fishing.

Posting Station.   *English and German Spoken.*

G. HELLSTRÖM

Jeweller

22 KIRKEGADEN, STAVANGER

(Near the Quay, beside the Post Office).

Manufacturing Gold and Silversmith. Norwegian Antiquities and Curiosities.
Wood Carvings, Photographs, Etc. Money Exchange.

Branch—Own House, Odde, Hardanger.

ROSENBERG'S MEKANISKE VÆRKSTED

STAVANGER

Cable Address—'VŒRKSTEDET.'

Steamship Repairs of every description.
Good Situation opposite the Quay.
Machine Shop, Foundry, and Smith Shop.

C. MIDDLETHON

STAVANGER, NORWAY

Depots Best Qualities of COALS for Bunkering

OFFICE—SKANDSEKAIEN.

OLUF YENSEN

Furrier

44 KIRKEGADEN 44

STAVANGER

Larges Collection of Norwegian Furs.

NORWAY & SWEDEN.
LAND OF THE MIDNIGHT SUN.

The **Wilson Line** of **Royal Mail Passenger Steamers**, luxuriously fitted and lighted by electricity, present the quickest and best opportunities of visiting the magnificent Fjords and Mountain Scenery of **NORWAY**, at very reasonable cost.

These Steamers have been specially built for Passenger Service, with their Saloons and Sleeping Accommodation in the *centre* of the ships—this position giving passengers the *maximum of comfort*. INTENDED SAILINGS ARE

HULL TO STAVANGER AND BERGEN.—Quickest Route to Norway.

During Passenger Season (middle May to middle September) Steam Ship '**ELDORADO**' every **Tuesday**. **Bergen** and **Stavanger** to **Hull**, Steam Ship '**ELDORADO**' every **Saturday**. During the remainder of the year every **Thursday**.

N.B.—The '**ELDORADO**' is of very high speed, and has superior accommodation for Passengers in the centre of the Ship, and a limited number of Deck Cabins, and also of Cabins for one Passenger only. Lighted by Electricity. Her Dining Saloon and Drawing Room have been considerably enlarged, more State Rooms added, and her whole Passenger accommodation extensively improved; the Promenade Deck over the Drawing and Smoke Rooms has also been improved and extended to the full width of the ship.

HULL TO CHRISTIANSAND AND CHRISTIANIA.

The magnificent Steam Ship '**MONTEBELLO**,' or the splendid Steam Ship '**ANGELO**,' every **Friday** evening; leaving **Christiania** for **Hull** every **Friday** afternoon (calling at **Christiansand** every **Saturday** morning). Both these Steamers are of high speed, and have Saloons on Deck and State Rooms amidships, are lighted by Electricity, and have been specially built and fitted for the Christiania service.

HULL TO DRONTHEIM.

Landing Passengers at **Aalesund, Christiansund** (and at **Molde** when specially arranged). Steam Ships '**JUNO**' or '**TASSO**' every **Thursday** to and from **Drontheim**, during the Drontheim Passenger Season. These Steamers are of high speed, and have been specially built and fitted for the Passenger Service with their Saloons and State Room accommodation in the centre of the ship. Lighted by Electricity. During the remainder of the year weekly.

LONDON TO CHRISTIANSAND AND CHRISTIANIA.

The splendid Steam Ships '**ROLLO**' or '**DOMINO**,' elegantly fitted and lighted by Electricity, from Millwall Docks, every **Friday** morning during the season. **Christiania** to **London** every **Thursday** afternoon (calling at **Christiansand** every Friday morning).

SPECIAL HOLIDAY TOURS.

Have been arranged by these steamers, including Return Saloon Tickets, with Victualling on Board and Hotel and Travelling expenses in Norway. An Illustrated Handbook of these Tours may be had separately.

HULL TO GOTHENBURG.

The Route to **STOCKHOLM** (BY RAILWAY OR CANAL) AND ST. PETERSBURG. The Royal Mail Steam Ships '**ARIOSTO**' or '**ROMEO**,' with spacious Saloons amidships, and State Rooms separated from the Saloon, lighted by Electricity, every **Saturday**, as soon after 5 P.M. as tide permits. Leaving **Gothenburg** for **Hull** every **Friday** at 1 P.M.

GRIMSBY TO GOTHENBURG.

The Royal Mail Steam Ship '**CAMEO**' or other Passenger Steamer, every **Thursday** noon. Leaving Gothenburg for Grimsby every **Wednesday** at 1 P.M.

FIRST-CLASS PASSENGER STEAMERS, mostly having their accommodation amidships, are also despatched from

HULL TO ST. PETERSBURG.—EVERY SATURDAY.
Leaving ST. PETERSBURG for HULL WEEKLY.

HULL TO COPENHAGEN.	GRIMSBY TO MALMO.
EVERY FRIDAY.	EVERY WEDNESDAY.
Leaving COPENHAGEN for HULL every Thursday.	Leaving MALMO for GRIMSBY every Thursday.

RATES OF PASSAGE:	Single Fares.		Return Fares.		Victualling.	
	1st Class.	2nd Class.	1st Class.	2nd Class.	1st Class.	2nd Class.
Hull to Gothenburg, . .	£3 3 0	£2 2 0	£5 5 0	£3 3 0	6s. 6d. per day.	4s. 6d. per day
„ Christiansand or Christiania, .	4 0 0	2 13 4	6 0 0	4 0 0	6s. 6d. „	4s. 6d. „
„ Stavanger or Bergen,	4 10 0	3 0 0	7 0 0	4 10 0	Included.	
„ Drontheim, . .	6 10 0	4 4 0	9 15 0	6 6 0	Included.	
„ Copenhagen, . .	3 3 0		5 5 0		6s. 6d. per day.	
„ St. Petersburg, .	5 5 0		7 17 6		6s. 6d. „	
London to Christiania or Christiania, .	4 0 0	2 13 4	6 0 0	4 0 0	6s. 6d. per day.	4s. 6d. per day.
Grimsby to Malmo, .	3 3 0	2 2 0	5 5 0	3 3 0	6s. 6d. „	4s. 6d. „
„ Gothenburg, .	3 3 0	2 2 0	5 5 0	3 3 0	6s. 6d. „	4s. 6d. „

A great advantage by the '**WILSON LINE**' is the issue of tickets available, upon payment of difference, to return by '**WILSON LINE**' Steamers from ports other than those for which the return tickets were originally issued.

For Passage and Freight apply to THOMAS WILSON, SONS & CO., LIMITED, Owners, HULL; or to W. E. BOTT & CO., 1 East India Avenue, Leadenhall Street; GELLATLY, HANKEY, SEWELL & CO., 51 Pall Mall; SEWELL & CROWTHER, 18 Cockspur Street; HY. GAZE & SONS, LIMITED, 142 Strand; or THOS. COOK & SON, Ludgate Circus, London.

DET STAVANGERSKE DAMPSKIBSSELSKAB

The Royal Norwegian Mail Steamers of this Company maintain regular lines of communication between

CHRISTIANIA and BERGEN

The Company's Steamers also ply on the Ryfylke Fjords, and leave Stavanger for SAND and SAUDE on Sundays and Wednesdays at 9 A.M., Mondays at 7 A.M., Thursdays at 1 P.M., Fridays at 3 P.M., Saturdays at 2 P.M.; also for SAND on Mondays at 2 P.M., and for SAND and HYLEN on Tuesdays at 8 A.M.

1896
STAVANGER — SAND — SAUDE
Summer Time-Table for S.S. 'ROBERT,' 1st June to 31st August, both dates inclusive.

Monday	. dep.	Saude, . .	6 a.m.	arr.	Sand,	7¾ a.m.	arr.	Stavanger, 1½ p.m.
Tuesday . .	,,	Stavanger,	2 p.m.	,,	,,	8 p.m.	,,	Saude, . 10 p.m.
Wednesday .	,,	Saude, . .	12 noon.	,,	,,	1½ p.m.	,,	Stavanger, 7 p.m.
Thursday .	,,	Stavanger,	12 noon.	,,	,,	5½ p.m.	,,	Saude, . 7½ p.m.
Friday . .	,,	Saude, . .	6 p.m.	,,	,,	7½ a.m.	,,	Stavanger, 1 p.m.
Friday . .	,,	*Stavanger,	2 p.m.	,,	,,	6 p.m.		
Saturday .	,,	*		dep.	,,	8 a.m.	,,	Stavanger,12 noon.
Saturday .	,,	Stavanger,	2 p.m.	arr.	,,	7½ p.m.	,,	Saude,. . 9½ p.m.

N.B.—S.S. 'ROBERT' runs in connection with the steamer on the Suldal Lake.
* Direct Route.

GRAND HOTEL

STAVANGER

OLAF PERSSON.

LARSSEN'S FAMILY HOTEL

4 NORDBÖGADEN, STAVANGER

Situated close to both Steamer Quays.

40 PRIZE MEDALS.   3 Factories: PARIS, LONDON, STRASBOURG.

COMPAGNIE FRANÇAISE

Purveyors by special appointment to H.R.H. the PRINCESS OF WALES.

GUARANTEED ABSOLUTELY PURE.

£10,000 REWARD!
See Conditions in every Packet, 6d., and Tin, 7d. ¼ lb.,
1/- ½ lb., 2/- 1 lb.
Delicious aroma and dietetic sustaining properties.
Vide ANALYSTS.

SUPERIOR CHOCOLATE.
9d. per ¼ lb. Packet. (Yellow Wrapper.)

CHOCOLATE WAFERS.
6d. and 1/- per Box. A delicious eating Chocolate.

CHOCOLATE HORSESHOES.
(REGISTERED.)
A superior eating Chocolate in handsome horseshoe boxes, 6d.

'SOUVENIR' BOXES.
(REGISTERED.)
The success of the season. Filled with Chocolates or Confectionery from 6d.

HIGH-LIFE BONBONS.
The most tasteful Dessert Sweetmeat. Elegant Boxes, 3/- each.

Of all first-class Grocers, Stores, or direct from

LONDON WORKS: BERMONDSEY, S.E.

NIELSEN'S HOTEL.

NEDRE VASENDEN, IN JÖLSTER, NORDFJORD, built in the summer of 1891, and containing a large Dining- and Drawing-Room, Smoking- and Toilet-Room, and twenty-two Bedrooms with forty beds, is recommended to Tourists. Excellent Trout Fishing in the Lake Jölster and the River Jölstra. The Hotel is situated half way between Faleide and Vadheim. The steamer *Skjold* starts from the pier close to the Hotel for Skei every morning between 7 and 8, when the fare is paid for at least three persons, and when notice is given beforehand through the telephone.

N. NIELSEN, *Proprietor.*

NOW READY.

NEW WORK ON NORWAY.

IN THE NORTHMAN'S LAND.

Travel, Sport and Folk-Lore in the Hardanger Fjord and Fjeld.

By MAJOR A. F. MOCKLER-FERRYMAN
F.R.G.S., F.Z.S., Oxfordshire Light Infantry, Author of 'Up the Niger,' etc.

With Map, Illustrations, and Appendix.   With 16 Full-Page Illustrations.
Crown 8vo.   320 pp.   7s. 6d.

London: SAMPSON LOW, MARSTON & COMPANY, Ltd.
AND ALL BOOKSELLERS.

GAUTHUN'S HOTEL

NÆSFLATEN, SULDAL

E. GAUTHUN,
Proprietor.

HOTEL FOLGEFONNEN
SELJESTAD
Between Odde and Röldal

OLE JOHANSEN,
Proprietor.

HOTEL ALEXANDRA
LOEN, NORDFJORD

POSTAL ADDRESS—'Loen, Nordfjord.'   TELEGRAMS—

First-class Hotel. Beautiful Situation. Sea Bathing. Warm and Cold Baths. Good Fishing in Private River, as well as Sea and Lake Fishing. Posting Station. Post Office and Steamer calling-place. Centre for many interesting Excursions and Mountain Ascents.

Moderate Terms.   Board and Lodging for Week or longer, K.4.00 per diem.

The Hotel is managed by Mr. M. A. LOEN, who has been in America for eight years.

English well Spoken.

ALEXANDRA HOTEL
MOLDE, NORWAY

First-class Hotel, conveniently situated close by the Quay, and in the finest and most healthy part (the west-end) of the town. From here the most charming view is had of the Mountain Panorama of the Romsdal. Hot and Cold Baths at the Hotel. Sea-baths near the Hotel.

RESTAURANT—CHARGES MODERATE.   GOOD ATTENDANCE.

HANEVOLD, *Proprietor.*

N.B.—The Hotel has lately been greatly enlarged.
The Hotel's steam launch 'Alexandra' carries passengers to and from steamers, and calls at Vestnes when telegraphed for from S holt for a limited number (up to twelve) passengers, at a charge of Kr. 10.00.   HANEVOLD.

LOW'S STANDARD NOVELS BY POPULAR WRITERS

WILLIAM BLACK'S NOVELS

Uniform Post 8vo Volumes, cloth 6s. each. New and Cheaper Edition, Crown 8vo. Volumes, cloth, 2s. 6d. each.

A Daughter of Heth. With Portrait of the Author.
The Strange Adventures of a Phaeton.
A Princess of Thule.
In Silk Attire.
Kilmeny.
Madcap Violet.
Three Feathers.
The Maid of Killeena.
Macleod of Dare.
Green Pastures and Piccadilly.
Lady Silverdale's Sweetheart.
White Wings.
Sunrise.

The Beautiful Wretch.
Shandon Bells.
Adventures in Thule.
Yolande.
Judith Shakespeare.
The Wise Women of Inverness.
White Heather.
Sabina Zembra.
The Strange Adventures of a Houseboat.
In Far Lochaber.
The Penance of John Logan.
The New Prince Fortunatus.
Donald Ross of Heimra.
Stand Fast, Craig Royston!

By the same Author. Uniform Post 8vo Volumes, cloth, 6s. only.

The Magic Ink.
Wolfenberg.
The Handsome Humes.
Highland Cousins. | Briseis.

STORIES BY W. CLARK RUSSELL

New Issue in Uniform 8vo Volumes, bound in cloth, 2s. 6d. each; or in half-roxburghe, gilt edges, 3s. 6d. each.

The Wreck of the 'Grosvenor.' With Photogravure Portrait of the Author, from a Painting showing Clark Russell at the age of seventeen, when in the merchant service.
An Ocean Freelance.
The Emigrant Ship.
The Frozen Pirate.
A Sea Queen.
Little Loo.

The Lady Maud.
My Watch below.
John Holdsworth, Chief Mate.
Jack's Courtship.
A Strange Voyage.
A Sailor's Sweetheart. With Portrait.
Betwixt the Forelands.
Mrs. Dines' Jewels.

NOVELS BY R. D. BLACKMORE

New Uniform Edition, Crown 8vo Volumes, bound in cloth, 2s. 6d. each.

Lorna Doone. 41st Edition. With Photogravure Portrait of the Author, specially prepared for this New Issue. Also Illustrated Edition for Presentation, gilt edges, 7s. 6d.; and Edition de Luxe, 21s.
Tales from the Telling House. 5s. only.
Perlycross. 6s. only.
Cradock Nowell.

Clara Vaughan.
Cripps the Carrier.
Tommy Upmore.
Christowell.
Alice Lorraine.
Mary Anerley.
Erema.
Kit and Kitty.
Springhaven. (Also Illustrated Edition, 7s. 6d.)

NOVELS BY GEORGE MACDONALD

New Issue in Uniform Crown 8vo Volumes, bound in cloth, 2s. 6d. each.

Mary Marston. Revised Edition. With Photogravure Portrait of the Author.
Adela Cathcart.
Vicar's Daughter.

Weighed and Wanting.
Guild Court. | Stephen Archer.
Essays by Dr. MacDonald. With Portrait.

LONDON: SAMPSON LOW, MARSTON & COMPANY, LIMITED,
St. Dunstan's House, Fetter Lane, Fleet Street, E.C.

WILLIAM BLACK'S NEW NOVEL.

The WORLD says:—

'The perfectly delightful heroine of his latest, simplest, most captivating novel, "Briseis," will, we think be adjudged a high place of honour among his pictures of young womanhood.... Remarkable for its literary excellence.'

A Third Edition
IS
READY
OF
BRISEIS
BY
WM. BLACK.
1 vol. cr. 8vo. **6s.**
At all Libraries and Booksellers.

PUNCH says:—

'"Briseis" is a perfect work of art.... A delightful book,'

The SCOTSMAN says:—

'As fresh and charming a story as Mr. Black ever wrote.'

LIFE OF
'THE AUTOCRAT
OF THE
BREAKFAST TABLE'
AND HIS LETTERS.

ALL ADMIRERS OF

OLIVER WENDELL HOLMES

SHOULD READ HIS

Life and Letters.

In **2** *vols. crown* **8vo.** *charmingly Illustrated. Price* **18s.** *Now ready at all the Libraries and Bookstalls.*

'So much that is charming, so much that is fresh.'—*Standard.*

'An elaborate and pleasing picture of Oliver Wendell Holmes. The Autocrat, the Professor, the Poet of the Breakfast Table—the wit, the novelist—the brilliant man of letters.'—*Scotsman.*

LONDON: SAMPSON LOW, MARSTON & COMPANY, LIMITED,
St. Dunstan's House, Fetter Lane, Fleet Street, E.C.

NEW WORK ON NORWAY. NOW READY

With 16 full-page Illustrations.   Crown 8vo. 320 pp.   7s. 6d.

IN THE NORTHMAN'S LAND

TRAVEL, SPORT, AND FOLKLORE IN THE HARDANGER FJORD AND FJELD

BY

MAJOR A. F. MOCKLER FERRYMAN,

F.R.G.S., F.Z.S.
OXFORDSHIRE LIGHT INFANTRY
AUTHOR OF 'UP THE NIGER,' ETC.

With Map, Illustrations, and Appendix.

This work is the latest addition to Norwegian literature, and should be read by all who have visited Norway, or who intend doing so. The author has devoted several years to the study of the manners and customs of the people, their old legends and traditions, their occupations and their inner life. The chapters contain a full and minute description of the scenery, and of the places of interest in the Hardanger District—justly considered the most beautiful part of Norway—with accounts of travel amongst its fjords, valleys, mountains, waterfalls, glaciers, and snowfields, whilst a particular feature of the book is the narration of nearly a hundred quaint old tales of folklore, ancient customs, and superstitions. Fishing and shooting are treated of at length, and special attention has been given to the habits of the wild animals and birds of the lowlands and of the mountains.

The book is well illustrated, handsomely bound in cloth, and is supplied with an excellent map, historical and other appendices, and an index.

LONDON : SAMPSON LOW, MARSTON, & COMPANY, LIMITED,
St. Dunstan's House, Fetter Lane, Fleet Street, E.C.

LOW'S POPULAR LIBRARY

OF

TRAVEL AND ADVENTURE

Uniform crown 8vo volumes, fully illustrated, bound in cloth, HALF-A-CROWN each.

Ten Years' Captivity in the Mahdi's Camp, 1882-1892. From the Original Manuscripts of Father Joseph Ohrwalder, late Priest of the Austrian Mission Station at Delen, in Kordofan. By Major F. R. WINGATE, R.A. Fully illustrated.

How I found Livingstone: including Four Months' Residence with Dr. Livingstone. By HENRY M. STANLEY, D.C.L., etc. With Maps and Illustrations.

The Cruise of the Falcon: a Voyage to South America in a Thirty-ton Yacht. By E. F. KNIGHT, Barrister-at-Law. With numerous Illustrations and Map.

The Great Lone Land: a Record of Travel and Adventure in North and West America. By Col. Sir W. F. BUTLER, K.C.B. With Illustrations and Route Map.

Men, Mines, and Animals in South Africa. By Lord RANDOLPH CHURCHILL. With Numerous Illustrations.

Our Hundred Days in Europe. By Dr. OLIVER WENDELL HOLMES.

The River Congo: from its Mouth to Bólóbó. By H. H. JOHNSTON, C.M.G. With numerous Illustrations.

Clear Round! Seeds of Story from other Countries: a Chronicle of Links and Rivets in this World's Girdle. By E. A. GORDON, Member of the Japan Society. With Maps, Illustrations, and Introductory Letter by Professor F. Max Müller.

The Cruise of H.M.S. 'Challenger': Scenes in Many Lands, Voyages over Many Seas. By W. J. J. SPRY, R.N., F.R.G.S. Twelfth Edition. With Map and numerous Illustrations.

Through Masai Land: a Journal of Exploration among the Snow-clad Volcanic Mountains and Strange Tribes of Eastern Equatorial Africa. By JOSEPH THOMSON, Gold Medallist of Royal Geographical Society. With Map and numerous Illustrations.

The Land of an African Sultan: Travels in Morocco. By WALTER B. HARRIS, F.R.G.S. With numerous Illustrations.

The Wild North Land. By General Sir WM. F. BUTLER, K.C.B. With Illustrations.

Coomassie: The Story of the Campaign in Africa, 1873-4. With Map and numerous Illustrations.

Magdala: The Story of the Abyssinian Campaign of 1866-7. With Map and Illustrations.

LONDON: SAMPSON LOW, MARSTON & COMPANY, LIMITED,
St. Dunstan's House, Fetter Lane, Fleet Street, E.C.

SAMPSON LOW, MARSTON & CO.'S
NEW BOOKS

A FOURTH EDITION IS NOW READY
In Two Royal 8vo Volumes of about 800 pages Fully Illustrated, Price 30s., of

IRONCLADS IN ACTION
1855 to 1895
By H. W. WILSON. With Introduction by Capt. A. T. MAHAN

'Has been an unqualified success.'—*Army and Navy Gazette*.
'A trustworthy record. . . . The manner in which it has been brought out reflects great credit on the publishers, Messrs. Sampson Low, Marston & Co.'—*Broad Arrow*.
'Students of naval warfare and all who concern themselves with naval questions in their actuality, must acknowledge themselves greatly indebted to Mr. H. W. Wilson.'—*The Times*.
'A full, accurate, informing, and well-written work—as interesting as any romance.' —*Glasgow Herald*.
'The naval world will be wiser for this book, which will take its place as a standard work, and will long retain that position.'—*Standard*.
'Deserves to be studied by every naval officer.'—*Morning Post*.
'Will be of the greatest use to all who are interested in sea power.'—*Daily News*.
'In a word, the work is worthy of the subject.'—*Daily Chronicle*.
'Admirably provided with maps and plans, and with a large number of drawings of notable warships.'—*The Times*.

THE 'PALL MALL MAGAZINE LIBRARY'

Field Marshal Viscount Wolseley's 'Decline and Fall of Napoleon.' Third Edition. Crown 8vo, cloth, fully illustrated, 3s. 6d.
    'A rare combination of military insight and literary skill.'—*Times*.

Field Marshal Lord Roberts' 'Rise of Wellington.' Second Edition. Crown 8vo, cloth extra, fully illustrated, 3s. 6d.
    'A very interesting study of Wellington.'—*Spectator*.

General Sir Evelyn Wood's 'Cavalry in the Waterloo Campaign.' Second Edition. Crown 8vo, cloth extra, fully illustrated, 3s. 6d.
    'Spiritedly and vividly written.'—*Daily News*.

Ready next week, uniform with the above, fully illustrated, 3s. 6d.
Major E. S. May's Guns and Cavalry: An Account of the United Action of Cavalry and Artillery.

Works by Captain A. T. MAHAN of the United States Navy.

The Influence of Sea Power upon History. 1 vol. Demy 8vo. Maps and Plans, 18s.

The Influence of Sea Power on the French Revolution and Empire. Two vols., demy 8vo. Maps and Plans, 30s.
    'No living writer is so well qualified to do this great theme justice as Captain Mahan.'—*Times*.

Life of Admiral Farragut. By Captain A. T. MAHAN. 8vo, cloth, 6s.

LONDON: SAMPSON LOW, MARSTON & COMPANY, LIMITED,
St. Dunstan's House, Fetter Lane, Fleet Street, London, E.C.

JULES VERNE'S WORKS

THE ONLY COPYRIGHT EDITIONS.

'Jules Verne, that Prince of Story-tellers.'—*Times.*

New and Cheap Edition. Illustrated. Crown 8vo, cloth lettered. 1/- each.

Adventures of Three Englishmen and Three Russians in South Africa.
Five Weeks in a Balloon.
A Floating City.
The Blockade Runners.
From the Earth to the Moon.
Around the Moon.
Around the World in Eighty Days.
Dr. Ox's Experiment.
Martin Paz, the Indian Patriot.
A Winter Amid the Ice.
Mysterious Island. Part I.—Dropped from the Clouds.
——— Part II.—Abandoned.
——— Part III.—The Secret of the Island.
Child of the Cavern.
Begum's Fortune.
Tribulations of a Chinaman.
Green Ray.
Steam House. Part I.—Demon of Cawnpore.
——— Part II.—Tigers and Traitors.
The Giant Raft. Part I.—Eight Hundred Leagues up the Amazon.
——— Part II.—The Cryptogram.
Kéraban. Part I.—Captain of the Guidara.
——— Part II.—Scarpante the Spy.
The Archipelago on Fire.
The Vanished Diamond.
Godfrey Morgan.
Mathias Sandorf (2 vols.) 1s. each.
The Lottery Ticket.
Clipper of the Clouds.
The Flight to France.
Burbank the Northerner } North against South
Taxar the Southerner } (2 vols.).

New Cheap Edition. Illus. Crown 8vo, cloth lettered, double vols. 2/- each.

Twenty Thousand Leagues Under the Sea.
Fur Country.
Survivors of the Chancellor. | Dick Sands.
Michael Strogoff. | Hector Servadac.

Another Edition. Large imp. 16mo, cloth extra, with many full-page Illustrations. 3/6 each.

Adventures of Three Englishmen and Three Russians in South Africa.
Survivors of the Chancellor.
Abandoned.
Child of the Cavern.
Begum's Fortune.
The Demon of Cawnpore.
Tigers and Traitors.
Eight Hundred Leagues up the Amazon.
Captain of the Guidara. | The Lottery Ticket.
Scarpante the Spy. | North against South.
The Vanished Diamond. | Flight to France.

In handsome cloth, gilt binding, gilt edges. Illus. Crown 8vo. 2/- each.

Adventures of Three Englishmen and Three Russians in South Africa.

Five Weeks in a Balloon.
A Floating City.
The Blockade Runners.
From the Earth to the Moon.
Around the Moon.
Around the World in Eighty Days.
Dr. Ox's Experiment and Master Zacharius.
Martin Paz, the Indian Patriot.
A Winter Amid the Snow.
Mysterious Island. Part I.—Dropped from the Clouds.
——— Part II.—Abandoned.
——— Part III.—The Secret of the Island.
Child of the Cavern.
Begum's Fortune.
Tribulations of a Chinaman.
Green Ray.
Steam House. Part I.—Demon of Cawnpore.
——— Part II.—Tigers and Traitors.
The Giant Raft. Part I.—Eight Hundred Leagues up the Amazon.
——— Part II.—The Cryptogram.
Kéraban. Part I.—Captain of the Guidara.
——— Part II.—Scarpante the Spy.
The Archipelago on Fire.
The Vanished Diamond.
Godfrey Morgan.
Clipper of the Clouds.
The Flight to France.

In Crown 8vo vols., cloth gilt. Full-page Illustrations. 2/6 each.

Five Weeks in a Balloon.
A Floating City. } In one vol.
The Blockade Runners. }
Around the World in Eighty Days.
Dropped from the Clouds.
The Cryptogram. | Cæsar Cascabel.
Godfrey Morgan. | A Family without a Name.
Adrift in the Pacific.
Purchase of the North Pole.
Mistress Brannican.
Castle of the Carpathians.
The Secret of the Island.
Tribulations of a Chinaman.
The Archipelago on Fire.
Clipper of the Clouds.

In handsome cloth, gilt binding, gilt edges. Illustrated. Double vols. 3/6 each.

Twenty Thousand Leagues under the Sea.
Fur Country.
Survivors of the Chancellor. | Mathias Sandorf.
Michael Strogoff. | Hector Servadac.
Dick Sands. | Green Ray.

Large Post 8vo Edition, green cloth gilt Latest vols. 6/- each.

Green Ray (gilt edges, crown 8vo.).
Adrift in the Pacific.
Purchase of the North Pole.
A Family without a Name.
Cæsar Cascabel.
Mistress Brannican.
Castle of the Carpathians.
Claudius Bombarnac. | Foundling Mick.
Captain Antifer. | Floating Island.

LONDON: SAMPSON LOW, MARSTON & COMPANY, LIMITED,
St. Dunstan's House, Fetter Lane, Fleet Street, London, E.C.

HUNTING.

SHOOTING.

FISHING.

EXPEDITIONS
FITTED AND PROVISIONED

For all Parts of the World at the

MILITARY EQUIPMENT STORES

AND

TORTOISE TENTS CO., Limited,

7 WATERLOO PLACE, LONDON, S.W.

The Company have just completed the equipment of Sir William Martin Conway's Spitzbergen Expedition. The Jackson-Harmsworth original and auxiliary Expeditions were also equipped by this Company; and Mr. J. Russell-Jeaffreson, F.R.G.S., has obtained from the Company the whole of his Arctic equipment for many years past.

SOLE AGENTS IN LONDON FOR HARDY BROS., ALNWICK.

Customers are reminded that all the various patterns of Rods and other specialties of the famous Alnwick firm can be obtained here as at the manufactory.

CARTER & CO.

137 ST. JOHN STREET ROAD, LONDON, E.C.

(Near the Angel, Islington.)

Outfits for Norway are not complete without our

PATENT FLIES WITH SPINNING HEADS

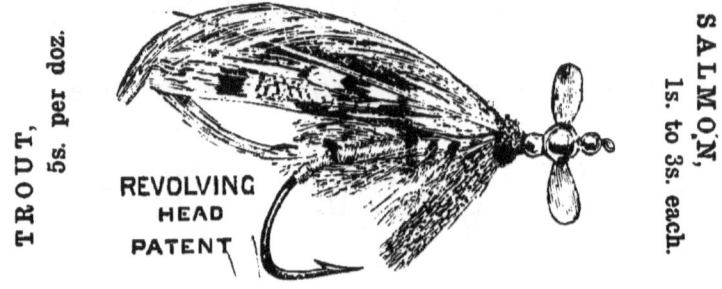

Our Gold Medal

BUILT CANE RODS

are the best in the world.

DOUBLE BUILT, 2 TOPS, SPIRAL LOCK JOINTS.
SALMON, £5, 5s.   TROUT, £2, 2s.

Price List of every description of Rods and Tackle Post Free.

Fishing Gazette:—'Undoubtedly do one of the largest trades in the world.'

www.ingramcontent.com/pod-product-compliance
Lightning Source LLC
Chambersburg PA
CBHW051728300426
44115CB00007B/508